Beyond Bear's Paw

ALSO BY JEROME A. GREENE

Evidence and the Custer Enigma (Kansas City, 1973)

Slim Buttes, 1876: An Episode of the Great Sioux War (Norman, 1982)

Yellowstone Command: Colonel Nelson A. Miles and the Great Sioux War, 1876–1877 (Lincoln, 1991; Norman, 2006)

(ed.) *Battles and Skirmishes of the Great Sioux War, 1876–1877: The Military View* (Norman, 1993)

Lakota and Cheyenne: Indian Views of the Great Sioux War, 1876–1877 (Norman, 1994)

(ed.) *Frontier Soldier: An Enlisted Man's Journal of the Sioux and Nez Perce Campaigns, 1877* (Helena, 1998)

Nez Perce Summer, 1877: The U.S. Army and the Nee-Me-Poo Crisis (Helena, 2000)

Morning Star Dawn: The Powder River Expedition and the Northern Cheyennes, 1876 (Norman, 2003)

(with Douglas D. Scott) *Finding Sand Creek: History, Archeology, and the 1864 Massacre Site* (Norman, 2004)

Washita: The U.S. Army and the Southern Cheyennes, 1867–1869 (Norman, 2004)

The Guns of Independence: The Siege of Yorktown, 1781 (New York, 2005)

Fort Randall on the Missouri, 1856–1892 (Pierre, 2005)

(ed.) *Indian War Veterans: Memories of Army Life and Campaigns in the West, 1864–1898* (New York, 2007)

Stricken Field: The Little Bighorn since 1876 (Norman, 2008)

Beyond Bear's Paw

The Nez Perce Indians in Canada

Jerome A. Greene

University of Oklahoma Press : Norman

Publication of this book is made possible through the generosity of Edith Kinney Gaylord.

Library of Congress Cataloging-in-Publication Data

Greene, Jerome A.
    Beyond Bear's Paw : the Nez Perce Indians in Canada / Jerome A. Greene.
        p.   cm.
    Includes bibliographical references and index.
    ISBN 978-0-8061-4068-1 (cloth)
    ISBN 978-0-8061-6045-0 (paper)
    1. Bear Paw, Battle of, Mont., 1877.   2. Joseph, Nez Perce Chief, 1840–1904.   3. White Bird.   4. Nez Perce Indians—Government relations.   5. Nez Perce Indians—Relocation—Canada.   6. Nez Perce Indians—Canada—Migrations.   I. Title.
    E83.877.G738 2010
    971.00497'4124—dc22
                                                                    2009005074

The paper in this book meets the guidelines for permanence and durability of the Committee on Production Guidelines for Book Longevity of the Council on Library Resources, Inc. ∞

*To the memory of those Nimiipuu
who sought sanctuary in Canada in 1877,
and to their descendants,
past and present*

CONTENTS

ILLUSTRATIONS

Preface and Acknowledgments

The history of the Nimiipuu people who entered Canada during the closing stages of the Nez Perce War in 1877 and who either remained there or returned to the United States (some to be incarcerated in the Indian Territory) signifies a bitter yet poignant chapter in Nez Perce tribal existence. It is a story that has been difficult to chronicle because of the paucity of available source materials relative to those of the war itself. There are few official documents, American or Canadian, explaining with any precision the events framing the story of the Nez Perces who crossed the "Medicine Line" to survive the devastation of Colonel Nelson A. Miles's command at Bear's Paw, Montana Territory, that resulted in the surrender of Chief Joseph's followers. It is clear from Nez Perce and Canadian sources, however, that a relatively large number of the people managed to escape the tumult at Bear's Paw and make their way north, initially to find succor with Sitting Bull's refugee Lakotas and later to find their own way forward—either returning to Idaho or places in the surrounding region or staying in Canada for good. This is the story of those people, as derived from existing reminiscences of Nez Perce participants and gleaned from pertinent military, diplomatic, and legal records of both countries.

The study was challenging on several fronts. Materials detailing the people's life and activities in Canada were, for the most part, difficult to find because of that government's historical decision to confer on the Nez Perces alien refugee status (as it did the Lakotas).

In addition, I had difficulties with the Washington office of the National Park Service when it came to arranging programmed research in Canada that proved costly in time and funding and which immensely complicated the project schedule. These constraints and others ensured that that part of the work directed to help pinpoint sites in Canada—where aspects of this history played out—had to be postponed, if not canceled altogether.

I nevertheless appreciate the support from those offices and visionary individuals who comprehended the importance of this study to the mission of Nez Perce National Historical Park. Among those I would most like to thank for their commitment during inception of the work and/or throughout its progress are the staff members—particularly former superintendent Doug Eury—at Nez Perce National Historical Park, Spalding, Idaho, and its collateral sites; former Big Hole National Battlefield Unit Superintendent Jon G. James (currently serving at George Washington Memorial Parkway, Virginia), who conceived the project; Tami DeGrosky, former superintendent of Big Hole; Jason Lyon, Integrated Resources Manager, Nez Perce National Historical Park; Robert Applegate, Park Librarian; Robert Chenoweth, Park Curator; and Robert West, former manager, Bear Paw Battlefield Unit. I must especially acknowledge Sandi McFarland, Administrator, Nez Perce National Historic Trail, Orofino, Idaho, for her continued interest and support and for providing U.S. Forest Service funding for foreign travel. Further, I am indebted to a select few who stepped forward at critical junctures to help facilitate this work. In this regard, I must especially thank Gary T. Cummins, former manager, Harpers Ferry Center, Harpers Ferry, West Virginia; Kathy Tustanowski-Marsh, Deputy Associate Manager, Programs and Budget, Harpers Ferry Center; and Rick Frost, Associate Regional Director, Communications, Legislation, and Partnerships, Intermountain Regional Office, Lakewood, Colorado, for direct help, for good counsel, and for persevering in their constructive efforts to make this project succeed. I thank Selma Fleming, Media Services, Harpers Ferry Center, for handling the peculiarities of travel management associated with this effort with her usual aplomb.

I received critical guidance in the location and use of Canadian archival materials, as well as general assistance regarding the Fort Walsh site (including road directions!), from Royce E. W. Pettyjohn and Clayton T. Yarshenko, Heritage Preservation Specialists; and David Rohatensky, Site Manager—all of Fort Walsh National Historic Site, Parks Canada, Maple Creek, Saskatchewan. The staff of the Glenbow Museum Library and Archives, Calgary, Alberta, proved extremely helpful and generous with their time, as did the staff of Library and Archives Canada, Ottawa, Ontario. It was indeed a pleasure to work with such dedicated professionals and the resources in their charge. I would like to particularly acknowledge Joanna Crandall, Reference Clerk, Library Information Service, of the latter institution, for her thoughtfulness in putting me in contact with appropriate parties.

Other individuals and offices that helped in this endeavor and deserve my gratitude include David Louter, National Park Service, Seattle, Washington; Ronald J. Papandrea, Warren, Michigan; Patsy Tate and Katherine Paxton, Library and Archives, Washington State University, Pullman; Robert G. Pilk, Lakewood, Colorado; Faye Morning Bull, Brocket, Alberta; Robert M. Utley, Georgetown, Texas; James S. Brust, San Pedro, California; Gordon S. Chappell, San Francisco, California; L. Clifford Soubier, Charles Town, West Virginia; Paul L. Hedren, Omaha, Nebraska; Paul Harbaugh, Englewood, Colorado; Bob Rea, Fort Supply, Oklahoma; Elliott West, University of Arkansas, Fayetteville; National Archives, Washington, D.C.; U.S. Army Military History Institute, Carlisle, Pennsylvania; Denver Public Library, Denver, Colorado; Lilly Library, Indiana University, Bloomington; Little Bighorn Battlefield National Monument, Crow Agency, Montana; Western History Department, University of Oklahoma, Norman; Montana Historical Society, Helena; and Brigham Young University Library, Provo, Utah.

To all of these people and institutions, I extend my heartfelt appreciation.

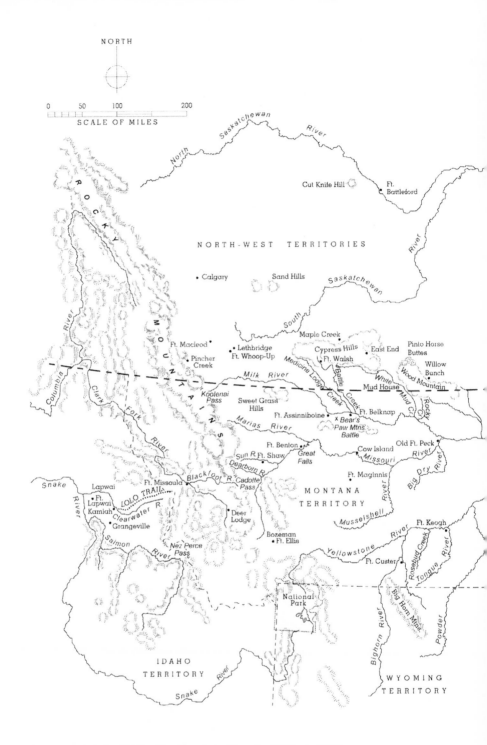

Area associated with the Nez Perces in Canada, 1877–ca. 1900.

Beyond Bear's Paw

CHAPTER 1

THE NEZ PERCE WAR AND
THE CANADIAN OPTION

Among the numerous wars fought between the United States Government and indigenous peoples during the late nineteenth century, the one pitting the army against the non-treaty Nez Perce—or Nimiipuu—Indians was in many ways most daunting for either adversary. For the Nez Perce people, who under military pressure chose to leave their homeland, the war became an epic of human endurance under duress; for the troops who pursued them over the course of sixteen weeks, it proved repeatedly disastrous, exhausting, seemingly interminable, and, as events played out, without satisfying conclusion. In fact, the Nez Perce War of 1877, of which the Canadian sojourn was of direct consequence for many Nimiipuu participant survivors as well as for the people as a whole, followed a familiar pattern in the history of Indian-white relations in the United States.

Briefly stated, the Nez Perces occupied territory in present eastern Oregon and central Idaho coveted by white Americans drawn into the region by economic prospects during the years following the Civil War. Specifically, land and minerals attracted farmers and miners who, in the course of their entrée, ran roughshod over the Native inhabitants. According to treaties in 1855 and 1863, many of those people had been placed on a reserve and targeted by missionaries in the country drained by the Clearwater River. Eventually, however, following more than a decade of mistreatment by white intruders, the federal government demanded removal onto this Lapwai Reservation of several remaining bands of non-treaty Nez Perce people in order to free up their lands for settlement by whites.

In May 1877, as the peoples of White Bird, Toohoolhoolzote, Joseph, and others assembled preparatory to submitting to the government, something of a cultural reaffirmation occurred, sparked by several youths fortified with liquor who set out to avenge past grievances against the tribe. The raiding of the white settlements along the Salmon River between June 14 and 15 by approximately twenty young Nez Perce warriors, and the resulting response by army troops from nearby Fort Lapwai to put down the trouble, had a polarizing effect among the non-treaty bands, uniting them against all past transgressions by whites and inspiring in their leadership a course of resistance over the ensuing several months. These events, and the decisions made by Nimiipuu leaders in their immediate aftermath, held major implications for the future of the non-treaty Nez Perce people.

Following the Nez Perces' killings of whites during the raids, the leadership did not conduct the non-treaty people onto the Lapwai Reservation. Instead, tribal elements headed by Joseph, Ollokot, Toohoolhoolzote, and others withdrew south to camp in traditional lands along Salmon River with the people of Chief White Bird. There, at dawn on June 17, soldiers from Fort Lapwai found them and approached their village to attack. Divining their purpose, the Indians skillfully preempted the strike, shooting the cavalry trumpeters and driving the mounted troops back in disorganization before they reached the encampment. Thirty-three U.S. soldiers—fully one-third of the attacking command—were killed at the Battle of White Bird Canyon; Nimiipuu casualties were virtually negligible. Moreover, coming on the heels of the previous year's defeat by Lakota Indians of Custer's command at the Little Bighorn River in Montana, the soldiers' loss to the Nez

Perces created an institutional paranoia that gripped the army through much of the subsequent fighting in 1877.

Immediately following White Bird Canyon, the non-treaty Nez Perces, fearful and uncertain with realization of their deed, awaited the course of events. When Brigadier General Oliver O. Howard renewed the campaign against them, the Indians withdrew into the highlands below the Salmon, then emerged north of the stream. Meantime, soldiers from Howard's command ineptly attacked the village of Looking Glass on Clear Creek, near the Middle Clearwater River, killing three of the people and driving that chief—who had previously aligned himself with the reservation people—to support White Bird and the others. Soon after, at the tiny community of Cottonwood, a body of non-treaty Indians ambushed an army detachment of eleven, killing them all before turning on a party of volunteers and killing three of them. Within days, General Howard approached the combined non-treaty village on the south fork of the Clearwater, sending howitzer fire against the people and instigating a two-day confrontation that cost fourteen army and four Indian lives before finally yielding an army victory. While the Nez Perces largely abandoned their village in their flight, they significantly withdrew from in front of Howard's command and began an eastward advance away from the soldiers and over the Lolo Trail, the umbilical leading from Idaho into Montana Territory. By then their numbers included about 750 people, together with 2,000 horses and several hundred dogs, so that the column stretched out for several miles. The strategic failure of General Howard to prevent their movement over the Lolo following the Battle of the Clearwater constituted a blunder of major proportion, permitting the Nez Perce conflict to proceed.

In their course east, the Indians circumvented an extensive log barrier ("Fort Fizzle") raised by soldiers stationed in western Montana in the canyon near the east end of Lolo Creek. The people then headed south, up Bitterroot Valley, largely believing that their troubles were over since leaving homeland behind. En route to the Yellowstone region, they bartered with white settlers as they passed through various communities. While Howard trailed on the Lolo trying to overtake them, however, additional troops from the army's Department of Dakota entered the campaign. As the Nimiipuu paused along the Big Hole River in southwestern Montana Territory, Colonel John Gibbon's soldiers were not far behind, and in the morning darkness of August 9, as the people slept, the troops attacked the camp. Yet at the Big Hole the Nez Perces overcame the initial surprise, fighting vigorously to drive the attackers back into a defensive position west of the stream. They surrounded Gibbon's command through the following night, finally departing on August 10 as word came of Howard's advance on the trail. The Battle of the Big Hole was a horrendously bloody engagement that yielded the deaths of perhaps ninety Indian men, women, and children—and the wounding of perhaps another hundred—while army losses totaled thirty-one killed and nearly forty wounded. Beyond the enormous casualties, at the Big Hole the Nez Perces learned the reality of their flight—that they were not yet free and would be hounded unmercifully by the army until they either surrendered or somehow escaped the ever-constricting military cordon.

From the Big Hole the Indians angled southeastwardly, going briefly into Idaho and then into Wyoming. Frustrated following the devastation of the Big Hole attack, they rallied actively to strike Howard's soldiers during the predawn hours of August 20, then aggressively besieged a body of cavalry sent after them, perhaps losing several warriors in the encounter. The Nez Perces' raid at Camas Meadows, Idaho Territory, netted them some two hundred army horses and mules with which they prolonged their journey. Then they entered the National Park (present-day Yellowstone National Park), and for two weeks—in comparative safety from Howard's struggling army—the Indians explored and puzzled over where to go next. Their tenure in the park disclosed internal dissension within the multi-band tribal group, likely evidence of building pressures and mixed temperaments. The range of their treatment of tourist parties encountered by the Nez Perces perhaps reflected varying stress levels within the body following Big Hole. (Groups of Indians operating seemingly independently from the main body killed several whites in the park, yet their treatment of captives eventually released was humane.) The record of much of the Nez Perces' odyssey in Yellowstone remains muddled, and their course through the park after leaving the shore of Lake Yellowstone remains at best speculative.

Pursued by Howard's command, now slowed to a ponderous march because of supply and medical needs, the tribesmen by early September emerged northeast of the park at Clark's Fork, a north-running stream that fed into the Yellowstone River at present-day Laurel, Montana. By then, additional army forces under Colonel Samuel D. Sturgis had gained the area from their station down the Yellowstone, but Sturgis's efforts to block the Nimiipuu as they came out of the park failed, and they headed down Clark's Fork to the Yellowstone River. Howard meantime joined Sturgis, and the latter pressed on the Nez Perces' trail, finally meeting them in protracted combat at Canyon Creek on September 13. The engagement amounted to long-range dueling with few casualties on either side, but the Indians succeeded in gaining a critical egress onto the plains and thus succeeded once more in thwarting Sturgis and the army. After Canyon Creek, the people headed due north with Canada the primary objective—their only apparent recourse for escaping the troops lay in passing over the international boundary into the British Possessions.

At the Missouri River the Nez Perces encountered an army detachment guarding freight on the north bank opposite Cow Island. There they begged food, then after sundown September 23 ignited the army stores before departing north. In Cow Creek Canyon they met a wagon train, raided its contents and set it afire, then briefly fought a contingent of armed volunteers just arrived from Fort Benton. The Indians continued north, oblivious of a new force closing on them from the southeast—the command of Colonel Nelson A. Miles from the Tongue River Cantonment far down the Yellowstone River. Responding to Howard's entreaties for help, Miles had departed his post on September 18, moving swiftly and diagonally in a southeast-to-northwest trajectory to head off the Indians either at the Missouri or points north.

On September 30, Miles's troops crested a ridge overlooking the Nez Perce camp near the northeast end of the Bear's Paw Mountains, just forty miles south of the Canadian line. The colonel quickly opened a charge on the people, his cavalry sweeping in from the south to capture the pony herd while storming the encampment. But the Nimiipuu reacted swiftly, inflicting heavy casualties among Miles's men and causing him to pull back and instead to surround and lay siege to the Indians' position. Over the course of the next five days, two artillery pieces destroyed much of the Nez Perces' defenses. Moreover, firepower from these weapons joined with that of the soldiers' small arms in killing several of the chiefs, including Looking Glass and Toohoolhoolzote. Nimiipuu casualties at Bear's Paw numbered perhaps twenty-five killed and fifty wounded, whereas army losses totaled twenty-four killed and forty-three wounded. On October 5, following the arrival of General Howard and his staff, negotiations prompted the Indians' submission. At Bear's Paw, the Nez Perces' trek of twelve hundred miles from Idaho to northern Montana ended with the Nimiipuu leader Joseph—one of the few chiefs to survive—delivering his carbine to Miles. The people who surrendered were trundled off to the Tongue River Cantonment for eventual transfer to the Indian Territory, far from their homeland.[1]

Throughout most of the non-treaty Nez Perces' trek, following the outbreak along the Salmon River in Idaho and through the entry of the people into Montana Territory, there appears to have occurred intermittent discussion within the inter-band leadership regarding escape to British America, an option that figured ever greater as the army pursuit wore on. Based on Nimiipuu recollections, the earliest dialogue regarding Canada apparently took place at Weippe Prairie, twenty miles northeast from Kamiah on the Clearwater River, where sometime around July 15 the leaders paused to council and to consider their situation, objectives, and choices. The meeting reportedly brought forth diverse views. Joseph and his brother Ollokot of the Wallowa band desired to cross into Montana via the Lolo Trail, head south through the Bitterroot Valley, then double back into the Salmon River region of

Idaho by passing along the Elk City Road through Nez Perce Pass, in the area of modern Darby, Montana. Looking Glass, of the Alpowais, and the principal military leader among the senior chiefs, wanted to continue east to reach the buffalo plains where the Nez Perces' longtime friends, the Crow Indians, might assist them. White Bird, of the Lamtama band, wanted to go directly north into Canada, but his view did not prevail, and the consensus was to follow Looking Glass's counsel to go to the plains and join the Crows. At Weippe, all the leaders present—Looking Glass, White Bird, Toohoolhoolzote, Joseph and Ollokot, and the Palouse chiefs Hahtalekin and Husis Kute—signified their concurrence despite certain individual disagreement.[2] Under the circumstances, the decision reflected their confidence in Looking Glass's seniority and experience, and his opinions regarding junction with the Crows therefore likely carried substantial authority.

Yet friction among the chiefs lingered after the Weippe council. The next time they assembled to deliberate their circumstances appears to have occurred two weeks later, on the evening of Saturday, July 28, following the tribesmen's passing around the barricade of Fort Fizzle and their arrival in Montana's Bitterroot Valley. The meeting was promoted by Joseph and Toohoolhoolzote, and it probably marked the first time that the leadership considered the reality of their likely having entered another army jurisdiction. For even though the chiefs could not fathom the intricacies of the new conditions they faced, three Nez Perce warriors who had recently traveled to the Crow country brought warnings of the presence of troops to the east, and perhaps told of permanent military stations in the Bighorn–Powder River region established by the government during recent army operations against the Lakotas and Northern Cheyennes.

Even though Grizzly Bear Youth, leader of the trio, reported that the Crows had been providing scouts for the army against the Sioux and Cheyennes, Looking Glass's belief that the Nez Perces would be welcomed by their old friends persisted. Yet Grizzly Bear Youth advised the chiefs to avoid going east where the army troops operated, and instead travel north through the

Flathead Reservation via Flathead Lake and cross into Canada. Concern was registered that the Flatheads, who were longtime friends of the people and had intermarried with them, had supported the troops behind the Fort Fizzle barricade, and therefore might attack the Nimiipuu north of Missoula. White Bird subscribed to this recommendation to go to Canada, since it conformed largely to his own thoughts on the matter, and he was joined in this by Red Owl, an Alpowai headman of Looking Glass's band. In the council, White Bird and Looking Glass debated the question. Other leaders also spoke up: Pile of Clouds disputed Looking Glass and advocated that the people return to the Salmon River country. Joseph eventually took a position against further fighting, perhaps still holding to his idea of returning to the Snake and Salmon rivers via Nez Perce Pass through the Bitterroot Mountains. Although Ollokot's position remains unknown (he likely sided with his brother, Joseph), Toohoolhoolzote and two prominent warriors, Rainbow and Five Wounds, sided with Looking Glass. In the end, the majority of the chiefs seem to have clung to the belief that their troubles with the army were behind them and that their long friendship with the Crows and other tribes on the plains would sustain them—perhaps permanently. Again, the Alpowai chief's experience and abilities in war matters overcame resistance in the leadership group, and the members yielded to Looking Glass's preference. White Bird at length counseled unity, fearing fragmentation of the group. "If we go to the Crows, we must all go," he said. At this meeting it appears that although the Canadian option received a thorough airing, mostly through Looking Glass's influence it remained merely an alternative.[3]

Following the disastrous Big Hole encounter, however, Looking Glass's leadership came into question. He had convinced the band leaders to camp in the Big Hole Basin despite warnings by some tribesmen that danger was imminent; some had even reported seeing soldiers scouting the area of the camp. In any event, security was lax—a factor that no doubt contributed to the heavy casualties sustained by the Indians. Following Big Hole,

Looking Glass lost favor; his role in coordinating the daily marches was given to Lean Elk, also known as Poker Joe. Although Looking Glass retained military authority among the people, he was clearly chagrined at his operational demotion regarding the daily march.[4]

The next discernible major development affecting the Nez Perces' thoughts regarding Canada and the Crows came in the wake of the devastation of the Big Hole combat, where so many of the people had been killed and wounded. In the weeks following that engagement there was much striking out against whites and white-owned property. Word that large numbers of Crows were now scouting for the army threatened to complicate and perhaps nullify the Nimiipuu plan. By the time the people entered the National Park, it is likely that their future course was as unknown to them as it was to the army command, and the amount of time passed in the park by the tribesmen suggests the possibility that they remained unsure where to go. During the two weeks they stayed in the park, they certainly ruminated over what to do, and likely one or more inter-band leadership councils took place. A discharged soldier, captured and held by the Indians for six days before escaping, told General Howard that the leaders had dispatched emissaries to the Crows seeking their support. It is possible that Looking Glass was among those who journeyed to meet the Crows, perhaps in the vicinity of their agency on the Stillwater River. One source, a white scout who lived with the Crows, stated that he met the chief under such circumstances. It is likely that the meeting proved beyond doubt the Crows' allegiance to the government troops, and that that knowledge ultimately translated into a disposition among the Nez Perce leadership to break for Canada. The scout, the reliable Thomas H. Leforge, indeed said that he told Looking Glass that he would attempt to discourage the Crows from trying to stop the Nimiipuu from crossing the Crow Reservation in their drive north.[5]

When the Nez Perces emerged from the mountains east of the National Park and headed down Clark's Fork toward the Yellowstone River, they had come to grips with the futility of trying to unite with the Crows, who out of tribal interest remained steadfast in their loyalty to the government. With military pressure from army columns closing variously from the south, east, and west, the people turned north to leave the park. In the Nez Perces' desperation to find refuge, the once least-favored Canadian option became the most viable; simply put, they had nowhere else to go.[6] If there remained any doubt as to the position of the Crows vis-à-vis the Nez Perces, the action with Sturgis's force at Canyon Creek and its aftermath settled the question once and for all. Although the Crow scouts did not participate in the engagement in a major way, they nonetheless captured numbers of Nez Perce horses in the wake of the fighting, and according to Nez Perce accounts, one of their elderly men was killed by the Crows. And to compound matters, on the day after the Canyon Creek skirmish, as Sturgis and Howard briefly consolidated their commands, about 150 Crows, seeking more ponies, attacked the Nez Perce column. They harassed the people and caused them to lose several hundred more animals, though unable to stop the Indians' movement north over the plains. The attack by the Crows proved unsettling to the Nimiipuu, and they grew angry and frustrated that their former friends had treated them so badly; in short, the Crows' betrayal provoked quarreling and dissension in the ranks. "I do not understand how the Crows could think to help the soldiers," remembered Yellow Wolf. "They were fighting against their best friends! Some Nez Perces in our band had helped them whip the Sioux who came against them only a few snows before. This is why Chief Looking Glass had advised going to the Crows, to the buffalo country. He thought Crows would help us." If anything, the fight with the Crows on September 14, 1877, must have quashed any doubt in the minds of the Nez Perce leaders about their settled course: to reach the British Possessions.[7]

Although direct evidence is tenuous, the prospect of Canadian sanctuary for the Nimiipuu—perhaps from the moment that it was first proposed—was influenced by recent occurrences involving another neighboring tribe, the Lakotas, or Teton Sioux, hereditary enemies of the Crows. In 1876 and early 1877, the Lakotas and their Northern Cheyenne allies—who had previously invaded Crow lands, and had faced largely the same incursions of whites experienced by the Nez Perces in Idaho—fought back against the army in a wide-ranging series of engagements that came to be known as the Great Sioux War. Fighting between the army and the Sioux and Cheyennes climaxed with the defeat of the Seventh U.S. Cavalry under Lieutenant Colonel George A. Custer at the Little Bighorn River in Montana. Thereafter the army waged a relentless campaign against them, and following a number of army victories, some of the tribesmen looked to Canada as a means of avoiding the alternative of death or surrender to reservation life. Most notably, Sitting Bull, the influential medicine man and political leader of the Hunkpapa Lakotas, had crossed the international border with his followers in May 1877, intending to remain there for all time. Given grapevine communication among the northern Plains tribes—and that many of the Nez Perces could read, write, and speak English (and knew something of the jurisdictional demarcation between the United States and Canada as well as its location) as a result of their missionary education—the passage of Sitting Bull and his people into Canada was likely well known among the Nimiipuu by the time of their departure from Idaho, and the consequence of that event must have gained significance to them as the weeks passed and the matter of their own survival became clear.

Four days after the Nez Perces fought with the Crows—and unknown to them as they continued their advance across the plains toward the Missouri River—the soldiers under Colonel Miles departed the Tongue River Cantonment, traveling northwest and seeking to intercept the unwary people somewhere in the vicinity of the Missouri or north of it. Since shortly after the Big Hole, Poker Joe had set the pace of the daily marching—much to the distress of Looking Glass, who believed that his position as chief should determine his right to govern movement of the procession. Poker Joe had insisted on hurrying the caravan forward, but amid the post–Canyon Creek discord, and after the Indians had passed Cow Island and had engaged the volunteers, Looking

Glass reasserted his authority. According to Nez Perce sources, the chief questioned the need for haste now that Howard's command was far behind; he argued that the horses were weak—many afflicted with a debilitating illness—and the elderly and children were weary from the march. With the approval of the inter-band council, authority for the march reverted to Looking Glass, and from that point forward the Nimiipuu slowed their advance to help maintain their strength. They passed around the eastern side of the Bear's Paw Mountains, then settled into camp at Tsanim Alikos Pah (Place of the Manure Fires) along Snake Creek on September 29, just forty miles from the Canadian line.[8]

That part of the international border between the United States and Canada, running thirteen hundred miles from western Minnesota to the Pacific Coast, is an entirely political construct that relies on no natural geographical features to influence its course. The 49th parallel as a political boundary derived from the 1713 Treaty of Utrecht, which divided New France from British North America. In 1803, following the Louisiana Purchase, President Thomas Jefferson recalled the article specifying the latitude and—through his ambassadors in Europe—proposed this line as the northern boundary of the new territory, which ran to the Rocky Mountains. This marked (on paper, at least) the beginning of the longest continuous straight international border in the world, ultimately stretching from approximately the 95th meridian on its east end to approximately the 123rd meridian on its west. Formal acknowledgment of the 49th parallel as the demarcation between British America and the United States awaited the conclusion of the War of 1812 and the Treaty of 1818; an Anglo-American accord of 1846 extended the border west from the Rocky Mountains to the Strait of Georgia, along the west coast of Washington Territory.

Political change prompted further fixing of the border's location. Following the foundation of the Dominion of Canada in 1867, whereby that nation attained political autonomy from Great Britain, and the accession three years later of the vast former holdings of the Hudson's Bay Company—which included lands comprising parts of present Saskatchewan, Alberta, and the Northwest Territories—both countries saw the need to determine the boundary line through survey. From 1872 through 1874, Canadian and American survey teams grittily labored through oppressive summer heat and frigid winter climes to formally plot the border along the 49th parallel west from Lake of the Woods. Marking parties followed the surveyors, spacing large iron pyramids along the parallel through Manitoba, and thereafter erecting stone cairns or earthen mounds—each five to eight feet high—at three-mile intervals on the line separating Dakota and Montana territories from the North-West Territories.[9]

Completed by August 1874, the demarcated boundary thereafter became a visibly recognizable entity for people in its proximity on either side. In large measure, these included the Native occupants—both large and small bands of tribesmen who had variously occupied the region for decades and who included members of the Blackfoot Confederacy; the Crees, Chippewas, Teton Sioux (Lakotas), Assiniboines, and Crows; as well as the Métis, the French-Canadian mixed-bloods (so-called "half-breeds") whose migrant camps stood along either side. Even before it was marked, however, these people were all aware of the border and the differences it signified. At the approximate midpoint of the line, a hundred-mile length of mostly treeless plain touching both present Blaine County, Montana, and the Cypress District of Saskatchewan, came to be regarded as a "Medicine Line" by Native peoples crossing from either direction. The line came to possess "magical political power" among the tribes, representing to some degree, at least, their perceived differentiation regarding the accessibility of liquor in each country. After 1874, the North-West Mounted Police monitored alcohol traffic in Canada. At first, the boundary was known as the "medicine road," meaning a route or way, until the more broadly encompassing term "Medicine Line" superseded it and was commonly used thereafter.[10]

Earlier generations of Native people were oblivious to the international boundary and traversed it in either direction as the need for game and sustenance dictated. By the 1870s, however, although they likely remained unaware of its overall significance in a geopolitical context, the Indians understood that the line represented a mystical power of change, as mirrored in their respective treatment on either side; in time its presence came to generate among certain peoples the promise of renewal on the Canadian side as opposed to the cultural stagnancy that generally followed their long-term contact with white Americans. One Lakota man named Robert Higheagle recalled that as a child his people called the line "holy" and that "things are different when you cross from one side to the other." They assumed "that in the absence of any agreement between the two Governments relative to crime, they were perfectly safe on one side of the line with regard to what had been done on the other." In the wake of the Indian conflicts on the northern plains of the United States in the 1870s, the Canadian option and its "difference" held real significance—especially regarding pursuit by U.S. troops. By then the "Medicine Line" promised relief, hope, and sanctuary for troubled tribal populations particularly to its south—for them it afforded an alternative in a world of danger and quickly diminishing options.[11]

By the 1870s, the two large nations on either side of the boundary represented distinct contrasts as they affected relationships, including settlement and control policies, respecting the tribes. The United States first encountered the northern Plains Indians in sustained fashion following the beginning of Anglo-American migration into the trans-Mississippi West during the 1840s. The increasing presence of white Americans intent on settlement and exploitation of fur and mineral resources affected the tribes by gradually constricting their hunting territory and by increasing competition among them for more limited game resources, thereby aggravating existing intertribal schisms and promoting new ones. In the decades following the war with Mexico, the United States government negotiated treaties with the tribes, attempting without success to restrict them to designated reservations, and thus remove them from areas of principal white migration and settlement. Many of the agreements were unclear to the Indians. Some tribes, or elements of them, forcibly resisted the encroachment of white Americans and the army troops sent to protect them, while others, hoping to benefit thereby, aligned with the government forces against hereditary enemies. The continued traffic west, interrupted by the U.S. Civil War, ushered in a period of contention and conflict between certain tribes on the one hand, and the army as instrument of the federal government on the other. Although the uprising against government treatment by eastern, or Santee, Sioux Indians in 1862–63 affected long-term U.S.–Indian relations throughout the plains country, the ultimate manifestation of the northern Plains Indian wars was the Great Sioux War of 1876–77, during which a coalition of Lakota tribes and their Northern Cheyenne allies succeeded in destroying the army command of Lieutenant Colonel George A. Custer at the Battle of the Little Bighorn in Montana, an event followed by prolonged military prosecution of those people by commands of the U.S. Army. By the close of the major warfare with the Sioux in 1877, settlement by American citizens had reached the area of the Medicine Line, much of it as yet sparsely scattered along Milk River and its tributaries in Montana.[12]

Although in Canada there were similarities with the American experience during the same period, there was also much that remained different. By 1870, white settlement was still comparatively thin in the region of the North-West Territories (affecting land in present-day Saskatchewan and Alberta). Indian policy in western Canada after creation of the Dominion in 1867 consisted largely of the domestication of tribal groups that had heretofore experienced little contact with whites and who maintained their unfettered buffalo-hunting lifestyles, of continuation of the formulation of British-style treaties to ensure "civilization" and assimilation of Indians into the broader Canadian society (a policy termed "enfranchisement"), and of designs to free up the acreage necessary for construction of the Canadian Pacific Railway, which would attract European settlers to the area. In some respects, the paternalistic Dominion government's economic objectives for the region were similar to those pursued below the

49th parallel, and between 1871 and 1876 six treaties were variously negotiated and ratified with resident tribes in Canada affecting the disposition of their lands and the establishment of Indian reserves in modern Manitoba, Saskatchewan, and Alberta.[13]

Although there existed parallels in the two countries' policies with regard to treaties, reservations, and assimilation, the similarities did not extend to military control mechanisms. The U.S. Army provided security to white settlers and travelers through the Indian country, occupying strategic stations throughout the western territories, including that land in the region of the international line. The army aggressively campaigned against tribesmen who refused the proffered reservation life, and over the years U.S. soldiers fought many costly battles with them. As a body, the army totaled approximately 25,000 officers and men during the 1870s, and a goodly number of them served in the West. In Canada, concerns that U.S. citizens' economic interests transcended the border, particularly in the area of present-day southern Alberta—where a lively illicit liquor trade had an impact on Native peoples—promoted the need for a regulating presence in the region. Canadian militia were not available for such service, and in response, another means of control appeared in western Canada, as represented by the arrival in 1874 of the North-West Mounted Police, a newly conceived force whose tempered presence would carry influence during proceedings at some of the Canadian treaty councils and beyond. Previously, the Hudson's Bay Company had maintained peace and established rules of comportment observed by both Indians and whites. Unlike the U.S. Army commands imposed in the region for enforcement and punitive reasons, the North-West Mounted Police, numbering but 335 officers and men in 1876, sought through consultation and negotiation to avert conflict rather than seek it. Given that no large-scale westward emigration had occurred as it had in the United States (there were but approximately 10,000 whites in western Canada in 1870), as well as the government's sluggish execution of its treaty responsibilities among the tribes, the police conducted no immediate enforcement activity respecting the Indians. Ever cognizant of American interests and influences in the area, however, they assumed mostly preventive duties: monitoring conditions on the Canadian frontier and enforcing law and order, rather than promoting armed confrontation. Thus, the police sought a semblance of fairness in their dealings with the tribes, and of neutrality in their relations with Americans along the border, intent on not giving Indians any cause to fear a collaboration with American army officials, or in any sense foster their forceful removal for punitive purposes. Anything else would not have worked, for as Canadian Prime Minister John A. MacDonald asserted, "We might as well try to check the flight of locusts from the south or the rush of buffalo from the north."[14]

By late 1875, the Mounted Police operated out of four stations and collateral outposts established in the North-West Territories. Two of them, Fort Macleod and Fort Walsh, factored most significantly in terms of police activity throughout the course of relations with the United States over Indian matters between 1876 and 1881. Fort Macleod, headquarters of the force from 1876 to 1878, was built in present southern Alberta to offset American incursions in the whiskey/fur trade. Constructed of cottonwood pickets, "it [was] well chosen for shelter from the winter winds, for wood and water, and for agriculture, but it [was] faulty as a military site.... [However,] there [was] little prospect of the post being attacked by any body." Soon after, the police under Inspector James Morrow Walsh established a new station, which eventually became the headquarters post in 1878. Fort Walsh stood approximately 160 miles east, barely across the modern provincial line in Saskatchewan. It was raised in a watered valley of the Cypress Hills, a rolling grass-, pine-, spruce-, and aspen-covered tract stretching some 100 miles east to west and incorporating hunting lands of multiple tribal bands, who often camped in the post's shadow. As erected, the post consisted of a 12-foot picketed stockade of spruce logs running 314 feet east to west on its north perimeter and 239 feet east to west on its south; it measured 239 feet along its east side and 192 along its west. In the center and along the four interior sides of the palisade stood single-story log buildings, including quarters, administrative facilities, and a guard house—all whitewashed inside and out, notched at the corners, and with interstices chinked with clay. Complementary bastions stood in the northwest and southeast corners, and two double-hinged gates secured the east entrance (one of them was fitted with a small doorway for individuals to pass through), which faced the incoming road from Fort Benton in Montana Territory in the south, over which supplies arrived via bull train. Another double gate on the west side permitted access to nearby Battle Creek. Completion of Fort Walsh also provided the nucleus for a nearby community of the same name, based largely on the enterprise of Fort Benton merchants and traders. Together, the presence of Forts Macleod and Walsh virtually ended the liquor traffic within a year.[15]

Within a short time, Fort Walsh assumed importance in Canadian officials' dealings with American Indians who sought sanctuary north of the boundary, as well as with U.S. authorities charged either with militarily prosecuting the tribesmen or with settling other matters related to them. The Lakotas, who began to arrive late in 1876, even as the army campaigns against them and the Northern Cheyennes proceeded in the United States, were followed later in 1877 by the Nez Perces. However, both groups had been preceded years earlier by a body of Dakota Indians composed of migrants from the 1862 Dakota uprising in Minnesota and Dakota Territory, some of them participants in that conflict, but also many from outlying areas drawn into present-day Manitoba and Saskatchewan by the prospect of game. These Santee, or Eastern Sioux—comprising parties of Sissetons, Wahpetons, Mdewakantons, and Wahpekutes—first came to Fort Garry at the Red River Settlement (later Winnipeg, Manitoba) in late 1862 and during 1863 and 1864. Despite the Dakotas' pronouncements that they had allied with Great Britain during the French and Indian War, the Revolutionary War, and the War of 1812, British officials considered these nearly 3,000 people (the figure "about 1,500 or 2,000" was given in 1877) to be displaced persons from the United

States and not claimants to Canadian territory. In Canada, they experienced armed clashes with Plains Ojibwas, who competed for game with the Sioux, and attempts by the American government to return them to the United States were for naught. Canadian authorities in time agreed to care for the Dakotas, and in the 1870s the so-called "resident Sioux" were assigned designated reserves by the government, thus assuming a "treaty" status much like that applied to Canada's own aborigines.[16] The precedent thus established by the Dakota refugees living in Canada was known among the Western Sioux because of existing family, band, and tribal affiliations and interrelationships; most likely it was known also among the Nez Perces, because some of those people had lived and doubtless hunted in the region north of the Missouri River, where interface with other area tribes must have supplied them such knowledge. In any event, what happened with the Lakotas in Canada in 1876–77 and thereafter held far-reaching ramifications for those non-treaty Nez Perces who reached Canada in 1877. For those reasons, elements of the Lakota expatriation are discussed at length below.

Because of their past experience regarding the entrée of Dakotas in 1862, 1863, and 1864, when warfare between the Lakotas and the U.S. Army erupted in 1876, Canadian authorities anticipated potential incursions from the south. In May 1876, even as army columns began mobilizing far below the border, the Canadian State Department notified the North-West Mounted Police of "the possibility of the United States' operations against the hostile Indians of Dakota and Montana, on the Yellowstone and Bighorn Rivers, resulting in their being driven for shelter into the Territories, and [the Indians'] using Canadian soil as a base for predatory and hostile operations." Canadian Governor-General Lord Dufferin termed the likelihood "a most undesirable contingency." Such "an influx of armed, warlike, and exasperated Indians will be anything but an agreeable addition to our population," he notified British Minister Sir Edward Thornton, who represented the Canadians in the American capital. Dufferin warned that if they "make our territory a base of operations for reprisals against their enemies, international complications of a very difficult character may ensue." The authorities surmised (correctly, as events would prove) that any Indians fleeing into Canada would likely head for the vicinity of Wood Mountain. Consequently, the police were instructed to pay particular attention to that area in their watch over the border country.[17]

Following the Battle of the Little Bighorn, wherein the combined Lakota and Northern Cheyenne warrior coalition defeated and destroyed the Seventh Cavalry command of Lieutenant Colonel George A. Custer, the attention of Canadian officials heightened in regard to Indian activity along that part of the international line touching northern Montana Territory immediately north of the principal combat zone. For example, in mid-August 1876, a French-Canadian mixed-blood named Gabriel Solomon claimed that he had been contacted by a scout from Sitting Bull's Hunkpapa camp in the wake of the Custer battle. The Lakota leader told this man, named Laframboise, that "there were only two ways of escape—one to the country of the Great Mother [Canada], the other to the Spaniards [Mexico]." Sitting Bull reportedly vacillated as to which course to pursue, although certainly Canada, by virtue of its immediate proximity, must always have been his primary choice of refuge. Moreover, Laframboise claimed that the chief told him "that as soon as he put his foot across the line on the Canadian soil he would bury the hatchet [that is, be peaceful]." Yet the police remained alert for trouble from the Lakotas. As a precautionary move, one hundred additional men were dispatched to Forts Macleod and Walsh, and an artillery complement arrived at the latter post. In November, word came that the Sioux had proposed an alliance with the Canadian Blackfoot to fight the Crow Indians and the Americans: "After they had killed all the Whites [in the U.S. territories] they would come over and join the Blackfeet to exterminate the Whites on this [Canadian] side." Although the Blackfeet, longtime enemies of the Lakotas, spurned this invitation, the perceived threat, whether true or not, was not lost on Canadian officials, including the Mounted Police. The Blackfeet, as well as most neighboring tribes in Canada, acknowledged the declining numbers of buffalo on which their subsistence depended, something an influx of Sioux now promised only to compound. In addition, rumors circulated among the Canadian mixed-bloods that the Lakotas were coming to Wood Mountain and Milk River and had sent word that they would steal horses and kill the people they found there.[18]

In the weeks and months following the Little Bighorn battle, as bolstered U.S. commands ranged over the Yellowstone and Powder River wilderness to seek and destroy the Lakotas and Cheyennes, the likelihood of some of those Indians striking for Canada grew more pronounced. Colonel Nelson A. Miles headed major operations from the Tongue River Cantonment at the mouth of Tongue River on the Yellowstone. They intensified in the fall of 1876, following Miles's meeting with Sitting Bull and other chiefs at Cedar Creek, in the divide country between the Yellowstone and Missouri drainages. In October, his troops fought Sitting Bull's warriors at Cedar Creek; two months later they routed the chief's camp at nearby Ash Creek, and in January defeated a force of Lakotas and Northern Cheyennes under Crazy Horse, Two Moon, and other leaders in the Wolf Mountains below the Yellowstone. Although many of the people began heading for the agencies established for them in Dakota Territory and Nebraska, Sitting Bull and his followers, many of whom had never subscribed to such agreements with the U.S. government, looked elsewhere. As pressure increased from American soldiers, many of these Indians, facing starvation and abject destitution, now turned to the north for relief of their condition.[19]

CHAPTER 2

Lakota Precedent

What happened to the Nez Perce contingent that ultimately managed to flee into Canada from the engagement with Colonel Miles's soldiers at Bear's Paw Mountains would draw significance from the previous arrival there in 1876–77 of the refugee Lakotas. In many ways, the Lakotas' experiences provided a prototype for what awaited the Nimiipuu. Moreover, the Nez Perces' appearance there in October 1877, fresh from Bear's Paw, seems to have had a directly consequential bearing on the Lakotas' determination to stay the course in Canada, at least for the immediate future. And over ensuing months (and in some instances even beyond that timeframe), as long as the majority of the Nez Perce escapees remained above the "Medicine Line" and in orbit of the Sioux, their existence was inextricably linked to those people.

The Canadian authorities' concerns that the Lakota Sioux targeted by the U.S. Army in the aftermath of the Battle of the Little Bighorn would seek refuge on Dominion territory were first realized in the fall of 1876. In August, rumors circulated about Sioux already having been observed in the vicinity of Wood Mountain, some 120 miles southeast of Fort Walsh and immediately north of the international line (in present-day Saskatchewan). Alerted by the Gabriel Solomon report, Superintendent James Morrow Walsh at Fort Walsh communicated with Major Guido Ilges at Fort Benton and learned that while many of the Indians were expected to turn themselves in at the Dakota and Nebraska agencies, Sitting Bull and his followers would likely remain in the north, their disposition uncertain. Walsh notified the State Department in Ottawa that Sitting Bull would probably "come over into our territories and seek peace."[1]

In the North-West Mounted Police hierarchy, it would be Superintendent Walsh and his superior, Commissioner James F. Macleod, who dealt most assiduously with the Tetons and later with the Nez Perces. The most direct interface belonged to the thirty-six-year-old Walsh (1840–1905), a native of eastern Canada who had seen militia service during the Fenian raids of the 1860s and the Red River (Métis) turbulence of 1869–70. His leadership skills won him appointment in the new police establishment in 1873. He built Fort Walsh, and by force of temperament would prove his mettle dealing with the Indian transients from the United States. The Scottish-born Macleod (1836–94) shared a militia background and served during the Red River Expedition of 1870. He joined the leadership of the North-West Mounted Police in 1873, becoming assistant commissioner in the following year, when he built Fort Macleod. Macleod became commissioner in 1875. He adopted a policy of treating Native peoples respectfully, and his special relationship with the Blackfoot fostered good relations that facilitated his negotiation of an important treaty with those people. It was the duo of Walsh and Macleod, former military officers now vested with civil authority, which monitored Canadian-Indian relations in the territory. Over the next few years, both men significantly ensured peace, not only as regarded their own Native peoples but with the Lakotas and Nez Perces from below the "Medicine Line."[2]

The Lakota eminence proved just a matter of time. The first body came over in late November, 1876, and consisted predominantly of Brulés under Lame Brulé from north of the Yellowstone, totaled fifty-seven lodges, and comprised perhaps 400 people.

Another mixed Lakota group—of fifty-two lodges—arrived on December 19 under Black Moon, a major Hunkpapa chief, together with leaders Little Knife, Long Dog, and Man Who Crawls. Superintendent Walsh reckoned the total Lakota assemblage at Wood Mountain at that time to number approximately 2,900 people (500 men, 1,000 women, and 1,400 children), besides some 3,500 horses and "30 United States Government mules." In council with the Tetons, who camped near a village of peaceful Santees who had been in Canada since the 1860s, Walsh learned the Indians' rationale for coming north: they had "been driven from their homes by the Americans, and had come to look for peace. They had been told by their grandfathers that they would find peace in the land of the British; their brothers, the Santees, had found it years ago, and they had followed them." On his superiors' authority, Walsh instructed the Indians in British law as it affected their stay in Canada, drawing assurances from the chiefs that they would not use the country as a basis for renewing "hostile operations against the United States." The officer also permitted the Lakotas to trade for a small lot of ammunition with which to hunt. Walsh stationed several Mounted Police at Wood Mountain to monitor ammunition arrival and disbursement. He further established a communications network—"lookout posts"—between the Cypress Hills and Wood Mountain so that he could keep better informed of the situation regarding the Sioux.[3]

Perhaps motivated by the reception of their kin at Wood Mountain, other Lakotas arrived within weeks. On March 3, 1877, Four Horns, leading spiritual and political leader of the Hunkpapas, appeared near Wood Mountain with fifty-seven lodges, along with a band of disgruntled Yanktonais under Medicine Bear from the Fort Peck Agency on the Missouri. They were destitute, and reported having had to consume the flesh of their horses during their march to Canada.[4] Again in council with the leaders Walsh spelled out the conditions under which the tribesmen might remain in Canada, a litany repeated yet again in early May when the Hunkpapa leader Sitting Bull, a principal in the Native coalition against the U.S. Army in 1876, appeared in the vicinity of Wood Mountain with 135 lodges of people and sixty mules. These included his own Hunkpapa following besides smaller bodies of Sans Arcs and Minneconjous under Spotted Eagle and Swift Bird, respectively. The people had lost many tepees when the level of the Missouri River rose suddenly the day after they crossed. Contemporary estimates of the total number of Lakotas in Canada following Sitting Bull's arrival vary significantly, ranging from a low of between 4,000 and 4,200 people in 600 lodges (including 1,800 warriors) to a high of 5,000 (including 1,000 warriors).

The presence of so large a body of Lakotas caused a certain unease among Dominion officials, beginning with Commissioner Macleod, who knew of the enmity between the Sioux and the Blackfoot as well as that between the Sioux and the Crees.[5] In March, Macleod notified David Laird, lieutenant governor for the North-West Territories, of his concerns, and proposed measures for dealing with the Lakotas, and in a missive to Prime Minister Alexander Mackenzie, he summarized what would become, in essence, immediate British policy regarding the presence of the Lakotas from the United States on Canadian soil:

> I would respectfully suggest that communication be opened up with the United States Government to ascertain upon what terms they would receive them back, and I fancy that they would only be too glad to have them return, as their presence so near the boundary line cannot but be a source of continual anxiety and trouble, and it would be impossible for the police to keep them in check over such an extended frontier; that the Indians be then told of the terms of the United States Government, that they cannot be recognized as British Indians, that no Reserves will be set apart for them, and no provision made for their maintenance by our Government; that by remaining on our side they will forfeit any claim they have on the United States, and that after a few years their only source of support— the buffalo—will have failed, and they will find themselves in a much worse position than they are at present.[6]

Over the next several years, the recommendations contained in Macleod's letter of May 30, 1877, embracing what one historian has described as a policy of "benign discouragement," guided negotiations between Canada and the United States concerning the Sioux and any other Indians (including the Nez Perces), who might cross the "Medicine Line" seeking sanctuary. British officials were cognizant of the general bad treatment American settlers and politicians had shown to the Indians; a committee of the Privy Council went on record to urge the U.S. government to adopt "a humane and prudent policy [that] may induce the Indians to return to their Reserves and pursue a more peaceable life in the future." For the present, however, concerns centered on Sitting Bull, who had received substantial media attention in the United States, especially following the Custer defeat. In early June, Walsh and Assistant Commissioner Acheson G. Irvine met the chief 140 miles east of Fort Walsh. Irvine described him as "a man of somewhat short stature, but with a pleasant face, a mouth showing great determination, and a fine high forehead. When he smiled, which he often did, his face brightened up wonderfully." In council on June 2, Sitting Bull expressed his reason for crossing into Canada: "I came to see the English, where we are going to raise a new life. . . . I saw that they [the Americans] were running us in every direction. That is the reason I came to see you." Irvine listened, then told the chiefs that they "must not cross the line to fight the Americans and return to this country." Further, he promised only enough ammunition to maintain subsistence through hunting. Sitting Bull acceded to the conditions and declared his intent always to stay north of the line. Referring to the recent sale of the Black Hills by the reservation Sioux under pressure from the U.S. government, he concluded, "What would I return for? . . . Once I was rich, plenty of money [wealth], but the Americans stole it all in the Black Hills. I have come to remain with the White Mother's [Queen Victoria's] children."[7]

The taking of the Black Hills by a commission negotiating with the agency Sioux in Dakota and Nebraska had occurred in September 1876, and satisfied an early objective of the U.S. government's war with Sitting Bull's and Crazy Horse's followers. Commanding General William T. Sherman had regarded these tribesmen as a "band of outlaws," and now noted that Colonel Miles, from his post on the Yellowstone, was "very anxious to go to the border with a sufficient force to demand of the British Agents that these Indians, now reduced to absolute want, and almost devoid of ammunition, be surrendered to him as prisoners." Sherman believed that the British should either "adopt these refugee Indians as their own or force them back to our side of the line before they recuperate their ponies and collect new supplies of ammunition." As did Dominion authorities, he feared the Lakotas would use Canada as a base of operations from which to repeatedly strike into the United States then withdraw north of the line. Sherman urged a mission to the Sioux to induce their return and offer them safe conduct south to various agencies "subject to the same terms and conditions of the others of the Sioux tribe who have surrendered, viz., to give up their arms and ponies . . . and thereafter live at peace on their Reservation."[8]

By midsummer 1877, while the Nez Perce War proceeded below the border, there were already mounting fears among Canada's own Indians above the "Medicine Line" (Crees, Assiniboines, Blackfoot, Piegans, Bloods, Saulteaux [Plains Ojibwas] and Sarsis) that the presence of the Lakotas meant competition for food, principally in the form of buffalo. These tribesmen generally hunted buffalo in the southern part of the territory where the herds ranged; coincidentally, it was the same area occupied by the Lakotas in 1877, and their competitive threat for the dwindling food resource was thus front and center. Mainly because of the effects it would have on Canadian Native peoples, British authorities feared "embarrassing consequences" if the Lakotas remained or enticed other American Sioux to follow them north. There were also underlying fears that Sitting Bull might orchestrate other disaffected tribes, including at least one attempt involving Nez Perce impetus (see chapter 4), into a hostile coalition that might trend to violence. Therefore, Canadian Secretary of State Richard W. Scott believed "it would be unwise to lead them to believe that they will be allowed permanent residence and treated as Canadian Indians," a position that translated into a need to convince U.S. government officials to try and persuade the chiefs to return south. To that end, dialogues proceeded in Washington between British and American diplomats, including Secretary of State William M. Evarts, to resolve the issue.[9]

According to Evarts, the Lakota tribesmen were considered "political offenders seeking asylum in a foreign country," and under existing treaty provisions the United States could not pursue their extradition. He believed that "Canada would not probably tolerate that American troops should cross the frontier to drive the American Indians back into the territory of the United States. Neither probably would she agree to drive them back with her own police into the arms of the American troops." The dilemma might be resolved, proposed British chargé d'affaires in the United States Francis R. Plunkett, if "the United States Government will be so good as to use their best endeavours to induce those Indians to return to their own country." He urged the United States to propose to the Sioux "tolerably favorable terms on which to return," while Canadian authorities would seek to persuade their acceptance of such terms and to otherwise promote their return. When Plunkett allowed that the Lakotas were not citizens but wards of the U.S. government without political privilege, Evarts countered that his government should not be expected to "hold out great temptations [for them] to return," as they were "savages whom they were only too happy to have got rid of, and who had committed all sorts of crimes before quitting the United States."[10]

From these conversations, as well as from the appearance in Washington, D.C., of Canadian Minister of the Interior David Mills, came direction and attempted resolution of the issue regarding the Sioux. Mills arrived August 8 unannounced from Ottawa (but at the behest of Prime Minister Alexander Mackenzie) to introduce himself at the British legation and to consult personally on the topic with President Rutherford B. Hayes, and with Acting Assistant Secretary of State Frederick W. Seward, Secretary of the Interior Carl Schurz, and Secretary of War George W. McCrary. The Americans advanced a proposal whereby the Sioux would be withdrawn some four hundred miles back into Canada from the boundary so as to remove the threat of their crossing back into the United States, but Mills explained that this was impossible because of Canada's "insignificant mounted force" and the large number of warriors. The stage was thus set for formulation of what became known as the Sitting Bull Commission (also known as the Terry Commission, after Brigadier General Alfred H. Terry, commander of the Department of Dakota in Saint Paul, Minnesota, who would chair the body). The cabinet approved such a course on August 10, 1877. Since Great Britain normally handled Canada's foreign affairs, Mills's maverick action eventually brought a reprimand from London and an apology from Canada for circumventing proper authority.[11]

The issue involving Sitting Bull's people (and later the Nez Perces) with the United States and Canada held implications under existing international law. Accordingly, each government was responsible for protecting the neighboring government's territory from the hostility of armed refugees who had crossed the border seeking asylum. The imminent commission, said Secretaries McCrary and Schurz (both of whom believed the State Department should properly oversee such a diplomatic endeavor), would seek accord with the Indians because "the President recognizes the difficulties which, in dealing with a savage population, may attend its [Canada's] fulfillment" of its international responsibility. In light of its concurrence regarding the need for a commission, the United States would strive to "avert a disturbance of peace on the border, even to the extent of entering into communication with an Indian chief who occupies the position of a fugitive enemy and criminal." While the Canadians were most interested in ensuring the commission's success in convincing the Indians to return to the United States, American officials were less enthused about that prospect than in determining "what danger there may be of hostile incursions on the part of Sitting Bull and the bands under his command upon the territory of the United States, and, if

possible, to effect such arrangements . . . as may be the best calcu-
lated to avert that danger." In fact, as the *National Republican* concluded, "It would be pleasing to this [U.S.] government if the
proposition did not succeed, as Sitting Bull is not a denizen desired
by any country." If the Indians refused to return to the United
States, the commissioners would be charged "to break off all communication with them, and the Government of Great Britain will,
no doubt, take such measures as may be necessary to protect the
territory of the United States against hostile invasion."[12]

With the concurrence of the War Department and General Sherman, who had favored such a course, Canadian Secretary of State
Scott accordingly proposed that the American commissioners
convene at Fort Benton, Montana Territory, around October 1,
1877, and that North-West Mounted Police Lieutenant Colonel
Macleod formally greet them at the international boundary the
next day. Scott telegraphed Macleod to "co-operate with [the]
Commissioners, but do not unduly press [the] Indians." At a cabinet meeting at the White House on August 15 (one of three in
which the mission was discussed), General Terry emerged as the
War Department appointee to the commission; Canadian-born
John McNeil of Saint Louis, Missouri—a brigadier general of that
state's troops during the U.S. Civil War—was also named. Moreover, the proposition was advanced (in accordance with international law stipulating that "foreign territory cannot be made the
basis of hostile operations") that should the Sioux initiate attacks
in the United States, the Canadian government, as protector of the
people, must be prevailed upon to remove the offending tribesmen from within American borders.[13]

In retrospect, the selection of Terry proved colossally porten-
tous. As overall commander of the troops who had fought Sitting
Bull and Crazy Horse, his physical presence could do nothing but
remind the Sioux of the recent past and steel their resolve against
returning. The following weeks were dedicated to logistically
organizing the commission and preparing its members to meet
the Sioux. In the North-West Territories, the Mounted Police kept
watch over the tribesmen to see that they did not go below the

line. All remained quiet. "The latest intelligence," wrote the American consul in Winnipeg, "was that Sitting Bull and his band were busily engaged in killing buffalo and preparing pemmican near Wood Mountain." In Ottawa, Minister Mills anticipated that the Indians would reject outright terms calling for them to surrender their arms and ponies in return for complete immunity, a position that would doom the mission to failure. In addition, he feared a backlash in the United States toward Canada: "These Indians," he wrote Macleod, "were reported to be guilty of acts of such barbarous cruelty that should they again return for the purpose of scalping women and children, their conduct could not fail to excite the indignation of the government and the people of the United States against this country." He instructed Macleod to "use your influence to promote, so far as you well can, the object of the United States Commissioners in securing the return of those Indians to their own Reservations." Further, and contrary to Secretary Scott's admonition not to "press" the Indians, he conveyed a blunt admonishment of the Sioux: "You will also inform those Indians that, should they go for any hostile purpose into United States territory, the Government of the United States may be permitted to follow them with their army into Canadian territory; and that in such an event they must not look for the friendship or protection of the Canadian Government." This statement was considered confidential information and at all events was not to be communicated to the American commissioners.[14]

Although British and Canadian officials hoped to expedite the commission's business and thus resolve the Lakota situation as soon as possible, and repeatedly urged such a course in Washington, its appointment and implementation was repeatedly delayed over the late summer of 1877. At the outset, finding suitable volunteers for such a sensitive mission took time; moreover, although sponsored by the Bureau of Indian Affairs, there was no congressional appropriation with which to fund the trip, so those selected at least initially had to consent to absorb their own expenses. Illness postponed the arrival of General Terry in Washington; sickness soon compelled General McNeil to resign his appointment altogether. Retired Colonel Francis A. Walker, a brevet brigadier general of volunteers during the Civil War, was contacted to replace McNeil, but he declined the position. Even more setbacks could be expected in the course of the commission's reaching the Sioux camp—depending on the state of navigability of the upper Missouri River to Fort Benton, which would become increasingly difficult as the season progressed—and determination of the point on the 49th parallel at which the commissioners would meet a Mounted Police escort to accompany them north. As well, unsubstantiated reports (later proved untrue) that Sitting Bull with thirteen hundred warriors had recrossed the boundary into American territory, and that Colonel Miles was mobilizing to receive him, compounded the matter as to whether the commission would be one of peace or war. Certainly there existed some hope that the reports were true, for, as Washington's *National Republican* reported, "[I]t will save our Government the humiliation of sending Commissioners to that untamed barbarian, who has twice badly defeated our military forces." For a moment, at least, depending on Sitting Bull's location above or below the border, Plunkett suggested the issuing of two sets of instructions to the commissioners—one to apply if the Sioux had remained in Canada, and the other if they had returned to the United States.[15]

Miles—whose campaigns in the autumn of 1876 and winter of 1876–77 had been responsible for the Teton exodus from Montana Territory into British America to begin with—was at first uncertain whether Sitting Bull had indeed returned to U.S. territory, or even had contemplated such a return. It is clear that the colonel was no diplomat. In messages forwarded to the Hunkpapa leader, Miles did nothing to ease the situation and, if anything, probably exacerbated things. In a communication dated August 19, Miles threatened him: "I told you when I saw you last year [at Cedar Creek, Montana,] what I should do if you remained hostile. I say the same now. If you come back to fight, the soldiers will fight you and follow you until you are destroyed." Two weeks later he warned: "If you return for war, the English Territory will no longer afford you a safe retreat, for the two governments have decided that you shall no longer disturb the peace of both." In both tidings, Miles extended the army's terms of submission— surrender of horses and arms and acquiesce fully to the will of the government "as the other Indians who have surrendered here." Despite the supposed proximity of Sitting Bull's Indians had they, in fact, crossed back into the United States, Miles's attention was shortly thereafter directed to the Nez Perces who were then making their way through Yellowstone National Park and ultimately toward Canada. On Tuesday, September 18, he departed Tongue River Cantonment with a command over five hundred strong to begin a movement northwest that would culminate twelve days later in his attack on the Nez Perces near the Bear's Paw Mountains. Indeed, Miles's operations against the non-treaty Nez Perces would produce important implications for the Terry Commission's work affecting its schedule, besides having a profound impact on its outcome.[16]

In early September, however, amid constant prompting by British and Canadian officials, efforts proceeded to assemble the commission and get it into the field before cold weather set in. Since fears existed among the Americans that the commissioners might be exposed to Indian treachery—as had resulted during a council with Indians in California four years earlier when Major General Edward R. S. Canby had been murdered by the Modoc leader Captain Jack—a body of Mounted Police was deemed necessary to accompany General Terry's party. In response to this request, Canadian Deputy-General William B. Richards promised "to have a strong escort at whatever point on the boundary the American Commission may designate." He added: "We have no fear of treachery on Canadian soil." It was agreed to meet at the point where the road between Fort Benton, Montana, and Fort Walsh transected the line. On September 8, the final commission was named. Besides General Terry as chairman, it consisted of Albert Gallatin Lawrence, a diplomat from Rhode Island who had previously served as U.S. attaché in Vienna, as Minister to Costa Rica, and, in 1875, as a commissioner to treat with the reservation Sioux over the Black Hills;

and Captain Henry B. Corbin, Twenty-fourth Infantry, only recently of the White House staff, as secretary. The members would convene September 11 in Saint Paul and three days later travel via Omaha on the Union Pacific Railroad to Corrine, Utah Territory, then north by stagecoach to Helena and Fort Shaw. From that point, two companies—one each of the Seventh Cavalry and Seventh Infantry—under Captain Henry B. Freeman would escort them to Fort Benton. The plan then called for them to journey from there to the border and be escorted north to meet Sitting Bull in late September.[17]

In the meantime, Colonel Miles's expedition against the non-treaty Nez Perces proceeded. Troops earlier en route to conduct General Terry's commission to the Canadian line were recalled after Miles learned that the Nez Perces had crossed the Missouri northbound. These troops—Companies F, G, and H under Captain George L. Tyler—instead joined Miles in the initial attack against the Nez Perces' camp near the Bear's Paw Mountains on September 30, an engagement that ended in severe casualties for the army and caused Miles to prosecute the people in siege fashion for five days, until the majority surrendered on October 5, 1877.[18] Miles's involvement in the Nez Perce War brought a sudden yet temporary halt to the commission to meet Sitting Bull. By early October, Terry, Lawrence, and Corbin, along with newly hired Saint Paul stenographer Jay Stone—all sufficiently outfitted for cold weather—had reached Fort Benton, where there were rumors of Miles's fight and where the exigencies of his campaign soon eclipsed their request for an escort to the line, and the members were forced to wait indefinitely at the river port while their wagons and escort instead bore provisions to aid Miles. Meantime, the Mounted Police escort ordered by Commissioner Macleod had arrived at the designated point on the line on October 4 (and was scheduled to meet the American delegates the next day) but was subsequently recalled to await word from Terry.[19] During the interim, Superintendent Walsh traveled 120 miles from Fort Walsh to Sitting Bull's camp at Pinto Horse Buttes, 40 miles from Wood Mountain, but learned that the Hunkpapa leader was not interested in meeting the commission from the United States. Walsh experienced difficulty convincing Sitting Bull of the importance of meeting the commission. For one thing, disease had taken his nine-year-old son, and the Hunkpapa leader was mourning his loss. Making Walsh's mission even more difficult was the proximity of the Nez Perce Indians ensconced at Bear's Paw, just 40 miles below the line. Some Nez Perces had already reached Sitting Bull, beseeching the Hunkpapa leader for help against Miles's soldiers, who had laid siege to the Indians' position. Many of the Sioux hoped to respond in aid of the Nez Perces, but Walsh cautioned them on that course, explaining that if they did so they would forfeit their privilege to live peacefully in Canada; the government would prevent the warriors' return into Canada and would drive their families south of the line. Above all, and finally complicating his effort to bring Sitting Bull to Fort Walsh, was the coincidental arrival of a large body of Nez Perce refugees from Bear's Paw. Walsh described their appearance at length, as follows:

> [During our meeting] one of the scouts came up, reporting a large party coming from the direction of the boundary line. In a few minutes more another arrived, stating they were whites. This aroused the whole camp; horses were driven in, warriors mounted their horses and started off in the direction of the approaching party, and the women commenced taking down the lodges and packing up. I tried to convince them that it was foolish to act as they were doing, as no white men would come to do them any injury. They said it might be their enemies. At this time the excitement was intense, so I told them I would ride out myself and ascertain who the party were. This appeared to please them very much. I mounted my horse and started in the direction of the advancing party. About two hundred warriors followed me. When about two miles out we met another scout, who informed me it was a party of Nez Perces who had made their escape from the line of the battle on Snake Creek [near the Bear's Paw Mountains]. I awaited their arrival and found the

party to consist of fifty men, forty women, and a large number of children, besides about three hundred horses. Many of them were wounded—men, women, and children. Some were shot badly through the body, legs, and arms. They were conducted to the [Sioux] camp by a number of Tetons and distributed through the lodges. When I returned I found the horses packed and the camp in readiness to move. On hearing it was the Nez Perces, the Indians met again in council and addressed me as follows [respecting the meeting with the Americans at Fort Walsh]: "Why do you come and seek us to go and talk with men who are killing our own race? You see these men, women, and children, wounded and bleeding? We cannot talk with men who have blood on their hands. They had stained the grass of the White Mother with it,"—meaning by the arrival of the Nez Perces.[20]

Despite this development, and to his credit, Walsh managed to convince the Lakotas not to aid the Nez Perces and to travel with him to Fort Walsh: "The Indians about concluded that it would be suicide for them . . . to render any help to the Nez Perce[s]."[21] "They asked me to remain one more night and they would go with me, [and] I consented."[22] Next morning, together with Sitting Bull and perhaps twenty-five of his followers, Walsh started for the post in the Cypress Hills. En route, some sixty miles from the post, he encountered Commissioner Macleod, who himself had set out for the Indian camp. As Macleod later wrote Interior Minister Mills:

Walsh reported to me that he had great difficulty in inducing them [the Sioux] to leave their camp, and that they were continually stopping to smoke and reconsider their decision to come. The fact that about 100 Nez Perces men, women, and children, wounded and bleeding, who had escaped from the United States troops, had come into their camp the day before they had left, appeared to have a great effect upon them, and they were evidently afraid that the American soldiers would not be prevented from crossing the line to attack them.[23]

What had happened at Bear's Paw and in its aftermath ultimately profoundly influenced the outcome of the commission sent to induce Sitting Bull and the Lakotas to return to the United States. Although the Sioux were already disinclined to accept the overtures of the United States representatives, the presence of battered Nez Perce refugees fresh from the encounter with Miles reinforced their disdain and effectively preempted any result favoring the Canadians' wishes. Macleod forwarded to Terry word of Sitting Bull's presence at Fort Walsh. The courier bearing the news also told of the arrival of White Bird and "twenty-four [Nez Perce] bucks and about thirty squaws and children" among the Sioux. In addition, he mentioned the presence of other Nez Perces who had been "constantly arriving" even while the Bear's Paw engagement proceeded to urge the Hunkpapa leader to send warriors to help fight the soldiers.[24] This was likely the first direct news Terry gained of the presence of the Nez Perces among the Lakotas.

Following his delay, General Terry notified Macleod at Fort Walsh, forty-five miles above the line, that the commission would be at the international boundary around October 14. Thus informed, the Canadian officer accompanied the police escort to the line, where Terry; Lawrence; Corbin; Stone; Freeman; Captain Edward W. Smith, Eighteenth Infantry (Terry's aide); and Baptiste Shane, commission interpreter, appeared on the afternoon of Monday, October 15, near Kennedy's Crossing of Milk River. On American soil Terry, with Corbin and Smith, approached the scarlet-clad Macleod and his constables on horseback near a boundary marker at the left of the road; Lawrence and Freeman followed in an army ambulance. The general saluted Macleod, and the officers shook hands all around. Leaving their American cavalry escort behind (Captain Tyler's three bedraggled companies of the Second Cavalry had joined them the night of October 13, arriving directly from the scene of the Bear's Paw engagement following the Nez Perces' surrender), the men, accompanied by three newspaper reporters (Jerome B. Stillson, *New York Herald;* Charles Sanford Diehl, *Chicago Times;* and John J. Healy, *Benton Record*), immediately started north, escorted by the police. Red-

suited Canadian lancers sat their animals and saluted the commissioners as they passed. Only the trailing infantrymen escorting the Americans' wagons crossed the line as servants of Terry's
commission, but their role was quickly superseded by Macleod's
own constables. (The men of the Seventh Infantry company, however, continued under arms and accompanied the group to Fort
Walsh.)[25] The delegation and escort passed through a tract called
Lonesome Prairie, blackened, said Diehl, for having been ignited
by the Nez Perces somewhere to the east, "but for what purpose
[was] insoluble." With Macleod and Terry in the lead, the party
quickly reached Fort Walsh near sunset on the 16th; there the
American troops went into bivouac. Walsh, who had remained
with the Indians, who occupied a "larger-sized room in one of the
log houses" at the post, reported to Macleod that the Sioux now
did not want to hear the Americans and wished to leave, "as they
could not believe anything they said." Yet their final disposition
to remain for the meeting was certainly due to the persuasive
powers of Superintendent Walsh, whom Sitting Bull believed and
respected.[26]

The commission met in Walsh's quarters at 10 A.M. Wednesday,
October 17, to prepare a statement for the Indians and go over it
with the interpreters (Shane plus interpreters from both Fort
Walsh and Sitting Bull's camp). Five hours later, the council
opened in the same room—evidently the largest at the post—with
the American commissioners, Mounted Police Commissioner
Macleod, and Superintendent Walsh; several other officers and
forty policemen also were present. Terry and Lawrence—with
Secretary Corbin, Stenographer Stone, and Walsh sat behind one
long table—while Macleod and reporters Stillson and Diehl sat
behind another. By all accounts, the meeting lasted one and one-
half hours and was to the point. Present for the Lakotas besides
Sitting Bull were Bear's Cap (Bear's Head), Spotted Eagle, Whirl-
wind Bear, Flying Bird, Iron Dog, Medicine Turns-around, The
Crow, Bear that Scatters, Yellow Dog, Little Knife, and a number
of lesser leaders. Initially Bear's Cap alone shook hands with the
Americans. Sitting Bull and his headmen refused.[27] The

Hunkpapa leader was perhaps indignant, too, about the presence of Terry, an officer largely responsible for command operations against the tribesmen before and after Little Bighorn. He and Spotted Eagle demanded that only the officers and reporters be present. "All seemed very angry," wrote an observer. The traditional pipe ceremony that normally accompanied such gatherings was absent. The Indians sat on buffalo robes spread on the floor and smoked individually throughout the proceedings. (Stillson reported that "until the finish all the Indians continued to smoke, smoke, smoke. . . . They smoked until the room reeked. They smoked as if they were smoking for their lives.") A brief initial interruption occurred when Sitting Bull protested one of the tables situated in front of (and apparently blocking view of) the commissioners. The chairs were immediately placed in front of the table so the commissioners were closer to the audience. The Indians then listened as Terry, through Sioux interpreter Constant Provost, read President Hayes's message explaining the purpose of their meeting—that he wanted a "lasting peace" with them with no further hostilities. The president, said Terry, offered them a "full pardon," and wanted them to return and join their friends and relatives at the agencies. "Of these bands [that have already surrendered], no single man has ever been punished for his hostile or criminal acts. Every man, every woman, and every child has been received as a friend . . . [and] has received sufficient food and clothing supplied for his support. . . . It is time that bloodshed should cease." The general also explained the only conditions on which they might return—surrender of their arms and ponies—terms anathema to the Sioux. Next, Provost translated the Sioux reaction. Sitting Bull rose from his seat on the floor and responded pointedly, telling of his affection for the Queen's land and the police (even pausing to shake hands again with Macleod and Walsh), and concluding with a statement to the Americans: "I did not give you the country, but you followed me from one place to another, so I had to leave and come over to this country. . . . You come here to tell us lies, but we don't want to hear them. Go back home where you came from." "When he cried 'You come here to

tell us lies,'" wrote Correspondent Diehl, "he advanced to the
commission and shook his forefinger at them with force and fury,
and stood there until the translation had been made." Nine, a
Yankton who had come to Canada with the Santees years earlier,
said: "You have got more lies than I can say." "These people sitting
around here, you promised to take good care of them . . . but you
did not fulfill your promises." "These people [indicating the
police], if they had a piece of tobacco, they gave me half, and that
is why I live over here." Before sitting down, Nine shook hands
with Terry and Lawrence. Several other subalterns then spoke,
followed by a woman, The One that Speaks Once, the wife of Bear
that Scatters, who stated, "I wanted to raise my children over
there, but you did not give me any time. . . . These are the people
that I am going to stay with and raise my children with." Her
words were duly interpreted by the baffled Provost, who was
obviously surprised by the deliberate insult of her orchestrated
appearance before the commissioners. Later, The Crow, a
Hunkpapa, asked, "What do you mean by coming over here and
talking that way [telling lies] to us?" When Terry inquired
whether he should tell the president that the Indians refused his
offer, Sitting Bull replied, "That is all I have to tell you." "This part
of the country does not belong to your people. You belong on the
other side; this side belongs to us." When Terry asked, finally, "Do
you refuse?" Sitting Bull turned abruptly and said, "I told you
what I meant. That should be enough." Soon after that, General
Terry, smiling, told them, "That's all," and the council ended.[28]

Immediately following the meeting, Commissioner Macleod
spoke to the Lakotas, emphasizing to them the imminent consequence of their answer to Terry and the others. He reminded them
that his government looked upon them as United States Indian
refugees on Canadian soil, and he told them,

> The answer you have given the United States Commissioners
> to-day prevents your ever going back to the United States with
> arms and ammunition in your possession. It is our duty to pre-
> vent you from doing this. I wish to tell you that if any of you or

your young men cross the line with arms in your hands that then we become your enemies as well as the Americans. . . . If you do this, that wall . . . will be broken down and the Americans may be permitted to cross the line as well as we can.

"I pointed out to them," Macleod wrote the commissioners of his post-council interview with the Lakotas, "that their only hope was the buffalo; that it would not be many years before that source of supply would cease, and that they could expect nothing whatever from the Queen's Government except protection as long as they behaved themselves." Sitting Bull had responded to Macleod: "To-day you heard the sweet talk of the Americans. They would give me flour and cattle, and when they get me across the line they would fight me. . . . I could never live over there again." Macleod was very interested in the Lakotas' grievances against the Americans—overrun lands, broken treaties, and so on, and for future reference in case of difficulties between the United States and Canada arising from the Indian situation on the border, he meaningfully dispatched Walsh to the refugee Nez Perce camp to solicit from them the same type of information that had impelled those people on the four-month travail taking them from Idaho to Montana and then into Canada.[29]

General Terry and his party departed Fort Walsh on October 18, the day after the council ended without success. An escort of Mounted Police accompanied them to the line, which they reached the next afternoon, when the U.S. troops took over and guided them south to Fort Benton, where they arrived on October 23.[30] By then, word had gone forward in the media that "the commission has met Sitting Bull and Sitting Bull has dismissed it abruptly and disdainfully. The expedition has failed in its purpose." "The plenipotentiaries," allowed the *New York Herald*, "were metaphorically tossed." From Fort Benton, the party journeyed down the Missouri in "two spacious and well-built mackinaws," gained Fort Buford on November 3, and from that point traveled to Bismarck in army ambulances. On the 8th, they rode the Northern Pacific cars to Saint Paul, Department of Dakota headquarters, where they adjourned, to reconvene in Washington three weeks later and file their official report. The outcome of the effort to orchestrate Sitting Bull's return to the United States frustrated both sides, but mostly the Canadians, who wanted the Lakotas gone. In December, Minister of the Interior David Mills became convinced from the newspaper reports that the Indians had not fully understood the American proposals. He wrote Macleod, advancing a strategy to induce the tribesmen to change their minds, telling his North-West Mounted Police commissioner to inform the Sioux leader that "should they be prepared to accept the offers made by the Commission, the President would, you are persuaded, be willing to assign to them a reserve out of the Indian territory, where the climate and the soil are both better than in the locality where their present reserve is situated"—a debatably untrue statement at best. Mills charged Macleod with "strictest secrecy" in broaching the topic with Sitting Bull, and to "prevent any notice of it from getting into the public papers."[31] However, this plan to re-engage Sitting Bull on the issue of returning to the United States seems to have fallen away over the course of time.

In the end, the so-called Sitting Bull Commission yielded mixed results. Although it did not convince the Lakotas to return to the United States as the Canadians desired, it did ascertain, according to its members, that because of the Indians' refusal of the commission's terms there would likely be no "hostile invasions" for the present. From the American perspective, remembrance of Colonel Miles's unrelenting operations against the Lakotas, which had in fact driven them north in the first place, would hopefully serve to continue to keep them above the line. Moreover, the Canadians' initial desire for the commission to woo the Indians back oddly created an extenuating effect that favored the Americans: "For some reason which they cannot fathom," noted the commissioners' report, "the Government of the United States very earnestly desires that they shall return. This belief has been confirmed and strengthened by the visit of the commission and the very favorable offers made to them. In their intense hostility to our government they are determined to contravene its wishes to the best of their ability."

Although the Americans did not want the Sioux back (an Interior Department entry simply noted, "Sitting Bull and his adherents are no longer considered wards of the Government"), officials worried that their pervasive influence on neighboring tribes below the boundary, like the Yanktons and Assiniboines, could spell trouble, stimulating among them disaffection and encouraging acts of hostility. The refugee Lakotas, stated the commissioners, would remain a bad influence: "We have already an illustration of this danger in the fact that more than one hundred of the Nez Perces defeated at Bear's Paw Mountain are now in Sitting Bull's camp." They concluded that Sitting Bull's people should indeed be removed far into the interior of Canada, there to be interned so that "they can no longer threaten, in any manner, the peace and safety of the state from which they have come." Furthermore, General Terry, on his return to Saint Paul, would urge construction of a new post on the Missouri River, or between the Missouri and the international boundary, to closely keep watch over the Indian situation with respect to the line. Meantime, the department commander also directed that another company of soldiers bolster the Fort Benton military station.[32]

In fact, however, the very real likelihood was that the Lakotas (and perhaps the Nez Perces) would indeed return to the American side when subsistence needs dictated. As the *Benton Record* averred, a Sioux presence was but a matter of time: "Notwithstanding his promises to remain upon Canadian soil, Sitting Bull will, in common with all the Northern Indians, follow the buffalo, no matter what direction the latter may take, and as the buffalo are almost sure to roam on this side of the line during the winter months, it is safe to say that hunger will frequently compel the Sioux Chief and his followers to come south of the line." That probability, furthermore, was rife with grave international import. While the Mounted Police represented an insufficient body to contend with the Sioux, "since the action of Sitting Bull [in rejecting the American terms] has compelled them to accept the responsibility, they will be held accountable for [any such] invasion of American soil, and very serious complications between the

United States and Canadian governments may be the result." On balance, opined the paper, "we consider it [that is, the outcome of the Terry Commission] a complete success, the advantages being all in favor of the American Government."[33]

Indeed, the Canadians feared that if they failed to control the Sioux they would reap the ire of the Americans; the British, meantime, feared that by extension they would be subject to the American disaffection toward Canada. Secretary of State Evarts, in temporizing things, called on Canada to keep the Sioux in check, yet held out hope that his country would yet induce the Indians to return to the United States.[34] As indicated, the results of the Terry Commission, as well as its aftermath among the Sioux, bore obvious impacts from the Nez Perce conflict. Likewise, in the wake of the Tetons' resounding rejection of the commission lay the premise of a similar course by those non-treaty Nez Perces who reached Canada during and following the concluding army operations against their kinsmen near the Bear's Paw Mountains in northern Montana Territory. That final struggle and its outcome would hold serious implications for all of the non-treaty Nez Perce people, as well as for the Tetons, the Canadian government, and the U.S. Army during the subsequent turbulent period as it affected operations and policy along the northern frontier.

CHAPTER 3

ESCAPE FROM BEAR'S PAW

The appearance of the Lakotas in Canada presaged by just eleven months the arrival there of refugees of the non-treaty Nez Perces. What had become a final flight for sanctuary for most of those people ended abruptly following Colonel Nelson A. Miles's attack on their camp along Snake Creek just northeast of the Bear's Paw Mountains in northern Montana Territory, forty miles below the Canadian line. Most of the principal Nez Perce leaders were killed during the six-day assault and investment by the army command; Chief Joseph and his people yielded at 2:20 P.M. on October 5, 1877, followed by others of the exhausted tribesmen. Over the following days and weeks, detachments of soldiers ranged through the surrounding country seeking out Nez Perces who had either eluded the fighting altogether before the attack commenced or had survived the initial assault and subsequent siege and managed to escape between September 30 and October 5, and afterward. Enemy Assiniboine and Gros Ventre (Atsina) warriors, recruited by the troops, also searched for the Nez Perces, sometimes killing or otherwise threatening with death those people who had fortuitously avoided or fled the combat at Bear's Paw.[1]

The Nimiipuu had set up their camp along Snake Creek on September 29, following their movement north from the Missouri

River. Their numbers approximated 700 or more people, including perhaps 250 warriors. It was ground well known to them as Tsanim Alikos Pah (Place of the Manure Fires), and they knew that Canada lay but forty miles away. Yet the dissension that had fairly permeated the convoy since the Big Hole battle and their passing through the National Park persisted, and many of the people were now further distraught over their treatment by the Crows, whom they had counted on to help them. After covering nearly twelve hundred miles since their trek began in Idaho, the families were worn out, especially the elderly and the young children. Many of their horses had become lame, too, their condition constantly aggravated by the unrelenting daily marches. Compounding all, disputes over leadership of the assembly had reappeared, as Looking Glass complained about Poker Joe's direction of affairs and his tendency to want to rush the people forward. Just days before, Looking Glass challenged the need for such a rapid pace and pressed his claim for leadership with the inter-band council, which presently restored his authority. Despite this, the Indians planned to stay at Snake Creek but one night and resume their way north the next morning.[2]

By the time that Colonel Miles's column of soldiers struck the Nez Perces some time after 9 A.M. on September 30th, the people were already busy with their daily routine and preparing to move out. Not everyone remained in the village: several men had gone hunting earlier, and a number of women had gone out on the prairie to skin and butcher buffalo killed the previous day before packing it for the day's journey. Still others had crossed the Snake Creek rivulet to the plateau west of the camp where most of the horses grazed, to select mounts to ride or be packed before pulling out. Among these were Joseph and his daughter, twelve-year-old Kapkap Ponmi (Noise of Running Water). Nez Perce informants later stated that scouts from the camp had by this time determined that soldiers were near and had shouted warnings. And Wottolen, who later became tribal historian, had dreamed during the night of an impending attack. Looking Glass largely discounted the concerns until other scouts rode in to raise an alarm that the troops were practically upon them, and by that time it was too late. In the sheer terror of the moment, however, fewer than two dozen quickly mustered Nimiipuu defenders hurriedly advanced and delivered a surprising and powerful counterblow to the cavalry assault, causing the troops to reel back with casualties, and forcing Miles to reassess his situation and by day's end to decide to lay siege to the position.

In the tumult of the attack, some of those Nez Perces who were away from the camp could not return. Others began to break away from the encampment in the opening moments following assaults by the army's Northern Cheyenne scouts who were operating in advance of the troops and approaching the herd. At least fifty and perhaps as many as seventy or more people on horseback evacuated the camp, driving a number of horses before them. Joseph, amid the herd when the attack commenced, told his daughter to catch one and join the others streaming north. He called to those out retrieving horses to hurry. Then, as they started north away from the advancing soldiers, he ran back to the camp through a hail of bullets that tore his clothing, grabbed a rifle, and took part in the defense.[3]

A number of Nez Perce accounts given decades later described the escape of those people from the village and the start of their movement toward Canada. Mrs. Wounded Head recalled:

> I had just returned from across the creek where the horse with sick feet was, and was standing barefooted by the fire and inside the poor shelter of canvas propped up on the windward side, when we heard Many Coyotes and one other man calling from the nearest bluff that they had seen the enemy—Indian scouts back of the hill—and had had a narrow escape from being killed, and that we would be attacked immediately. My mother told me to go out and see if it was true, what we heard. . . . Far up the rising slope to the south I saw the enemies coming, riding hard. I did not return to the canvas shelter. I heard the cry go up: 'Save the horses! Save the horses!' Barefooted and with only a shawl above my common dress, I ran

swiftly for the horses. The soldiers on us, I could not return for
my mother and sister. I found my father, Wat-tas-ine, there
watching the horses. I gave him my rope and he went to lasso
the horses. His son, my brother Peo-peo Ilp-pilp [Red Bird]
went with him. They caught four horses. Chief Joseph was calling: 'Get hurry! Get hurry! Get hurry and going!' We mounted
the horses and left. Only one blanket, I rode bareback as did the
rest. Going quite a distance, we stopped. We listened to the
guns back where they were fighting. I cannot tell the distance,
but we were outside the battle. There we stayed till the evening
drew on. The night darkness came about us and still we do not
travel further. Not only ourselves, but Chief Joseph's older wife
[He-yoom-u-yikt] and daughter are with us. But people are
scattered everywhere, hungry, freezing. Almost naked, they
had escaped from the camp when the soldiers came charging
and shooting. Thus, we remained overnight. We must not build
a fire. No bedding, cold and chilly, we stood or sat holding our
horses. We cried with misery and loneliness, as we still heard
the guns of the battle.[4]

Similarly, years later Reverend Mark Arthur recalled his experience as a thirteen-year-old Nez Perce boy in the Bear's Paw
camp: "That morning I went out to look for horses. One had
strayed off and when I had found him and returned to the herd I
heard shots fired and the bullets whistled near me. I kept on and
tried to get back to our camp, when some people came running
out and met us. About this time I looked and the high bank back
[south] of the camp was black with soldiers. The Indian scouts
with the soldiers had now got very close to us and we fled down
the creek. We camped that night—a small party of us—on the
same creek on which the battle was fought. . . . That afternoon we
killed two buffalo and roasted the meat that night and so had
plenty to eat. All of us were mounted."[5] And Black Eagle, visiting
the Bear's Paw field in 1928, recalled his own actions as a teen
there in 1877 in somewhat more detail:

The camp was getting ready to move. I left, going after the horses. . . . I saw our horses not far away. I heard at that moment a halloo in the camp. Turning, I saw everybody in confusion, those scattered rushing back to camp and getting their guns. I heard a rumbling like stampeding buffaloes to the south, and looking I saw troops galloping toward us. I knew well what that meant, and I ran for the horses. I had soldier shoes on which were too large and heavy for the soft going. I stopped and took them off, leaving them there on the ground. The horses were wise to the shooting, and all began stampeding. I have no rope, no bridle. I have a blanket, and I tear it to make the rope. I catch Peo-peo Tholekt's [Bird Alighting's] horse by overtaking him. I put my rope around his neck but I cannot jump on him as a man. I climb on him and follow a lot of horses down to the bottom where Chief Too-hool-hool-sute and others were soon to be killed. There are many Nez Perces, some on horses. I saw women and children, and Peo's mother was there. She asked for the horse I was on and I gave it to her. She handed me my blanket-rope and I soon caught my own horse. Another woman gave me a strap about three feet long which helped me to make the Indian bridle about the under jaw of my horse. Then we rode! We drove the horses down the creek and went up on the hill. . . . The Cheyennes [scouts] attacked us there, firing at us from some distance. Then soldiers appeared and shot one of our mules. We hurried, going a little farther, climbing the highest butte. I looked back and saw all the Cheyennes and soldiers had left, going back to the battle. This was the last I saw of them. We were now on the highest butte [Big Butte] where we watched the horses for some time before moving on.

Black Tail recollected that "there were about fifty who thus escaped, Peo-peo Tholekt among them."[6] Young Samuel Tilden also remembered being among the horses with his mother, having raced to the herd as soon as the soldiers appeared. "The foremost enemy I saw was a bonneted Indian [scout] on a spotted horse.

Our horses were ready saddled. . . . There were no pack horses ready. . . . Many people got away without moccasins, and no clothing worthwhile, and no blankets."[7]

In the initial charge on the camp by Miles's force, the Second Cavalry quickly diverged left, to the northwest toward the plateau where the large herd of horses, mules, and ponies were located. By the time that the troops reached the herd, the Nez Perces had commenced driving off the animals in two bunches. The cavalrymen succeeded in retaining one group of perhaps 500, but the Indians succeeded in driving away the other part of the herd, numbering some 250 animals, some already packed, following the sallies of the Northern Cheyenne scouts.[8] When the troops saw these people moving away distant about one-half mile north of the camp, Second Lieutenant Edward J. McClernand led a company of the Second Cavalry to head them off. A running encounter occurred over a distance of perhaps five miles that was altogether detached from the main engagement going on simultaneously at the camp, as McClernand's soldiers tried to halt the fleeing tribesmen and capture their animals. In this exchange, Nez Perce men held a front against the troops to keep the horses secure while the women followed. The soldiers and scouts repeatedly tried to get between and separate the groups, but the women stayed close and prevented that from happening. Moreover, as soldiers captured small numbers of horses, they pulled away to guard them, and McClernand soon found his effective numbers dwindling. Soon he broke off the pursuit and defensively postured his men while withdrawing back to the main command fighting at the camp. The cavalrymen evidently managed to capture the greater share of the herd taken north by the escaping Indians.[9] Among the people with this group of escapees was About Sleep, a boy who rode with his brother mounted behind him on the same horse. "Our warriors are passing shots with the cavalrymen," he recalled. "They are close together, mixing it up. Soldiers continue sending shots at us, but they cannot stop us. My little brother, holding right to me, has one braid of hair shot off close in his ear. Two soldiers pursue us but are driven back before they catch us."[10]

Besides this relatively large group of people (apparently between fifty and seventy in number), there were others who managed to either escape at the outset of the attack under different circumstances or had gone from the camp before the fighting started. The women who had left with pack horses to skin buffaloes killed by Nez Perce hunters were proceeding with their work when the shooting erupted in the distant camp. (One of these women was In-who-lise [Broken Tooth], who had been wounded at the Big Hole encounter in August.) The hunters approached them and together they ascended a ridge from which they saw the soldiers in the distance near the camp. The men told the women to continue their work while they tried to return and help defend the people. But they could not safely go back, and when they returned to the women they told them about the Cheyenne scouts and the troops and their inability to get into the camp. This group of men and women stayed hidden in the vicinity of the battleground until after October 5, when Joseph and the others surrendered. The five days were cold and wet, but the group remained to see what the outcome might be, and to decide whether to turn themselves in to the soldiers or go to Canada.[11] Elsewhere, a young unidentified Nez Perce girl somehow escaped the commotion of the attack and headed down Snake Creek. After going some distance, she encountered a body of horses and managed to catch one. She manufactured a bridle from her clothing, then mounted and rode the animal down a coulee where she encountered two Indian women who had likewise fled the camp. One had a broken arm, and when the girl attempted to help her on the horse she accidentally pushed her completely over the back and onto the ground and the woman cried in pain while the young girl in the sudden humor of the moment could not keep from laughing. The three sought help at a cabin along Milk River, and the two women eventually made it into Canada, while the girl apparently found relief at the then-abandoned agency of Fort Belknap.[12]

For the Nimiipuu who were away from the Bear's Paw camp or who managed to flee before or during the initial army attack on the morning of September 30, the next few days were uncertain if not totally confusing, as well as dangerous for several reasons. As mentioned, some of the men attempted to get back into the camp to help fight the soldiers and protect the people. (In fact, a few men succeeded in returning. Numb Fingers, No Fingers, and Yellow Head got back into the camp two days after they escaped the initial attack.[13]) But the likelihood of accomplishing such a measure faded after Miles's initial assault collapsed and his troops secured the perimeter preparatory to laying siege to the tribesmen's position. Instead, the refugees from the camp either remained in the area to see what was happening to their friends and families or started north toward the border. Those who took the latter course generally traveled in the dispersed pattern in which they had left the camp—groups large and small. One thing is certain—it was a fearful time for those ill-prepared Nez Perces venturing north amidst bad weather, roaming detachments of soldiers, and enemy tribesmen seeking reward or compensation from the army for tracking them down and killing them.

Surviving Nimiipuu accounts of the journey from Bear's Paw into Canada universally describe the travails the people encountered en route. The weather remained stormy with rain and snow, and the refugees—many without proper attire, including footgear, and some almost naked—suffered terribly. As noted, too, some delayed their departure from the camp/battlefield area and thus were exposed to the elements for longer periods. Black Eagle declared that "we were between three and four days reaching Sitting Bull [in Canada]." "It was two or three days before we reached some Crees who gave me moccasins and other clothing. Barefooted, I had no coat, no hat, no blanket. It was cold and stormy as we traveled. It was about all I could do keeping from death by freezing." Moreover, the weather was so "stormy, [that] part of the time we did not know which direction we were going. Cloudy, cold, and stormy, [with] nothing by which to be guided." Mrs. Wounded Head affirmed this view, stating that it was "stormy and snowing, the sun shut from sight and no stars at night, [and] we could not know which way to go." The people experienced little difficulty in crossing Milk River because the water was shallow at that time of the year. Also, Mrs. Wounded Head explained that "always somebody knew where the rivers were not deep for the riding."[14]

Mrs. Wounded Head remembered that following the first night, September 30, the people in her group ("about ten women, some children, and some men") moved on down Snake Creek but stayed in the general area: "About three days and nights we stayed off aways from the camp where the battle was being fought." On October 2, "we could still hear the cannon-guns. The battle was still going on. Nothing to eat all that day, all that night [that] we remained there. Though no food nor fire, I grow sleepy. All of us fall asleep. After a while we feel as if a blanket is covering us. It is snow!" On the 3rd they continued down the creek and met some Nez Perce men building a fire. The people warmed themselves and spent the night there. "It is still snowing," remembered Mrs. Wounded Head. "Four days in all we are hiding, no food, starving and cold. . . . I am barefooted." On the fifth day out from Bear's Paw (October 5), this group pressed on toward Sitting Bull's village and in the evening the warriors succeeded in killing a buffalo. The people built a fire and roasted and consumed the meat. Next day they encountered some Plains Ojibwa (Chippewa) Indians from whom they received food, clothing, and—in Mrs. Wounded Head's case—a pair of moccasins. "Then I feel better," she related. "But I never forget that I was five suns without food. I never forget how I suffered with cold and hunger." "We had no blankets when we escaped." "Only for the friendly Chippewas, I think I should have died with the cold." At the Ojibwa camp they also were given matches to use on their journey. Meantime, Mrs. Wounded Head's husband himself later escaped the soldier-cordoned camp at Bear's Paw attired in breechcloth and moccasins. "He was freezing that night," she recalled. "The daylight came and he killed a soldier and dressed himself in the dead man's clothes. He killed a second soldier, whose clothes he gave to Indians needing them. He kept both their horses. . . . [Later,] Plains Cree Indians traded him their own clothes for the soldier clothes he wore. The Crees told him it was not best to be found wearing soldier clothes and riding soldier horses."[15]

By far the largest body of Nimiipuu to escape from Bear's Paw did so on the night of October 5–6, following Joseph's surrender, when the Lamtama chief, White Bird (Peopeo Hihi), with a large number of followers somehow managed to clear the tightly posted army investment of the Nez Perce position and steal away in the darkness.[16] White Bird (or, more accurately translated, White Pelican), a respected medicine man among the Lamtamas, had been recognized as chief years before the 1877 conflict. Although his age in 1877 is debated (some say he was forty-nine years old, while others claim he was seventy or more), he stood nearly six feet tall and was muscular and broad shouldered with a strong, handsome face. White men who knew him said "he was of an agreeable disposition and exhibited a desire for fairness." He had been a major leader in the inter-band hierarchy at the inception of fighting near his village in White Bird Canyon in June, and he had played a significant role in turning the fortunes of the people following the army attack at the Big Hole. Yet all throughout the ordeal of the people's movement from Idaho into Montana, White Bird had been constant in his determination to reach Canada, and during the several councils in which the leaders deliberated over where to go, although abiding with each majority decision, he had remained steadfast in his advocacy for crossing the border, and at Bear's Paw his opinion remained unchanged. Evidently, Looking Glass by this time agreed with White Bird on the Canadian objective, despite Joseph's own decision to yield. On October 5, Looking Glass reportedly told White Bird, "We will leave here tonight," but he was killed by an army marksman within hours. The seeming disagreement between Joseph and White Bird regarding the former's decision to submit to Miles against the will of the latter has been repeatedly misinterpreted as resulting from a deep schism of authority within the Nez Perce ranks, when in fact it went to the heart of the people's tribal government dynamic. In emergency situations, individual chiefs spoke for their own followers and not for others, and it was understood that even individuals might set their own course, too. As Ollokot's wife recalled, "People were divided. Some would go with Joseph, some with White Bird. The fight was over and nothing to stay for." Thus, following Joseph's surrender, 87 men, 184 women, and 147 children accepted the terms and gave up the fight; fewer than 6 of White Bird's followers turned themselves in then. White Bird reportedly declared at the time that "What Joseph agrees to is all right," although it in no way signified his own submission or intent.[17]

Particulars of exactly how White Bird and his wife and such other of his people extricated themselves from within the military cordon supposedly surrounding the Snake Creek camp remain largely unknown. The surrenders initiated in the afternoon by Joseph's submission, however, continued until well into the night. The only plausible explanation is that the darkness and snowfall— as well as topography—amidst the movements and ongoing commotion, likely afforded a relatively easy opportunity for White Bird and his followers to pass unnoticed by the troops and outlying pickets, apparently at around 9 P.M.[18] (Indeed, Yellow Wolf, who [traveling alone] was probably the last to leave the camp for the north toward morning of the same night, stated that "during the night soldier guards [pickets] were all about us. Only the guards; all other soldiers sleeping.") It was after nightfall on October 5, remembered Mrs. Ollokot, "when I escaped with Chief White Bird and his band all afoot.... We walked out leaving many of our friends. Some were too bad wounded to travel and had to stay.... Night drew on as we left. We had blankets but not too heavy for the traveling. Not enough to keep us warm when camping. It was lonesome, the leaving. Husband dead, friends buried or held prisoners.... Strong men, well women, and little children killed and buried. They had not done wrong to be so killed." Another woman related that "we left in the night while many of the warriors were still giving up their arms."[19] And another who went remarked "that they crept out quietly. Soldiers saw them but did not fire."[20]

A statement by Lucullus V. McWhorter, who collected many Nez Perce recollections, indicated that the Indians escaped during "a blizzard-swept night."[21] According to Wottolen, who accompanied the chief, each man carried a gun and ammunition: "We carried only a little grub. We could not travel fast because of the women and children."[22] The precise number of people who departed with White Bird varies considerably in different accounts; most indicate that as many as fifty got away. One oft-cited account was that of Duncan MacDonald, who wrote of the Nez Perce War from the Nimiipuu perspective for the pages of *The New North-West*, published in Deer Lodge, Montana. Mac-Donald was part Nez Perce through his mother, spoke the language fluently, and managed to interview White Bird later: "In the escaping party were one hundred three warriors, sixty women, eight children. . . . One remarkable feature of the party was that there were no dogs with them. An Indian procession is usually considered incomplete unless there are in it a number of these latter animals. In a residence of thirty years in the Indian country, I have not heard of a parallel case."[23]

Whatever the number who went with him, the movement of White Bird and his followers over the ensuing several days until they reached Canada proved difficult in the extreme. The weather was brutal, with intermittent blizzard conditions attending the journey across the bleak scape to sanctuary in Sitting Bull's camp. According to accounts of participants in the fearsome trek, most of the people wore inadequate clothing, with some practically naked. Some endured wounds received in the Bear's Paw action. Because of the women and children and the wounded, they moved slowly afoot along the Snake Creek bottom to reach Milk River, which was shallow and forded with relative ease. Wottolen said that the movement lasted about ten days, and "we had but little to eat. We traveled slow. We stopped often and sat down to let the women and children rest." Ollokot's widow remembered that the trek was without food for the first two days, when some pronghorns were killed and eaten.[24]

Fully descriptive reports by observers of White Bird's party during its movement north have not been found, although two statements exist that mention this group. The Oblate Catholic priest and missionary Jean Baptiste Marie Genin wrote of his encounter with these Nez Perces at a "half-breed" camp near Milk River: "As we were preparing to enter our winter quarters, one very dark night, our camp was suddenly filled with Nez Perces Indians. Among them was White Bird, a Nez Perces chief. Nearly all except him were badly wounded. We had heard the cannon fire two days previous, but did not know anything about the Nez Perces' war. The fight could not have been over fifteen miles from us. I began at once the work usually performed in hospitals. How could a priest refuse his attention to suffering humanity? The good half-breeds fed these poor Indians, whilst I washed and wrapped their wounds."[25] Another missive describing something of White Bird's people, perhaps at the same camp, was written to Colonel Miles by John Howard, one of his scouts, who encountered them just before they entered Canada. "After leaving your command," he told Miles, "I met 'White Bird' (Nez Perce) and 14 warriors & about 7 women at the Half Breed Camp about 5 miles from the line En route to the Teton camp. They were at first willing to surrender but 'White Bird' dissuaded them, and in spite of all the inducements I offered I could not get the Halfbreeds to help me attack them."[26]

Those Nez Perces who escaped from Bear's Paw, or who were otherwise away from the camp during the course of the army attack and siege, quickly became the subjects of military pursuit in the aftermath of Chief Joseph's surrender. Realizing that those who fled north during the initial assault were bound for Canada, Colonel Miles hoped to preempt their arrival there, and on October 3 he wrote Terry asking "that information be sent to the British authorities to prevent any portion of the Nez Perces tribe crossing the line, or to disarm them should they take refuge on English soil."[27] Six days later, following the surrender, Miles directly expressed to Superintendent Walsh his concern regarding White Bird's group:

I have the honor to inform you that at the engagement with the Nez Perces on Eagle Creek on the 30 ulto., and prior to the surrender of that tribe on the 5 inst., some 30 or 40 warriors, with squaws, papooses and some 200 horses, ponies, &c. left the main camp with the prospective intention of taking refuge in the Canadian dominions. This band was, presumptively, led by "White Bird," he being of the party, and I would request that should this party cross the boundary line they be compelled to return to the United States, or be disarmed and held prisoners until communication can be had with the higher authorities and their pleasure in this matter be ascertained.[28]

In the immediate aftermath of the surrender, Miles dispatched at least three detachments of troops to range through the country and seek out the scattered parties of Nimiipuu. At the same time, he sought help from civilians and from Native enemies of the tribesmen—particularly auxiliaries drafted from among the regional Assiniboine and Gros Ventre tribes—to find these breakaway Nez Perces and kill or capture them. Reportedly, the colonel promised one local resident twenty-five horses from the Nez Perce herd, plus $500, for getting White Bird "dead or alive." One of the army detachments consisted of Second Lieutenant Marion P. Maus and ten men who were sent toward Milk River to head off tribesmen near the Canadian line. They were joined by a detachment of Seventh Cavalry, and over the course of fifteen days Maus and these men succeeded in capturing a dozen Nez Perces, who were delivered to the Tongue River Cantonment on the Yellowstone River.[29] In addition, forty mounted volunteers reconnoitered the western part of the Bear's Paw range and northeastward toward Milk River seeking "to pick up any outlying parties of the Nez Perces" who might still be in that area.[30]

Perhaps worse than the roaming army detachments seeking to find and capture Nimiipuu refugees from Bear's Paw were complicit enemy tribesmen who sought to kill them. Miles wrote, "the Assiniboines are killing the Nez Perces as I sent them word that they could fight any that escaped and take their arms and ponies."

Some camps of Gros Ventres simply refused to accept the Nez Perces, but in other instances the contacts proved deadly. Long-standing intertribal enmity now surfaced as Assiniboines and Gros Ventres, seeking to appease American army commands operating in their country, readily engaged in locating the people in their desperate circumstances, sometimes turning on them with deadly surprise. On October 3, even before the surrender, a party of Gros Ventres met some Nez Perces along the south fork of Box Elder Creek, killing five men and capturing one woman and one or two children. Soon after the surrender, a group of Assiniboines that included Moccasin, Thunder Bird, Speak Thunder, Prowling Dog, and Wetan, retrieved army mules and property from Nez Perces along Milk River, and during a thirteen-day scout captured four of the people and killed seven others. Elsewhere, more refugee Nez Perces were reported along the Marias River; some approached a Gros Ventre camp but were turned away by those tribesmen.[31]

In one of the worst incidents involving enemy people killing the refugees, five Nez Perces—reportedly scouts—went into an Assiniboine camp where they were disarmed before being "turned loose on the flat and chased and shot . . . like buffalo." The men were identified as Strong Eagle, Calf of the Leg, Hide Scraper, White Hawk, and Wamushkaiya.[32] In a similar instance, two women and three men seeking help approached Indians in the vicinity of Fort Belknap, where they were welcomed and given breakfast in a lodge. But afterwards the Gros Ventres and Assini-boines took them to a sandbar on Milk River—some five or six miles west of modern Chinook, Montana—where a Gros Ventre warrior named Long Horse shot them to death, reportedly because Colonel Miles had warned them against harboring fugi-tive Nez Perces.[33] Maneuvering in this area in the wake of Joseph's surrender, Lieutenant Scott came on the scalped bodies of the five Nimiipuu scouts killed by the Assiniboines. The Assiniboines told Scott that they gave the Nez Perces a good dinner. "After their dinner," he recollected, "they started toward the Gros Ventre vil-lage, and were allowed to get some miles away, when the young

Assiniboine braves saddled up and went out and killed them all, and their scalps were there hanging on a pole to dry in the wind."[34] A journal entry given by a private in Miles's command that might in fact elaborate on this same incident described two Canadian Frenchmen coming among the soldiers on the evening of October 7 to relay a report that Indians in a mixed camp of Gros Ventres and Assiniboines killed fourteen Nez Perces and captured many of their ponies. And when an officer wrote his mother about the casualties at Bear's Paw, he noted that "5 Indians were killed outside [the lines] and 11 more were killed over on Milk River by the Gros Ventres and Assiniboines, to whom these 11 had gone for assistance."[35]

These accounts seemingly applied to the people who fled Bear's Paw during the opening assault on September 30. But White Bird's followers also suffered at the hands of enemies. When apprised of White Bird's departure, Miles reportedly remarked, "I haven't got any use for White Bird. I've got all his traps [personal belongings; goods] and don't think he is worth a mule." He reportedly told local resident William Bent to get the word out at Milk River "not to kill any more Nez Perces." Yet the colonel later notified General Terry, "White Bird crept out of camp. He was reported wounded, and I have sent the Assiniboines for him." Duncan MacDonald stated via his interview with the chief that seven warriors were killed by Assiniboines and Gros Ventre as White Bird's party made its way north. They included Umti-lilp-cown, who helped commit the Salmon River murders in Idaho that had spawned the warfare with the army in June.[36]

There exist other isolated accounts of the killing of escaping Nez Perces by enemy tribesmen. Some fortunately evaded the seeming treachery of the Assiniboines. Such a group wandering the wrong way doubled up on horseback and lived on raw buffalo meat. One evening they approached a camp of Assiniboines who gave them a lodge and cooked buffalo meat. During the night a Gros Ventre woman informed them that the Assiniboines planned to turn them in to the troops, so most of them got away—leaving behind young In-who-lise, who was ill, and who remained in the camp through the winter and joined a band of Pend d'Oreilles. Gros Ventres pursued yet another group from Bear's Paw who presently managed to drive them away. A man, Kous-chute, had both legs severely wounded, and he insisted that his colleagues go on without him, which they finally did. Afterwards, more Gros Ventres found him and tendered aid, which he rejected. At Kous-chute's appeal, the Gros Ventres at last killed him. Still others— at least fourteen—met death at the hands of Crow, Northern Cheyenne, and Blackfoot tribesmen.[37]

Exactly when the first Nez Perce escapees from Bear's Paw crossed the "Medicine Line" and connected with the Teton Sioux is not known. Apparently, several warriors who were out hunting at the time of Miles's attack, or who somehow broke away and could not return to the camp, preceded any of the larger groups who made it into Canada. According to the Nimiipuu, at least three men identified as Half Moon, Left Hand (Wep-sus-whe-nin), and Wel-la-he-wit arrived to tell the Lakotas about the fighting at Bear's Paw below the line, perhaps with the hope of recruiting Sitting Bull's warriors to help counter the army there. These Nez Perces could not speak the language, nor were they adept at sign language. When they tried to sign for "water" and "stream"—to connote Snake Creek—the Sioux misunderstood it to mean the Missouri River, a considerable distance away and too far to travel for them to be able to materially assist the besieged Nez Perces. Soon after, perhaps on October 4, three more men (Peopeo Tholekt, Koo-sou-yeen, and James Williams) reached the Sioux and managed to straighten out the confusion.[38] Some Nez Perce accounts suggest that a sizable number of Sioux mounted an effort to go to Bear's Paw and help against the soldiers, but arriving refugees told them it was too late and they turned back.[39]

The arrival of the first large group of Nez Perces took place on October 8. That was the day that Superintendent Walsh met with the Sioux to convince Sitting Bull to go to Fort Walsh and meet General Terry and the commission sent to try to induce him to return to the United States. It is clear in Walsh's report that the advent of the Nez Perces startled the Sioux, almost as though they had not been previously apprised of their coming, which is in contradistinction to Nez Perce accounts, as those cited above, that specify an earlier arrival of some of those people. Walsh reported that the party consisted of "fifty men, forty women, and a large number of children, besides about three hundred horses." He said that many were wounded, "shot badly through the body, legs, and arms." The Sioux greeted them, and the timing of their arrival, as previously discussed, carried implications for Sitting Bull's subsequent meeting with the commissioners regarding the Tetons' future.[40] As Walsh commented years later, Sitting Bull "declared he could not comprehend the meaning of Terry's coming to ask the return of the Sioux" after having just driven the Nez Perces out of the United States:

> He was coming to offer him [Sitting Bull] a home for himself and people, and yet had just taken from Joseph and his people the home occupied by the Nez Perces for 200 years. What had Joseph and his people done to be treated so[?] Joseph and "White B[ird]" and their people had always been friends of the Whites. . . . They lived in wooden houses, had schools and churches, and believed in the white man's god. ["]They drive this man from them today, and tomorrow ask me, who they call a wild man, a hostile, a killer of white men, a hater of an American, to come back and they will give me & my people a home and clothe and feed us[?] With [such] evidence before me, can I be otherwise than suspicious of these men's purpose[?"][41]

A Lakota account speaks of an early meeting with Nez Perces that perhaps involved this first group. According to Black Elk, an Oglala youth who had recently been fighting the Crows in the border country, "Just as they came up there about the time I was going to pull the trigger I recognized them as tokas [enemies], but they were [in fact] friends. They were a bunch of Cut-noses (Nez Perces). One of them could speak Sioux, and he said, 'How!' They asked me what I was doing here. They all hollered not to shoot that they were friends. I told them that I thought they were enemies and I was ready to kill him. They asked me where we were going and we rode back with them to the band. When we got back to camp, everyone put their arms around the shoulders of the people and began to wail. I cried all day there. It was hard work crying all day, but this was the custom."[42] Walsh later wrote that "the Sioux were jubilant over the arrival of the Nez Perces & took them into their lodges and fed and looked after them, cared for the wounded, and finally gave [the] refugees new lodges."[43]

Within a few days of the first Nez Perce arrivals among the Sioux, White Bird and his followers reached the camp. The precise date of arrival of these people has not been confirmed, but it is likely that they showed up on October 11 or 12. Superintendent Walsh reported that "one party of thirty and another of ten persons arrived there two or three days after my leaving the camp with Sitting Bull and chiefs [on October 9]."[44] From this statement, it is not certain whether both parties arrived on the same day. It is certain that by the time of Walsh's return from Fort Walsh with Sitting Bull and his headmen on October 21, White Bird and his followers were present in the Sioux camp. Yellow Wolf was among one of the last Nez Perce parties to reach the Lakota camp, which they approached warily because in the past the two tribes had not been friendly. But the Sioux welcomed them and took them into their tepees. One of them told Yellow Wolf, "'Nez Perce Indian, you are now my friend. From this time on.' . . . They gave me everything I asked, just as if I were one of their children."[45] The Nez Perces were in bad shape. One reportedly had a broken arm in a sling; another had been shot and was still bleeding from a bullet wound in the chest. Sitting Bull's people treated them kindly, and gave feasts for them. Peo-peo Tholekt said that "Sitting Bull was a fine man. He was very kind to us and to his own people."[46]

On Monday, October 22, Walsh met with the newly arrived Nez Perces in a circle prepared at the center of the Lakota camp. White Bird was introduced as "chief of the escaped Nez Perces," and spent a considerable amount of time describing the travails of his people—doubtless as a rationale to explain the people's sudden presence seeking sanctuary in the Queen's country, as well as to verbally preempt any effort by the Canadians to turn them back. "They appeared very anxious to let me know (so that I might inform the White Mother)," Walsh wrote, "how badly they had been treated by the Americans." White Bird recounted the transgressions of the past, the mounting murders of Nez Perce people by whites with impunity, the problems with General Howard before the war broke out, and the difficulty that that officer had imposed on the people with his directive to remove themselves and their stock onto the reservation: "My brother and Joseph decided if the soldiers came to drive us from our country we would fight them; the soldiers came and we fought. We were informed we would find peace in this country, and came to it." Walsh's accounting of Nez Perces in Canada indicated that "there are 90 men and 200 women and children in the Teton camp." As for their future, he reported that the Nimiipuu "are divided as to what they will do—whether they will remain in the Teton camp or move to the Cypress [Hills]. They appear to have a desire to live with the whites. They speak a great deal about living in a house like the white man and going to church. They say they are very poor, and scarcely know what to do." Walsh thought that with a good interpreter the Nez Perces might be convinced to accept the terms given Joseph and go back, "as a great many of their wives and families are with Joseph."

In the meeting, Walsh further learned that on about October 16 a white man and a Nez Perce Indian sent by Colonel Miles had visited the Lakota camp to try to convince the Nez Perces to surrender. Fortunately for them, the Tetons had protected the two, who assuredly would otherwise have been killed by the irate tribesmen:

> The Tetons told the Nez Perces that no blood could be shed in their camp, that the law of the White Mother would not allow it, and persons wishing to remain in the Teton camp would have to obey it. The Nez Perces claimed that these men had assisted in killing their tribe. The Tetons replied, "If these men have done you any injury we will keep them here until one of

the White Mother's chiefs arrives. . . ." Two nights before my arrival the Nez Perce Indian escaped, and one night after the white man made his escape. The Tetons informed me they were not closely watched, but were permitted to go about the camp as they liked. I really believe the Tetons assisted them in making their escape.[47]

From this meeting Walsh gained an assessment of White Bird: "While not much of a speaker, [he was] a very intelligent man of fine and good judgment." He regarded the Lamtama chief as "less diplomatic than [Sitting] Bull, but more clear in perception and quicker in decision."[48] The meeting provided Walsh and the Canadian government valuable perspective on the Nez Perce presence on their soil; it also afforded clues into future actions by some of the Nez Perce people as they dealt with their situation far from familiar surroundings and absent friends and relatives they would come to miss very much.

Walsh's late October tabulation was probably close to the mark as to the total number of Nez Perces who entered Canada in the two major groups of arrivals from Bear's Paw. In addition, it probably included other smaller parties or individuals who reached the Lakotas between and after the arrivals of October 9 and October 11 or 12. Owing to his experience with the Teton Sioux and other tribes, Walsh was certainly practiced in counting Indian people, so from that standpoint his contemporary estimates appear credible. That of October 22—of 290 Nez Perce people ("90 men and 200 women and children") among the Lakotas—represents the most finite calculation of those present on Canadian soil, and while that figure was assuredly approximate, it was based on Walsh's accrued insights and knowledge. (The Nez Perce Black Eagle provided a careful estimate of as many as 234 "who reached the Sioux camp in Canada," a figure somewhat within tolerance of Walsh's 290.) The official tally of those who surrendered to Colonel Miles at Bear's Paw stood at 448. Yet that figure—along with 25 tribal Bear's Paw fatalities plus an estimated 30 for those killed en route north—subtracted from 700 (the approximate number of Nimiipuu in the Bear's Paw camp at the inception of the fighting), yields but 197—a sizable difference from Walsh's stated total of 290 for those reaching Canada. While the discrepancy is likely explained in part by continuing vagaries in numerical accuracy respecting the size of the non-treaty assemblage from the time of its departure from Idaho until it reached Bear's Paw, it is also possible that the count of 448 included some of White Bird's people who had surrendered and later fled the army cordon with the chief as darkness settled over the field. There are probably additional factors to explain the variance, and although Major Walsh's figure of 290 is doubtless close to accurate, the true number of Nimiipuu escaping to Canada most likely will never be known.[49]

According to White Bird, as recounted nearly a year later, the chief counciled with Sitting Bull on several occasions. In one instance, probably soon after the Nez Perces' arrival, the Hunkpapa reiterated the conditions imposed by the Canadians—strictures that must be abided by to insure the Indians' continued acceptance on British soil. "He strongly advised me," White Bird told Duncan MacDonald in July 1878, "to prevent my Indians from crossing the line, saying: 'We must do as the Police tell us— behave ourselves here and not go or allow our men to go into American . . . Possessions to commit depredations. Should we do so, we will surely get into trouble. The Police don't lie like the Americans, and we must respect them. Now mind what I say, we get our protection from them and we must respect our protectors!' To this I quite agreed."[50]

Nonetheless, there are statements that some time after the arrival of the Nez Perces among the Sioux, "after the people had rested a few days," Sitting Bull led a party of ten Lakota and nine Nimiipuu warriors, along with three Nimiipuu women, to the Bear's Paw battle site to see whether the soldiers had left. The Hunkpapa chief reportedly traversed the battlefield with these people and retrieved ammunition cached there before heading back. It is also possible that some Nez Perces and Sioux continued the journey to Cow Creek looking for caches of goods in that vicinity. Army letters documented such activity, and Father Genin recounted it also. While it is likely that this happened, it apparently took place in November or December, somewhat later than Nez Perce and Sioux reminiscences specify.[51] But if Sitting Bull and the Nez Perces indeed took part in such an adventure, they did so at the great risk of offending Superintendent Walsh and their Canadian hosts and of jeopardizing both tribes' continued sanctuary in the Queen's land.

In the wake of their victory at Bear's Paw, American army officials downplayed the escape of any of the Nez Perces, including White Bird's followers, after Joseph's surrender. Neither Colonel Miles nor General Howard fathomed that nearly three hundred of the people had escaped from the battle site, and references to a "few" of the Indians getting away—as were promulgated in contemporaneous army correspondence—thus never threatened the significance of the success. In official correspondence, initially, Miles continued to downplay the reality that a large number of the Nez Perces had managed to elude army sentinels posted around their position and subsequently made their way into Canada. Far from ignoring the escape of those people, General Howard twisted the knowledge to his own devices, referencing his request to Miles to help in the campaign against the Nez Perces as resulting in the "capture or *driving [of] the Hostiles* beyond the limits of the United States [emphasis added]." Later, commending Miles for his success (preceding the divisive rancor between them over credit for the achievement), Howard wrote him on October 7, while yet on the Snake Creek battlefield, and lauded the colonel for conducting "a forced march of nearly three hundred miles, a quick attack, [a] successful battle ending with capture of the main body of the enemy, their chief and their main camp, and the driving of the remnant across the boundary of the United States."[52]

CHAPTER 4

Nez Perce Expatriates and the Teton Ordeal

In their flight from the scene of the Bear's Paw attack, the refugee Nez Perces traveled north-northeast into Canada from Milk River. After meeting the Lakotas, they shared the lodges in Sitting Bull's village along Frenchman's Creek (also known as White Mud Creek), an affluent of the Milk some twenty miles above the line and a like distance west of the slopes of Wood Mountain. Here they stayed, many of them recuperating over the next days and weeks from injuries received during the fighting with Colonel Miles's command or resting from the ordeal of their months-long trek and escape. The Lakota people continued to embrace the Nimiipuu. Speaking generally of his people's time with the Sioux, Black Eagle remembered that "Sitting Bull was very good with the Nez Perces," he shared food resources with them, and the two tribes hunted buffalo together.[1] Initially, the Sioux scattered the people among their lodges, a move that was misunderstood and that at first worried Yellow Wolf: "I knew we never were friends to the Sioux Indians, and it must be they meant to kill us." Shortly thereafter, however, the Lakotas invited the Nimiipuu to smoke with them and allowed them to search for their relatives; when found, the newly arrived people were permitted to move into tepees shared by their kin and the Sioux families.[2]

Although they had difficulty communicating with the Nez Perces—both tribes often resorting to sign language in their exchanges—the Lakotas, at least at first, seemed genuinely glad to have them in their midst. One measure of extending hospitality to them was through the staging of "a great war dance," and a recollection of this event survives among Nimiipuu sources. According to Wottolen, the Sioux signed to one man, Mool-mool-kin, that they, the Lakotas, would dance first, followed by the Nez Perces. Following that, the Nez Perces would select a man to explain the warfare with the whites and tell the Sioux hosts what he personally had accomplished. Mool-mool-kin gave Wottolen a pledge stick, representing a spotted horse he owned that he wanted to present to honor their new friends. "Give this stick to whatever Sioux you select to take this horse," he told him. Wottolen agreed, and after the dance he explained his exploits, which another Nez Perce translated into English, and which a Sioux in turn translated into Lakota. But rather than give away the valuable horse, Wottolen instead stripped his only shirt from his body and presented it to the selected man, returning the pledge stick to Mool-mool-kin.[3]

The Nez Perces remained close to the Lakotas during their first few months in Canada, largely because of their desperate condition and their need to reconstitute themselves as an identifiable group entity following their ordeal. It appears that after several weeks in the Sioux tepees the Nimiipuu began to rebuild their own semblance of a camp community, with lodges and materials donated by their hosts. The mixed-blood trader Jean-Louis Légaré, who operated his post at Willow Bunch on the north side of Wood Mountain but twenty miles above the line, recalled that he saw relatively few of the people who came on horseback to his store late that autumn. Most stayed in their apparently restructured camp near Sitting Bull's village. "Never saw many of them Nez Perces," wrote Légaré, "[only] 10 or 12 lodges. [They] never mixed much with the other Indians." And furthermore, "they did not like much the Tetons. They had their camp away from the other."[4]

Miles's Yellowstone command continued to monitor the activities of the Sioux and their Nez Perce associates through the late fall and into the winter of 1877–78. Things remained tense along the line. In November, a report reached Colonel Gibbon at Fort Shaw stating that Superintendent Walsh and a force of Mounted Police had crossed the line and entered Lame Bull's Gros Ventre village where a number of Nez Perce refugees had been previously killed. They seized a Nez Perce woman held prisoner there and removed her to Sitting Bull's camp in Canada. In one unlikely account, Walsh told the Gros Ventres to give up the woman or he would "send the Sioux and Nez Perces across the line to wipe them out." In early December 1877, Lieutenant Colonel George P. Buell, commanding officer at Bighorn Post (soon to be named Fort Custer), announced the finding of two Nez Perces among the nearby Crows. One proved to be Meopkowit (Baby, or Know Nothing)—known among the whites as Old George—a Nimiipuu who had been with General Howard's command and who had been instrumental in the negotiations leading to Joseph's surrender at Bear's Paw. The two were brought to the post and George related that General Howard had given him permission to visit Sitting Bull's camp to search for his daughter, who was there. Accompanied by a white scout (see chapter 3), he gained the camp, but according to Old George the Sioux took them prisoner and beat them. George managed to escape, and reported "Sitting Bull and the remnant of the Nez-Perces were encamped either on St. Mary's-river or Milk-river." George stated that the people traded mostly with the Métis. "The Nez-Perces," he said, "want to get away, but the Sioux hold them." The two further reported that the Lakotas were planning to come into the Missouri country to kill soldiers and Crows, and that "the Nez-Perces [who presumably will come with them] will try and slip off a few at a time." Buell dispatched word to the Crows that they should not kill any Nez Perces coming from Canada, but bring them to the fort, where "I will receive their surrender."[5] Within weeks other intelligence brought additional word that the Nez Perces "wish to come back if their lives are spared and forgiveness extended to them. . . . The Nez Perces state they are badly treated by the Indians at Sitting-bull's camp—that they are whipped and treated as slaves." Miles later directed that Old George and the other Nez Perce be sent to Fort Keogh to be interrogated.[6] This information and similar reports, whether true or not, would subsequently influence an army initiative to induce the expatriate Nez Perces to return to the United States.

Despite his concern over the fact that some of the Nimiipuu had eluded his army at Bear's Paw, and his hopes of capturing and bringing back as many escapees as his roving detachments and allied tribes might find, Miles still evinced his longstanding concern over what he considered the threatening presence of the Tetons, so close to the border and the Montana frontier. Scout John Howard, who had encountered White Bird's followers along Milk River during their trek north, wrote Miles on October 20 that the Sioux had not yet learned of the death of Crazy Horse at Camp Robinson, Nebraska, more than a month earlier, and that the young Oglala war chief's last message to them had promised a renewal of warfare with the whites. In preparation, said Howard, Sitting Bull had sought a fighting alliance with Blackfoot Chief Crowfoot, who spurned the attempted union with age-old enemies and instead offered 2,000 warriors "to drive the Tetons across the line." More likely, Sitting Bull merely cemented ties of mutual amity with the Blackfeet, as well as with the Assiniboines, Crees, and other groups.[7]

Miles expressed concern over reports of late November and early December that placed the Sioux below the international line. One body of Indians reportedly hunted buffalo between the Marias River and the Sweet Grass Hills, and their presence was disturbing other tribes. Another report, cited earlier, placed Sitting Bull with Sioux and Nez Perce warriors at the Bear's Paw battlefield, their presence confirmed by "white traders, half-breeds, Crow Indians and others." Moreover, other information conveyed Sitting Bull's plan to move south across the international line during the winter months, with some evidence suggesting that many of his people (including Sitting Bull himself) plus at least some Nez Perces were already relocated on Rock Creek in a massive buildup below the line. In addition, in November more Sioux, under No

Neck, had left Red Cloud Agency in Nebraska en route to Sitting Bull's camp and were supposedly already near Porcupine Creek north of the Missouri. Still others, perhaps as many as 700 Oglalas and Minneconjous under Low Dog and Black Shield, were reported along the same route north from the Nebraska agencies in early January 1878. Miles further told his superiors that word of upcoming warfare scheduled for spring (possibly with an initial thrust at the new Fort Peck Agency at Poplar Creek) had been disseminated by the Sioux among the Gros Ventres, Piegans, Assiniboines, and Crows with the hope of their joining in a grand coalition against the whites. Miles estimated the number of Sioux (including allied Nez Perces) threatening the frontier to total 804 lodges of approximately 4000–5600 souls. While allowing that the information might indeed be erroneous, Miles averred that "it makes little difference whether Sitting Bull is individually north or south of the line; he is simply the exponent of a large body of Indians that have waged war against the Government of the United States and sought refuge in British Territory. . . . He represents a hostile element that is constantly drawing to itself strength, and, if not checked, is liable to disaffect all the Indian tribes in the North West, and should this camp remain even immediately north of the line, it will constantly threaten the peace of this section of country and be a source of annoyance and expense to the government."[8]

Miles also registered concern over the Milk River "halfbreeds" below the border who had abetted the Nez Perces and— he believed—repeatedly traded ammunition to the Sioux, and he requested authority to drive these people from the region north of the Missouri. In early November, reports noted the presence of a party of sixty Sioux and forty Nez Perces "well-mounted, armed, and painted for the war-path," in the area of the "halfbreed camp on Milk river, fifteen miles below Fort Belknap," either en route to locate caches of goods stowed in the country near the Missouri or looking for horses to steal. It is possible that this party was the same one reportedly headed by Sitting Bull himself that scouted over the Bear's Paw battleground in the weeks following that encounter.[9]

British authorities quickly provided documentation that allayed American fears. While certain of the reports regarding Sitting Bull's re-emergence south of the border had the ring of authenticity, some of them were likely trumped up and had in their purpose the manipulative ploy of certain Montana entrepreneurs and politicians bent on a lucrative objective. Their purpose was to heighten the need—as they saw it—for government construction and garrisoning of a new army post located along the frontier between the Missouri River and the Canadian boundary. While such an endeavor would offer greater security from Sioux and Nez Perces than that provided by Miles's troops along the Yellowstone and the small garrison at Fort Benton, it also meant that such an undertaking would come packaged with abundant economic benefits for citizens of the community of Fort Benton and the surrounding region. (These efforts eventually culminated in the construction of two stations: Fort Assinniboine in 1879 near present-day Havre, Montana; and Fort Maginnis [named for the territorial delegate to Congress, Martin Maginnis] the following year, below the Missouri near the Judith Basin and present-day Lewistown.)[10]

Nonetheless, the aggressive Miles utilized the reports for his own purposes, too, brazenly asking Sherman in personal correspondence (he was married to Sherman's niece) for a promotion to brigadier general, then suggesting the deployment of his troops to the border, citing the reports and rumors of Sitting Bull's arrival—or imminent arrival—below the line. He viewed the so-called "doctrine of hot pursuit"—then observed in regard to Mexico and the Apaches—as being applicable to Canada. But Sherman reined him in, warning Miles that he should not move north of the Missouri nor "without positive orders . . . cross the British line on the theory that the Canadian authorities are not acting in good faith." Muting the clamor somewhat was the report of Assistant Commissioner Acheson G. Irvine of the Mounted Police, who in January journeyed to Wood Mountain to find Sitting Bull and his people essentially occupying the tract they had before. The Nez Perces, now in seventy-five lodges, were reported to be associated with Spotted Eagle's Sioux. The rumored assembly of the tribes preliminary to a reopening of hostilities below the border had not, in fact, occurred. After a subsequent inspection, Irvine reported to the Canadian authorities that there was "no danger of Canadian Indians making an alliance with Sioux against whites." Despite this confirmation of conditions, the Fort Benton newspaper continued to cite accounts of the Sioux "swarming" on United States territory north of the Missouri, but by then Miles doubted the veracity of such accounts.[11]

Other events alarmed Canadian authorities. Commissioner Macleod had learned of an anticipated movement west by the Nez Perces into Blackfoot country: "It was their intention to supply themselves with what they wanted in the neighborhood of Fort Macleod, and make a dash through the mountains to their old homes on the other side [of the line]." A division of Mounted Police at Fort Macleod monitored this situation, "which did not appear improbable," but the expected Nez Perce movement did not occur. In the late summer of 1878, a large body of Northern Cheyennes, incarcerated in the Indian Territory (present-day Oklahoma) since 1877, broke away from their agency and headed north toward Montana, possibly—it was feared—to join the Sioux across the line. That union never transpired. Meantime, a few refugee Bannocks fleeing strife in their Oregon homeland seem to have made their way north to the Cypress Hills and Wood Mountain following a brief clash with Miles's soldiers near Yellowstone National Park. But it remained the congregation of tribesmen already in Canada—not only "American" Indians but those Canadian tribes jockeying for position relative to game availability—that brought changes in the distribution of the Mounted Police. Macleod, with approval of the Interior Ministry, concentrated the force at Fort Walsh to "strengthen the hands of our own Indians, who are very jealous of the intrusion of the Sioux," to insure against disturbances that might erupt.[12]

As for the Lakotas, their presence on Canadian soil posed a chronic problem as long as they remained. As Macleod explained,

The Sioux invasion and their continued residence in our territory have entirely changed the Indian situation, and completely upset the calculations upon which the different treaties were based, viz., that the Indians could subsist on buffalo until they became self supporting. Not only have the Sioux killed off an immense number of animals which would have been available for our own Indians; but by the continued presence of such increased numbers, they have prevented the northern Indians from securing their usual supplies, and have driven the large eastern herd south, to occupy the very gap left by the Sioux when they left their old hunting grounds. It is a matter of reasonable doubt whether the herd will ever return in anything like the same number as heretofore. I think that the straits to which the Sioux have been brought this winter will very likely soften down the antipathy to the American Government, and pave the way towards a peaceful return to the other side.[13]

Indeed, the situation of the Lakotas in Canada began to change markedly in the spring and summer of 1878. Sitting Bull may have lost prestige following the failure of the great Indian conspiracy that was to capstone his re-emergence below the line, and there are indications that his credibility was challenged by other Sioux chiefs, although such conclusions appear speculative at best. In any event, a request (initiated by Miles) by the United States to the British to have the Canadians intern the Lakotas several hundred miles from the border by April 10 was politely declined. Miles had planned to conduct operations against any Sioux found below the border after that date. Instead, he was accorded the opportunity to synchronize intelligence reports with the Mounted Police. Regardless, such a proposal proved unnecessary, for the real crippler—that began to appear in mid-1878 and to manifest pronounced change in the matter regarding the Sioux—was hunger, owing to the growing competition for declining buffalo herds.

According to a report by Assistant Commissioner Irvine in July, the Lakota Sioux and some Nez Perces were located as follows:

Spotted Eagle and Little Knife, with 35 lodges, are camped about two miles north of the boundary line, in a south-easterly direction from the east end of Cypress Hills. About twenty-five miles from this camp, north, Long Dog is camped with 13 lodges, and 20 miles south-east of Long Dog, Sitting Bull is camped with 11 lodges. About six miles north of Pinto Horse Butte, the Minacongo [Minneconjou] and 40 lodges, and six miles east of this there is a camp of 15 lodges. Twenty miles west of Wood Mountain, Bear's Cap and Pretty Bear are camped with 110 lodges, and about fifty miles east of this there is a small camp of 8 lodges. About 15 miles north of this post [Wood Mountain] there is a camp of 225 lodges, 25 being Nez Perces, the remainder being [of the deceased] Crazy Horse's [Oglala] Band.

That summer the large Wood Mountain assemblage began to scatter into smaller encampments, moving away from other bodies almost randomly to avail themselves of the dispersing herds. Some camps migrated north of the Cypress Hills and Fort Walsh. By autumn 1878 there were some 580 lodges of Sioux in Canada, mostly scattered close to the border along White Mud Creek and west and north of Wood Mountain. In time, the dispersal of those lodges affected the Lakotas' tribal cohesion, and tiny parties began to break away, some filtering back into the United States and heading to the Dakota Territory agencies for sustenance.[14]

Although by autumn 1878, the majority of the Nez Perces who had gone into Canada in 1877 had either departed for Idaho or were bound to join tribes in western Canada (see chapter 5), those who remained, along with other Nez Perces who had affiliated themselves with the United States government, would by their presence continue something of a peripheral relationship with the Lakotas. Miles remained alert to any and all possibilities of further Lakota collusion with the Nez Perces and other tribes. What subsequently happened to the Sioux therefore held real contextual pertinence for Nimiipuu fortunes as it affected their own dwindling presence in Canada. It also provided backdrop to a few rarely recorded incidents of Nez Perce history vis-à-vis the Lakotas, and, despite the fleeting nature of the intertribal liaison, the Nimiipuu story would be incomplete without relation of the close of the Lakotas' Canadian tenure.

In October 1878, Colonel Miles reported the arrival at Fort Keogh of three Sioux men who asked on what terms they might yield, to which he replied "unconditional surrender." "They represented that portion of the Ogallalla, Minneconjou, and Sans Arc tribes north of the line. . . . They stated that they had thrown away Sitting Bull and were desirous of returning . . . [and] that they were willing to surrender arms and ponies and receive cattle as the others had done that surrendered here." Miles stated that, in the wake of the Nez Perce War, he had come to regard Sitting Bull's camp as "an asylum and rendezvous for all disaffected and hostile Indians as well as a place where stolen stock has been and can be taken with safety. It is a constant menace to the peace of this region and neither life nor property is safe on this side so long as a horde of hostile Indians remain immediately across the border." He urged his superiors to consider establishing a reservation north of the Yellowstone, in the area of the Redwater and Big Dry Rivers ("an excellent Indian country filled with game [and] valuable for pasturage").[15]

Miles's recommendation was not acted upon, and must have been viewed by his superiors as most impractical because of the area's proximity to the international line and the likelihood of recurring incidents involving the Sioux and Canada. Furthermore, the colonel must have known that the game situation was changing rapidly, especially as regarded the declining numbers of buffalo. In fact, by 1878 continued competition over the herds among Canadian and American tribes had severely compromised availability of that staple. Considered foreign Indians, the Lakota and Nimiipuu refugees in Canada received neither rations nor annuities from that government. Their contest with the Canadian Blackfoot, Bloods, Piegans, Crees, Assiniboines, and others for available game promised only to compound the discord among all. When, in the autumn of 1878, Sitting Bull crossed the line for a week with a party seeking buffalo, it accelerated dissolution among the Lakotas that would culminate in their permanent return to American soil.[16]

Driven by hunger, Canada's own Indians also headed south for game, and in January reports described concentrations of Blackfoot, Bloods, Piegans, and Crees hunting in the Bear's Paw Mountains, although most later proved to be Assiniboines and Crees. Throughout late 1878 and early 1879, however, the visits by Lakotas to buffalo grounds below the international line intensified. The intermittent sojourns gained in frequency, and although they were designed for nothing more than seeking food, trouble often accompanied them. The sanctions these people had agreed to now were swept aside, and the Mounted Police were powerless to prevent the movements. In November, five Sioux hunting south of the border were fired on while they slept, and one was killed; Chief Spotted Eagle and perhaps fifty men journeyed below the line to retrieve the body and bring back meat.

Meantime, during the autumn of 1878, Sitting Bull entertained a Nez Perce–inspired notion to encourage the Crows—who themselves feared disarmament by the Americans—to join the Lakotas in exile, a concept fully alien to Canadian authorities. Sizing up their old friends, who had openly sided with Miles's command during the fighting with the Nimiipuu, six Nez Perces journeyed south in September to explore the possibility of such a union. They returned with news that both the Crows and the Gros Ventres would council with the Lakotas. At a meeting in Sioux lodges in mid-December, White Bird explained the Crow position and stated that if American troops stripped them of their guns and ponies, they would indeed head for Canada. Subsequently, the Sioux leaders decided that peace with their former Crow enemies would strengthen them should they have to face American troops moving north across the border. Yet a Nez Perce–Lakota delegation to the Sioux seeking that end failed altogether after a basic Crow propensity to take Lakota horses surfaced, and the Lakotas, in turn, plotted reprisals.

Walsh, learning of the collusion of White Bird and Sitting Bull, upbraided the latter, telling him, "You and the Nez Perces are to blame for this raid. . . . If you had not tried to plant sedition in the Crow tribe, . . . the Crows would never have sent their young men into the White Mother's country to steal horses from the Sioux." In seeming punctuation, early in February 1879, a party of Sioux hunters fifteen miles below the line was set upon by Crows while they slept. The Crows killed one warrior, severely wounded several others, and stole their horses. Mutual Lakota-Crow retaliations along the boundary continued well into the year. Furthermore, a report in March claimed that Sitting Bull and twenty-five hundred people were poised near the line, and that "his followers [were] to be found engaged in hunting buffalo at various points on the American side." However, a missive from Assistant Commissioner Irvine placed the Hunkpapa leader, with five lodges (along with White Bird and ten lodges of Nez Perces) at a place called Mud House just above the line and west of Wood Mountain.[17]

Beyond their frustration at seeing the Lakotas and Nez Perces violate their agreement not to go below the boundary, the matter regarding game prospects alarmed the Canadians, as was articulated by Prime Minister John A. MacDonald, who had assumed the portfolio of Minister of the Interior as his own: "The best authorities agree in representing five years as the maximum period for which the food wants of the Indians of the Plains may be to any reasonable extent supplied from the buffalo; and the situation is rendered all the more critical from day to day during this period, in consequence of the risk of a collision between our own Indians and those of the United States within our territory increasing, as that risk does, in exact proportion to the decrease of this means of sustenance." MacDonald suggested a revival of American diplomacy vis-à-vis the Terry Commission. "There is some reason to believe that a different spirit might be exhibited by Sitting Bull and the other leading chiefs, were they approached at the present time in a friendly way by the Government of the United States with propositions . . . of a more lenient character than those formerly rejected."[18] While Miles's scouts surveilled conditions north of the Missouri, Ottawa sought solution to the bigger issue. Hoping to stem competition among the

Canadian and American tribes in the North-West Territories, the
Privy Council asked the United States to promote the Lakotas'
return by modifying its terms to let those people keep their
horses and surrender only their arms before going on the reservation. This proposal came amid increasing reports of the Sioux
going below the line, some of which suggested they were instigating problems with other tribes.[19]

As Miles observed events developing north of the Missouri in
1878 and 1879, he watched the mounting unrest among the
American tribes of Assiniboines and Yanktonais around Fort
Peck as the Lakotas, Nez Perce hangers-on, and mixed-blood
confederates from Canada agitated and caused trouble with
those people. In addition to stealing horses and competing for
limited game, the Sioux and their followers repeatedly killed
American cattle, then butchered and took the meat. In late March
1879, a party reportedly composed of two Sioux and seven Nez
Perces killed one man and wounded another near Terry's Land-
ing on the Yellowstone. (It was later learned that but two Nez
Perces were involved, identified only as White Eye and Johnson.
White Eye was later killed by Crows; Johnson was found with
the Sioux thirty miles west of Wood Mountain. An eyewitness
exonerated Johnson of the crime.) Afterward, the Indians stole
fifty or sixty cattle and committed other depredations before
heading north across the line to Wood Mountain. In June, Miles
sent an officer (Second Lieutenant John C. F. Tillson, Fifth
Infantry) to accompany the aggrieved stockman into Canada to
identify the culprit Lakotas and recover his cattle. Walsh took
them through the Sioux camp, but found none of the animals.
That same month other warriors (possibly Gros Ventres) killed
one settler and wounded another, and Miles notified Commissioner Macleod of his intention, on Terry's direction, and with
Sherman's consent, to move troops into the region between the
Missouri and the line: "[I] will endeavor to arrest or drive back
any Indians who have been hostile and annoying our [Fort Peck]
Indians. In case they again return to your territory, I would be
thankful for any information as to their locality, or in case they

make any movement toward returning to this side of the line after having recrossed it."[20]

Further provocation occurred in 1879, when—amid rumors that a Chicago firm was shipping fixed ammunition to Winnipeg for delivery to the Hudson's Bay Company, then to be routed to the Sioux—word came that Sitting Bull had been camping with his warriors on Fort Peck Reservation lands between February and May while invading those Indians' special hunting tracts. Wellington Bird, agent at Fort Peck, wrote Commissioner of Indian Affairs Ezra A. Hayt as early as February that the "Sitting Bull Indians were scattered over this Indian reservation in camps of half a dozen to one hundred lodges, from the north of Milk River to Wood Mountain [Mounted] Police Station." In April, Bird notified Hayt that the situation had worsened:

> Our Agency Indians are coming in to the Agency now daily and complaining bitterly of the encroachments of these Indians on their hunting-grounds. They say they find Uncpapas [Hunkpapapas] from Sitting Bull's camp everywhere driving and scattering the buffalo and other game so that it has become a matter of real difficulty for them to obtain buffalo enough for their subsistence. They further complain that these Indians steal their horses and run them all over the boundary line. I believe there is no doubt at all that Sitting Bull is now on American soil, and has been camped south of the boundary line since the middle of February last, and that practically all his Indians are now south of the northern boundary, there being, as they claim, no game for their subsistence on the Canadian side. . . . A more unprotected condition than now exists of the buildings and property of the Agency, at both Poplar River and Wolf Point, cannot be conceived.[21]

The same month, soldiers from Fort Logan, Montana, cornered eight Sioux warriors near the Musselshell River and killed them all during a sharp engagement. In line with the prevailing military viewpoint, Secretary of State Evarts wrote Edward Thornton,

"Should these erratic movements continue, this government may at any moment be brought face to face with the necessity of suppressing the marauding operations of the hostile Indians under Sitting Bull's lead, or of even resorting to active military operations to repel open attacks upon the lives and property of its own people."[22]

Direct incentive for American military intervention against the Sioux continued through the late spring and early summer of 1879. In June, Agent Bird, "after much and careful deliberation," requested that troops be sent to the Fort Peck Agency. Colonel Miles had already received instruction from General Terry, on authority of Sherman and the Secretary of the Interior, to drive the Lakotas north of the boundary then set up a temporary camp north of the Missouri River from which to observe the border country. Miles enlisted scouts from among the Assiniboines near Fort Peck and sent troops to move those people and the Yanktonais south of the Missouri toward the Yellowstone in order to provide them access to game and to remove them from the proximity of his campaign. In early July, he set out from Fort Keogh with soldiers of the Second Cavalry and Fifth Infantry, besides a Hotchkiss detachment, his contingent of Indian scouts, and requisite wagons. Fording the Missouri to the previously abandoned Fort Peck Agency (Old Fort Peck), Miles headed north on July 15 with 33 officers, 643 men, and 143 friendly Indians and Indian scouts, including Crows, Northern Cheyennes, and some friendly Sioux and passed up the south side of Milk River. Two days later, along Beaver Creek, an affluent of the Milk, Miles's Indians located and impetuously attacked four hundred Sioux, the strike followed by a cavalry charge that drove them for a dozen miles. Near the site of a former fur-trading post called Old Fort Browning, the Lakotas made a stand and fought vigorously until the balance of Miles's command arrived, at which point they withdrew north of the Milk, leaving eight dead. Sitting Bull reportedly took part in the affair. Two soldiers received wounds; two Indian scouts died and two were wounded. Miles forded Milk River and kept on the trail until it crossed the line near Little Rocky Creek. Light skirmishing between the troops and Indians proceeded for a time on July 23.

One of Miles's scouts, a mixed-blood Nez Perce named Oliver Brisbo, took part in the Milk River affair and gave an account of the action in a period newspaper. Brisbo, from Oregon, "has a pleasant countenance," said the tabloid, "and talks rather good English." Brisbo was one of those who had reported to Miles about the Indians hunting below the line the previous spring, and the colonel recruited him as a scout. According to the newspaper account,

The reported great fight of Miles with the hostile Sioux . . . was a farce. The true inwardness, Brisbo thinks, never has yet been revealed. Miles was ambitious and wanted a chance to show his bravery. Two companies of soldiers and fifty-four Indian scouts, Brisbo being one of them, under [First] Lieut. [William P.] Clark, started out in advance of Miles' command. The engagement took place about fifty miles south of the line. . . . The Indians were going north and did not want to fight. They had come down to hunt buffalo, and were then on their way back across the line. Brisbo saw Sitting Bull in the distance accompanied by two Nez Perces and two Sioux. They were waving their hands, which signified the desire to talk with Miles. The Crow scouts with Clark wanted to fight and they began firing. Sitting Bull turned away and joined his band over the ridge. There were only twelve braves with their women and children with Sitting Bull, the main band being then on a retreat. They wanted to get their wives and children to a place of safety, so they showed fight. Selecting a favorable location, they began to fire back, the women and children retreating in haste. One squaw and child had already been killed by the scouts, who had kept up an incessant firing. The twelve warriors stood off the fifty-four scouts until the two companies came up. They then retreated, several of the scouts following them closely. One Crow had been firing at Sitting Bull throughout the skirmish. A Sioux told Sitting Bull and Bull turned and fired, saying, "you want to kill me, do you?" [The remainder of the account is missing.]

Miles bivouacked his men near the boundary. On July 23, Superintendent Walsh appeared to ascertain the purpose of the presence of the troops so near the border, and learned that they had responded to "the depredations and trespasses committed by Indians from the Canadian side." According to one source, Walsh and Miles lightly debated whether hunting buffalo constituted a hostile act. Miles told the major that the "American" Indians needed the beasts, and, besides, the Sioux had stolen horses and killed settlers. Walsh promised to help identify and return animals taken over the line. Miles specifically desired to arrest the murderers of the white men along the Yellowstone, and a U.S. marshal had accompanied his column for that purpose. He told Walsh of his intention to confiscate property from Canadian mixed-bloods and others who had traded ammunition to the Lakotas. After Walsh departed, Miles drew his force back down Rocky Creek and went into camp. Five days later, the inspector returned with Long Dog, a respected Hunkpapa, who told the colonel that the Indians intended to remain in Canada and would henceforth cause no trouble. Walsh assured Miles that further demonstrations by the Lakotas would not occur below the line. Subsequently, the army command divided to range west and east, and in a week's time had arrested and dispersed more than eight hundred mixed-bloods (called half-breeds) who had trespassed on the reservation. The soldiers then returned to their post along the Yellowstone.[23]

A civilian news correspondent on the expedition, John F. Finerty of *The Chicago Times,* accompanied Walsh back to Sitting Bull's village at Wood Mountain, and his notices provide one of the most vivid and comprehensive descriptions of the Lakotas at the halfway point of their sojourn in Canada, as well as mention of the Nez Perces yet remaining with the Sioux. According to Finerty, the Indians occupied "a large village of tepees covering the valley." It stood along Mushroom Creek, "and was shaped somewhat like the figure 8, the upper and larger side containing the Hunkpapas, Ogallalas, and Sans Arcs, while the lower held the Yanktonais, Santees, and Nez Perces, not to mention the ferocious Miniconjous." Mosquitoes, he wrote, were "a positive plague."

He met or saw many Sioux, including Long Dog, Big Road, Rain-in-the-Face, and Spotted Eagle. He described Sitting Bull with parted hair, broad face, and "with a prominent hooked nose and wide jaws." "I noticed he was an inch or two over the medium height, broadly built, rather bow-legged, . . . and he limped slightly, as though from an old wound." During a council with Walsh and the chiefs, an Oglala known as The Hero articulated the desperation now confronting the Indians: "When my young men go hunting over there, they are met with fire. My women are killed and my children starve. . . . My grandmother (the Queen of England) says I must not go to war, and I obey her. I see my people starving, and I go to kill the buffalo. The Great Spirit made no lines. . . . Why then do the Americans meet us with fire when we only wish to feed ourselves and our women and children? . . . I see the buffalo near the stone heaps [markers] and I must not shoot him, even while my children cry for his meat."[24]

General Terry overwhelmingly endorsed Miles's efforts against the Tetons: "The hostile Sioux . . . had been permitted by the Dominion Government to repair all the losses of arms, horses, and equipments [since 1877] . . . and to completely prepare themselves again for war. . . . They had invaded our territory almost as a body, and had covered with marauding parties the country between the boundary and the Yellowstone River." "Now it is believed that not a hostile Sioux remains south of the boundary." Yet despite Colonel Miles's expedition to the line, and despite the best promises of the Lakotas and efforts by the Canadian authorities to preclude future transgressions, the issue of hungry Indians seeking game would not go away. United States authorities also recognized the futility. As General Sheridan concluded in his annual report, "When the buffalo again return south of the northern boundary line, they will be followed by the Indians . . . , and it will be exceedingly difficult to establish any international conditions which will prevent such an invasion of our territory." While migration would indeed recur, the fact of increasingly declining herds would somewhat temper the reality of Sheridan's remark. On the other hand, in light of Miles's movement, Canadians now feared that the American Indians, foodless and pushed back north of the line, might now feel compelled to raid settlements in that country.[25]

For the foreseeable future, the Canadians and Americans remained fixed in their respective positions. As the former continued to call on the United States to take back the Sioux upon surrender of their firearms and not their animals, the latter continued to hold their northern neighbors accountable for Lakota actions below the border. Meantime, as expected, Lakota migrations below the line resumed late in 1879 and occurred intermittently through the following winter and spring. Again, the people, desperate with the rapid disappearance of the buffalo, were drawn to cattle ranches along the Yellowstone River. (It is not certain that any Nez Perces accompanied the Sioux raiders.) Army troops occasionally captured those transgressors, while others yielded outright to the soldiers. The Mounted Police encouraged the latter response, and even Sitting Bull indicated an intention to turn himself in to the Americans. Yet the United States would permit the people to surrender only as prisoners of war under the terms previously presented to them. When the Canadian cabinet proposed that the Americans drop the "unconditional surrender" requisite and permit the tribesmen to keep their mounts, and espoused the right of either nation's Indians to cross the boundary for game, the British Foreign Office opposed pressing the issue.[26]

Conditions for the Lakotas, as well as for Canada's tribes, continued to worsen. The Indian Commissioner of the North-West Territories, Edgar B. Dewdney, worked to stem imminent starvation among the Blackfoot, Crees, and other Canadian Indians, and to persuade the Sioux with Sitting Bull to leave the Dominion for good. The Canadian tribes, he reported, were so destitute that they were eating "mice, dogs, and even their buffalo skins." During the winter of 1879–80, they openly killed the stock of cattlemen, who were forced to drive their animals south into Montana. As most of these stockmen were squatters, they received no protection from the Mounted Police. Depredations continued below the line, too. In one instance in early February 1880, a war party of Hunkpapas attacked two citizens on Powder River. Following an exchange, a cavalry detachment killed one of the offenders and captured three others. Secretary Evarts asked that the consequent civil charges against the captives be broadcast among the Sioux in Canada "to discourage similar incursions from that quarter." Elsewhere, in March troops from Fort Keogh variously skirmished with Sioux along Little Porcupine Creek north of the Yellowstone and near Rosebud and O'Fallon Creeks south of the river. Two months later, the Crows fought a mixed party of Lakotas and Nez Perces; they killed four, including two Nimiipuu, and carried their scalps to the Crow agency. By and large, however, by this time the Nez Perces yet remaining in Canada had mostly dispersed away from the Sioux to congregate in the area below Fort Macleod (see chapter 7).[27]

In preparation for full-scale surrenders by the Lakotas, late in November 1879, Indian Commissioner Hayt reminded his agents close to the 49th parallel that surrendering Lakotas must turn in their arms and horses. Early in 1880, as the tribesmen were reduced to eating diseased horse carcasses, the edifice began to crack. Driven by hunger, groups of destitute Sioux began the trek south to submit as prisoners to the United States government. Some journeyed all the way to Spotted Tail Agency in Nebraska. Early in January, Sitting Bull and 450 lodges of Lakotas camped below the line on Frenchman Creek. Forty-one families submitted late that month at the Fort Peck Agency on Poplar River, where their Yanktonais friends and relatives lived. "From that time on to the last of April they kept coming in small parties and turning over their ponies and arms till there were 1,116 in all—109 men, 209 women, 424 boys, and 374 girls—and they had turned over 43 ponies, 40 guns, and 7 revolvers. Before coming here for two or three months they had been killing and eating their ponies, and most of them came on foot." More tribesmen arrived intermittently through the fall. Troops from Fort Custer helped oversee the people crowding into the agency, and in December 1880, soldiers under Major Guido Ilges marched from Fort Keogh to Fort

Peck to induce some of the more stubborn Sioux to surrender. On January 2, 1881, Ilges's infantrymen fired on Gall's and The Crow's Hunkpapas at Poplar River and captured some 300 returnees who were marched overland to Fort Buford.[28]

Sitting Bull refused to yield, although his crossing and recrossing of the line had now become irritatingly frequent. (He had come below the boundary on the verge of surrendering early in 1881, but Ilges's action at Poplar River had impelled him north once more.) Although he held out hope that the British would provide him a reserve and thus recognize his people as Canadian Indians, the Hunkpapa leader no longer had Major Walsh to intercede for him, as that officer had been transferred during the summer of 1880—his influence with and interest in Sitting Bull having been questioned by superior authority. In February 1881, Evarts informed his British counterpart that "many of the hostiles have accepted the terms offered them, and have been placed in a position to deprive them of the power of doing harm." "The frontier question . . . as respects Sitting Bull himself and his immediate following [is] still pending." Evarts called on the British government and the Canadians "in the fulfillment of neighborly comity and good will," to either "domicile him as a British Indian" and keep him from again entering the United States, or repel him altogether if he crossed again to the south with intent to return to Canada.[29]

Walsh's replacement, the Irish-born Lief E. F. Crozier, continued his predecessor's tactics of encouraging the Sioux to go south, but he also worked to undermine Sitting Bull's authority among his people, even convincing the Sans Arc Chief Spotted Eagle to yield; Chief Big Road and his people also went in, surrendering to Miles at Fort Keogh. American authorities also worked through their scouts to convince the Indians that submission was now the proper course. As more and more traveled below the line to the agencies, Sitting Bull's followers dwindled. Through the Mounted Police, even Sitting Bull himself initiated overtures to army officials at Fort Buford in Dakota Territory. One who counseled Sitting Bull during the early months of 1881 was the trader at Willow Bunch, near Wood Mountain, Jean-Louis Légaré. He recalled the conditions among the Sioux: "Many of them had not even a pony, and those who had, possessed very lean ones; and as the ponies died either of leanness or sickness, they ate it [sic] at once." Légaré assured Sitting Bull that he and his people would not be harmed by the Americans if they went in. He convinced him that only abject poverty and starvation awaited them in Canada and that the British wanted them gone. Légaré organized a group of Sioux willing to travel to Fort Buford to talk with Major David H. Brotherton, the post commander, but Sitting Bull instead set out for the Mounted Police station at Fort Qu'Appelle, 140 miles northeast of Wood Mountain, with a final appeal for status from the Canadians that brought him no satisfaction. (He received neither a reserve for his people nor permission to move them onto the Santee Sioux tract some 100 miles northeast of Qu'Appelle.) At Fort Qu'Appelle, an arriving Lieutenant Governor Dewdney explained the Hunkpapa's few remaining options. It became clear that the Canadian position toward the Sioux was quickly hardening. Sitting Bull had meantime sent envoys to Fort Buford to ascertain what treatment previously surrendering Sioux had received. Those who inquired for the chief were so impressed that they returned to Wood Mountain to bring their own families south. When Sitting Bull returned from Fort Qu'Appelle, he learned that Légaré had taken more people to Buford.

Scarcely two weeks later, and with Sitting Bull's reluctant assent, the French trader started south once again, this time accompanying the remaining aged and young among the Hunkpapa's followers. There is no doubt that Sitting Bull now feared for his life, but he had no recourse, and with Légaré's assurances he started with the others—the last to do so. Forty lodges—187 people—made the journey, mostly walking or riding forward in lumbering Red River carts, following wagons brimming with goods from Légaré's store to sustain them. They required more provisions, too, brought up from Fort Buford to see them through the trip. At noon on July 19, 1881, the ragtag caravan of impoverished men, women, and children trudged onto the parade ground at the post and surrendered to Major Brotherton, the final Teton Sioux refugees from

Canada to yield. In a council ceremony in the major's office, the Hunkpapa who had engineered the powerful Indian coalition that had resisted the soldiers so successfully for so long turned over his rifle forever; within days he headed down the Missouri River a prisoner of war.[30]

Among the bedraggled people who came in with Sitting Bull was Seeskoomkee (Cut Off), also known as Steps, or No Feet. His original name was Attween (translation unknown). He was possibly a Shoshoni-Bannock man who had reportedly come among the Yakimas as a purchased slave. At one point during his enforced servitude he was disciplined for thievery by being left outside one night in subzero temperatures, his hands and feet secured in metal traps, and Steps lost both feet and his right hand. Eventually freed from his obligations among the Yakimas, he came to live among the Nimiipuu, and during the Nez Perce War he fought the soldiers at White Bird Canyon, Big Hole, and Bear's Paw. Managing to flee the latter field and find his way into Canada with the refugee Nez Perces, he attached himself to the Lakotas. He stayed with them through Sitting Bull's surrender in 1881 and eventually married a Sioux. Steps was incarcerated with Sitting Bull's followers at Fort Randall, Dakota Territory, for two years, until the government permitted the return of those Sioux to their agencies in 1883. He later argued with and killed a young Lakota man, but was absolved of blame in the death. By late 1890, Steps, apparently known colloquially among the Sioux as "Stepps [sic] the Cripple," was living among Ghost Dance followers of Minneconjou chief Hump on the Cheyenne River Reservation. Yet pronouncing himself a Nez Perce, he repaired to Fort Bennett, South Dakota, amid looming conflict with the army that led ultimately to Wounded Knee.[31] The presence of this quasi-Nimiipuu man among those surrendering with Sitting Bull in 1881 represented something of a continuum of the Nez Perces' time of refuge with his people following their arrival in Canada in the wake of the debacle at Bear's Paw Mountains.

CHAPTER 5

BREAKING FOR HOME

With the known exception of Steps, the young Shoshoni-Bannock who had lived with and fought alongside the Nimiipuu, apparently few tribesmen from the Nez Perce encampment surrendered with Sitting Bull or other Lakota leaders in 1880–81.[1] By that time most of the people had moved away from the Tetons—some to return to their Idaho homeland, others to join temporarily or permanently with other tribes in Canada or the United States. Still others dispersed to other places in the North-West Territories and were contented to remain above the international boundary. A body of Nez Perces that included the family of Chief White Bird settled in the vicinity of Fort Macleod, in present-day Alberta, and largely stayed there, seemingly for a generation or more. As indicated, much of what ultimately happened to the Nimiipuu who escaped to Canada in 1877 hinged on the Tetons, who facilitated their entrée there and with whom they were to a degree inextricably connected, particularly over the months immediately following, and whose own experience is vital to fully comprehend the Nez Perces' existence north of the Medicine Line.

Significantly, the refugee Nez Perces were never bound by the same federal policy of unconditional surrender (that is, the giving up of all guns and horses) as was imposed upon Sitting Bull's people by the United States Government. The seeming altruism of the Americans toward the Nimiipuu likely reflected the comparative numbers of Sioux versus Nez Perces who crossed the line (approximately 300 Nez Perces versus 4,000 Lakotas) and the relative perceived threat consequently presented by each group; it also likely mirrored a more charitable disposition toward those people among white Americans historically as well as during the course of the war, as compared with punitive attitudes held against the Sioux and Cheyennes because of their destruction of Custer's command. Moreover, there were certainly latent racist attitudes that favored the Nez Perces among whites—many of those Indians had embraced tenets of white civilization in their government, religion, and culture since early in the nineteenth century when missionaries worked among them, and the people were perceived differently from other Indians of the time. By 1877, many had spent time in missionary schools and spoke English fluently and otherwise adapted to white practices; indeed, many bore Christian names. As a tribe, the Nez Perces were considered by many whites to be more acculturated, and thus more like themselves. They further possessed a tradition of friendliness toward whites that infused their society and had even been manifested on the battlefield by the non-treaty people, where mutilations of the dead by the warriors had been rare, and where instances abounded of their outright humanity to wounded soldiers.[2]

As previously mentioned, information brought south from the Sioux camp by visiting Nez Perces indicated that at least some of those relatives camping with Sitting Bull's people were not overly pleased with their association with their age-old enemies (some reportedly had been "whipped and treated as slaves"), even though their pitiable circumstances dictated that, for the moment at least, they remain with them. Whether these were truthful statements or simply words of the moment meant to mollify American authorities is not known. Late in 1877 the commanding officer of the army post on the Bighorn River nonetheless advised the Crows to bring returning Nez Perces to the fort where they might surrender. Yet no mass surrenders on the part of the "Canadian" Nimiipuu ever occurred. Instead, perhaps influenced by the existing game situation affecting themselves and their Lakota hosts, by the spring of 1878 there appears to have begun a tilt away from those people. Indications are that the shift occurred sporadically and did not involve all the Nez Perces at once, perhaps reflecting elements of band affiliation and inter-band societal alignment that existed.

The move from the Sioux lodges appears to have been gradual. The Lakotas had housed them following their arrival north of the line, and it was from those dwellings that Nez Perce hunters had reportedly traveled below the boundary with their hosts late in 1877 (although some of these reports might have been erroneous).[3] The Nez Perces eventually were able to raise their own tepees adjoining several of the Lakota camps. In February 1878, Assistant Commissioner Irvine reported some seventy-five lodges of Nez Perces camped with the Lakota chief Spotted Eagle about sixty miles east of Fort Walsh at the end of the Cypress Hills. In April, one of Miles's sources told of Nez Perces camped on White Mud Creek thirty miles north of the Sioux camp of Black Shield. "I only saw 10 Nez Perces," the scout commented, "and they were in Sitting Bull's lodge and expressed a desire to return to Joseph." And in July, some twenty or twenty-five Nez Perce tepees stood alongside a large Oglala assemblage of two hundred lodges located fifteen miles north of Wood Mountain. Within a month, these people had migrated west, near Pinto Horse Butte, en route to a buffalo herd spotted near Little Wood Mountain, and by late August, only White Bird and his immediate followers remained with the Sioux. The others had dispersed into several smaller camps through the region—several attaching themselves to area Blood and Piegan villages by mid-October. Meantime, during the early autumn six Nez Perces violated their agreement with the Mounted Police and journeyed below the line to visit the Crows. Their relationship with the Crows had become tenuous, at best, since the war, and apparently was further compromised by the Crows' killing of five more Nimiipuu in 1878 (see chapter 4, note 3). The Crows now welcomed them with kindness and, moreover, sent back with them the previously mentioned tidings to the Lakotas, apparently suggesting an end to the longstanding hostility with those people. The hint of a rapprochement between the Crows and the Sioux, with a Lakota–Crow–Nez Perce coalition in the offing, appears to have been grounded in Crow concerns over game availability and fears that the U.S. Army meant to strip them of their arms and horses. Instead, however, the Crows raided the hated Lakotas' horse herds, dashing any attempt at such a union and forcing Sitting Bull to conspire to retaliate. Walsh approached Sitting Bull and told him forcefully that he blamed him and the Nez Perces for the trouble, and warned the Hunkpapa that his intrigue would jeopardize his future in Canada. Walsh's strong rebuke following the Crows' raid ended Sitting Bull's war ardor. The Hunkpapa leader owned up to his scheming, and the attempted union eroded Walsh's trust in the Lakotas' promises to abide by the rules.[4]

Whether accounts of their dissatisfaction with their Sioux hosts were true (Yellow Wolf stated, "we got along fine with the Sioux"), it is clear from tribal sources that many of the Nimiipuu, no doubt homesick, had decided to head back to the United States, and principally to Idaho, as early as the onset of warm weather in spring 1878. Most likely, they did not know the full particulars of the movement of Joseph's people to eastern Kansas and eventually to the Indian Territory. (Again, Yellow Wolf claimed that the people had received word from Joseph to surrender and join him in exile.) Some of them set out in family units, or in small parties of two or three, with Idaho their objective, while others decided to remain among the Lakotas for the immediate future. Many of those who stayed in the north decided to leave in 1879, and perhaps even in 1880. As indicated, some camped among other tribes in their course and took several years to complete the journey home (evidently some also continued to wander until the return of Joseph's band in 1885, and then joined with them). Mark Arthur, who as a boy of thirteen fled into Canada from Bear's Paw, stated, "I was three years getting back to Lapwai. We returned part of the distance each year." For all, the trip back proved extremely risky, with encounters with settlers or soldiers always possible and death and injury ever imminent. Those who made it to Lapwai faced the possibility of arrest and shipment into exile with Joseph's followers (which some of them nonetheless sought), although lenient officers permitted others to reside with relatives among the treaty people there.[5]

Duncan MacDonald collected information from White Bird and, likely, other Nez Perces about the movements in the spring and early summer of 1878. A large party that left with Joseph's daughter "deserted White Bird's camp in the middle of the night and started for Idaho. . . . Some of them told the Indians remaining north that they were going to try to cross the Kootenai pass if they could find the trail." He added the following information about other departees:

About a week before the . . . above mentioned left White Bird's camp, Eagle of the Light's brother left. Joe Hill left with him. There were three men and two or three women in the party. I think they are [presently?] around Tobacco Plains, Kootenai— north of the line. Some time in June, after the twenty left, another small party deserted—four or five men and the same number of women and children. The day after I arrived at Fort Walsh, the well known scout Captain John, son-in-law, and wife and child, started for Idaho. I met them at Fort Walsh. This is all the information I have of Nez Perces moving this way.[6]

Specific and detailed accounts of the journeys home by groups or individuals appear to be rare, although some were delivered to historian Lucullus V. McWhorter early in the twentieth century. The widow of Ollokot, brother of Joseph who had been killed at Bear's Paw, told of spending two years among the Lakotas before moving on, eventually living with the Spokan Indians through the winter of 1881 before going to Lapwai. Mrs. Wounded Head likewise spent two years with the Sioux before joining with the Spokans, where she remained for two years before settling at Lapwai. A woman named Peopeo Hihhih (White Bird) recalled leaving Canada in about 1880, when she was ten or so. "We stayed up there three years," she related. "Was with the Blackfeet two years, and came to another place, maybe the Crees for one year. Was with the Flatheads one year. I was, maybe, six or seven years among the different tribes. Mother died among the Blackfeet." Meantime, the war leader Two Moon left the Lakotas in the spring of 1878 and lived two winters with the Flatheads in Montana before joining the Lemhi Shoshonis for a winter in southern Idaho. Then Two Moon, like others of the Nez Perces from Canada, went to live with the Spokans for "one snow." After the exiles' return from the Indian Territory, Two Moon joined Joseph's people at Nespelum, Washington, and the Colville Reservation. Another man, Red Wolf III, reported on his odyssey: "I stayed two years with Sitting Bull's people, then one year with the Blackfeet. Then one year with the Flatheads. Then I came to the Umatillas, then back to Lapwai." Red Wolf said that he and his party traveled by foot from Canada, and in Montana they traded their guns away because they felt it was too dangerous to retain them while on the journey. Some went back by themselves for intermittent visits on the reservation. Apparently, many of the returnees believed that they could return to Lapwai unmolested by authorities and remain there with relatives. Others, however, mostly men, feared that they would be hanged; they determined to wait in Canada until homes might be established for them at Lapwai. At least one group leaving in June 1878 consisted of seven warriors; another numbered four men and one woman. In Idaho, the former party was captured and imprisoned in the Fort Lapwai guardhouse, while the other went into the country of the Pend d'Oreille Indians. Possibly other small parties commenced the journey earlier.[7]

The general route for many of the Nez Perces leaving Sitting Bull's people in Canada to head directly for Idaho seems to have been diagonally southwest through the area of modern Chinook and Havre, then continuing southwest roughly paralleling the Missouri River to the Sun and Dearborn Rivers and through the Rocky Mountains via Cadotte Pass. They then followed down the Big Blackfoot River, tracing the future route of Montana State Highway 200 and approximating in reverse the course of Captain Meriwether Lewis and his party during their return in 1806. Perhaps seeking to avoid encounters with troops, some evidently negotiated Deep Creek Divide before passing south through Bear Gulch to the Clark Fork River (formerly Deer Lodge River). They continued to Willow Creek and crossed the divide separating the north and south branches of that stream, then followed the South Willow to Rock Creek. From there, some of the people angled northwest down the Clark's Fork to the area of Missoula, then traversed the Lo Lo Trail to reach their home country. Others apparently diverged south and west from the area of Rock Creek via the Big Hole and Bitterroot lands to reach Nez Perce Pass and the Elk City Trail, by which route they gained the Snake and Salmon River-lands in a circuitous trek to the same objective.[8]

White ranchers in the vicinity of the Dearborn River in present-day Lewis and Clark County encountered some of the tribesmen as they passed south and west toward their homeland. Sheepman Warren C. Gillette recalled meeting two of them in the late spring of 1878: "At first I thought they were cowboys, but as they came nearer I could see the red blankets." The encounter was not pleasant, as the warriors took his saddle, then one approached him and

suddenly grabbed my watch chain with his right hand, jerking the watch from the vest pocket. . . . As the watch was of great value, being a Jurgensen [product], . . . I would not let it go, so I grasped his wrist with my left hand, making him let go and shoved him back. He then drew his gun, a short Henry rifle, and threw a cartridge with the lever and aimed it at me; by that time I had concluded that I did not want the watch. . . . He lowered the muzzle of his gun and received the watch and chain. He then mounted his horse and rode away to the south, carrying the watch and chain in his hand. . . . The one that robbed me was a tall and fine-looking man, twenty-five years old, I should judge. . . . The other was older, shorter and not so good looking. I took the old saddle [discarded by the Indians], put it on my

horse . . . and went on to the camp. I found these Indians had
been there before me and had taken a gun, some cartridges and
food. . . . A few days after, two of my neighbors were killed on
the Dearborn river by this same tribe.[9]

The dead men on the Dearborn were A. L. Cuttle and John W.
Wareham; in fact, they were killed that summer—about July 6. A
neighbor told of the murders: "Cuttle was struck three times with
an axe in the head, but was probably shot first. Wareham showed
no marks. . . . The bodies were found in a creek that runs by the
house. A barn had also been broken open and the harness lines
and straps of the halters taken. The tragedy was discovered by
Mr. Charles Carey, of Sun River."[10]

There exist several miscellaneous and piecemeal references to
various other returnees that reflect the tenuous and difficult circumstances faced by the Nimiipuu who left the Sioux and re-
entered the United States. One account referenced a party of nine
Nez Perces (five men, two women, and two boys) who were captured by soldiers near the Blackfoot Agency at Chouteau, Montana, and ultimately delivered to the Indian Territory. And in 1879,
Umatilla scouts for the army, during operations against the so-
called Sheepeater Indians (Shoshoni-Bannocks), came upon a pile
of rocks that they interpreted to represent the passage back to Nez
Perce country of five men, three women, and three girls. A white
scout, John W. Redington, described the "memorial" as "a stone-
heap about knee high, with detached rocks of various sizes on the
ground close around it, two of the main ones showing the direction from which the Indians came and went."[11]

Reportedly the largest body of returnees to travel together back
into the United States was a party of twenty-nine people headed
by Wottolen (previously referenced by Duncan MacDonald).
These people mostly followed the course outlined above, leaving
Canada late in May 1878. Although they represented a mix of people from among the different Nez Perce bands, army authorities
referred to them all as being from White Bird's band because of
that chief's prominence as a refugee in Canada. Among this

group, as mentioned, was Joseph's daughter, Kapkap Ponmi, who had fled the Bear's Paw camp at the beginning of the attack; others included Yellow Wolf (of Joseph's band), Peopeo Tholekt, and Black Eagle, son of Wottolen.[12] Only about five, including several elderly men and some older boys, might have been considered fighters if needed. All rode horses, and each warrior had around ten cartridges for his weapon. One of their number, a woman named To-ton-mi, was lost en route in the vicinity of present Chinook, Montana, and it was feared that enemy tribesmen had taken her. (Some believed that she subsequently joined the Flatheads and died among them years later.) These people made their way south through Montana stealing and killing livestock here and there for subsistence, while enduring both unfriendly tribesmen and settlers along their route. The Assiniboines (the Nez Perces called them Walkarounds) and Lemhi Shoshonis seemed particularly willing to turn them in. In one instance, Yellow Wolf located a herd of cattle, and then led the others to it. "They were glad for those cattle," he explained. "We went down near the herd and unpacked. I had found them, so I shot the first steer. Then another man shot one. That was the time we had meat." That night the people butchered and dried the meat and next morning they were packed and ready to resume.[13]

Evidently, as circumstances dictated, they traveled sometimes together and sometimes in smaller groups. As they moved, several warriors rode in advance, scouting the way and seeking food and horses. In one incident, likely west of the Clark's Fork River in the area of Willow Creek, Yellow Wolf described taking a number of horses from a ranch to replace some Nez Perce animals that had gone lame. Accompanied by a young man named Soklahtomah (Ten Owl, also known as Fifteen Owl), Yellow Wolf approached a barn holding the beasts. As he recalled,

We tore down the board fence. It was a large barn. We got around above the horses. We saw no white man anywhere. It might have been forty steps we drove those horses, when they ran, playing. Could do nothing with them. All ran back to the

barn, racing around the barn. I saw one white man looking at
me. Then they came out with rifles and shot at us. The horses
ran away from the barn, scared of guns. We took the horses. We
looked back. The men had one saddle horse and came after the
horses. When we got to the top of the hill in the woods, the
white men did not follow us.[14]

These Indians, indeed, may have committed the two murders
on the Dearborn around July 6. On South Willow Creek, the
Indian men and women shortly encountered the cabin of Sam
Spence, X. Bennett, and another man, and took their food and provisions, but left them unharmed. Yet on July 11, while passing
through Bear Gulch to Willow Creek, they reportedly killed two
placer miners (Lynch and Meyers), and late that evening killed
another man named John Hays in McKay Gulch, taking his
revolver, food, money, and bedding. At 3 A.M. the next day, along
Rock Creek, twenty miles west of Philipsburg and southeast of
Missoula, eight or ten warriors looking for food, including Heinmot Tosinlikt (Henry Tabador), Peopeo Tholekt, and Tipyahlahna
Kikt (Alighting Eagle), confronted three white men near a house.
They were Amos Elliott, William Joy, and J. H. Jones. Jones broke
and ran away, as if he were going to find soldiers, and he managed
to elude the closely pursuing Nimiipuu, although they wounded
him in the right arm. Joy then became angry with the warriors,
and Tabador knocked him on the head, killing him; the Indians
then killed Elliott outside. On July 13, a party of locals from
Philipsburg found the dead.

The Indians had other encounters with local whites as they continued moving, taking (and later releasing) fifty-two horses,
killing cattle, and capturing various guns from settlers as they
went. Soon alarm spread among whites that these Indians would
join with the Flatheads in an uprising against them. "All was
excitement," remembered Jones. "Scouts were sent out in all
directions. People would come in and report seeing Indians on
every hill west and south of town. The town was fortified with
rifle pits." For two weeks a local mill became the temporary resi-

dence of women and children from outlying areas. "Then the Indian scare died down and the ranchers thought it safe to return to their homes."[15] However, the agent of the Flathead Reservation registered apprehension for his own charges: "The excitement of the past few months, . . . [including] the murders committed by the Nez Perces in close proximity to this reservation, has given me a great deal of anxiety, fearing that the settlers or military might mistake these people [the Flatheads] for hostiles, and by attacking them plunge the tribes into war. . . . The chiefs fear that the hostiles may commit murder on the reservation or in some of the neighboring settlements, which may be attributed to their people and hastily acted upon by the whites and cause trouble."[16]

Meantime, soldiers from Fort Missoula tried to block the Nez Perces' passage to Idaho, and skirmishing occurred at the headwaters of the Middle Clearwater River on Sunday, July 21, 1878, when a detachment under First Lieutenant Thomas S. Wallace killed six of the people and wounded three more (the casualty figures were disputed by Yellow Wolf), in addition to capturing thirty-one horses and mules and killing twenty-three more. Seeking the perpetrators of the recent killings, Wallace had left Fort Missoula with some citizen volunteers and Flathead auxiliaries who had turned back before the tribesmen were encountered. At 1:30 P.M., the dozen Third infantrymen charged the Nez Perce camp, "opening a rapid fire as we advanced." As Wallace reported:

> The position of the Indians was very strong on account of the ground which we necessarily had to fight over to approach them, having to charge down hill under full view for about 400 yards, having but few trees and no brush. The Indians numbered, so far as can be ascertained, 17 bucks and two squaws, and were undoubtedly the band who committed the recent depredations on Dearborn, Bear Gulch, Rock and Willow creeks, as many of the animals captured by me have been identified and claimed by citizens as having been stolen from them by those Indians.

Another report stated that "Among the killed was [Henry] Ta-ba-dor, their chief. . . . No casualties on our side except the wounding of a few horses. The fight lasted two hours."[17]

Years later, Yellow Wolf related incidents of this combat:

> I gave the war whoop. Whirling my horse, down the steep hill, over logs I went. Soldiers were ahead of me. Blocking the way! They fired from all around. I did not stop for anything. Only changed to a little different direction. . . . Wearing white shirts, some soldiers [citizens] ran toward me. They thought to kill me first. But I was not stopping for them. I did not try shooting. Only I must get away. A soldier was ahead of me, just to one side. He was waiting to shoot as soon as I came up. As I passed that soldier, he nearly poked me with his gun. He shot my horse through the withers. I did not fall with my horse. I lit on my feet and went out from there. That soldier got no other shot at me.[18]

The action with Wallace's troops created consternation among settlers in the area. Rumors circulated that White Bird and some forty warriors had returned to the area and were occupying the old Clear Creek battleground above the forks of the Clearwater, where soldiers had attacked Looking Glass's village on July 1, 1877. "The excitement . . . is great," trumpeted *The Oregonian* of Portland. "Sixty volunteers are in readiness to proceed against them. . . . Many apprehensions exist that White Bird is backed by some of Sitting Bull's men who are scattered through the mountains."[19] Eventually, troops from Fort Lapwai captured some of the Indians. One of them, a woman named Lucy (probably Lucy Williams), told Captain William Falck, Second Infantry, that the people had planned to live nearby with the Umatillas. According to Falck, Lucy detailed their treatment by the Sioux, as well as their journey of return, thusly:

> [Sitting Bull] treated them all very badly, excepting White Bird; owing to this treatment great discontent had arisen among them, and especially among those who were not members of White

Bird's band proper; for that reason many of them had made up their minds to escape and return to their native homes. . . . They left Sitting Bull's camp about the 20th of June; in ten days they struck Milk River in a southwesterly direction from the camp, and in five days thereafter the Rocky Mountains. They came through the Blackfeet country and saw no whites until they reached Bitter Root Mountains, thence they came in by the Elk City trail. The women all had horses when leaving Sitting Bull's camp; some of the men were dismounted until near Helena; north of there they stole two good American horses. When near the Hellgate River in the Flathead country three men of the party left, and the following morning drove in a large band of good horses; after selecting the best and gentlest, the balance were set adrift. The men and women of the party separated every morning and met in camp at night, when the men would bring in blankets, clothing, coffee, sugar, and plunder generally. When in the Bitter Root Valley the women were left in charge of two men, with directions to take the Elk City trail, while the men were to take the Lo Lo trail, but on the following day the women overtook the men and found the latter in possession of a large and fine band of horses and mules. They went in camp about 90 miles from Elk City, and while resting there the following day were overtaken in the afternoon by a party of thirty white men, who attacked them and fought them at long range until evening. The white men were successful in capturing all of the horses and mules, including the horses and saddles of the entire party, excepting six on which they mounted the squaws, the men marching until they reached the reservation, where they again provided themselves with mounts by stealing from Kamiah Indians. In this fight the squaw says one white man was killed and no Indians. The entire party camped near Clear Creek; when James Lawyer's first party [that had been sent from the agency] found them they all refused to surrender, and declared their determination to join the Snakes. During the night five squaws escaped and surrendered to Lawyer. Three women and children are still left with the party, who are probably gone to the Salmon

River, there to open some caches left by their people last year, containing money, blankets, provisions, &c.[20]

Black Eagle elaborated on the arrival into the homeland from his perspective:

We arrived in the Kamiah country, Clear Creek, a branch of the Clearwater, and stopped. One evening two Indian women spied on us, and met Peopeo Tholekt and Iskiloom. So these two women went back and told the rest of the Indians that they saw Peo and Iskiloom. Next day three men came to Wottolen. They were Kipkip Pahliwhkin, head of the three; besides he was one of the bosses from the agency. His escorts were Wuewooky-atakinneene and Tomma Kownah. When these three arrived, boss said to Wottolen, "We learn that you came here yesterday. I want you to come to the agency with us. The agency [agent?] will talk to you. . . ." Wottolen replied, "No, I am not going to surrender, or go to the agency. Even you, Kip, are one of the agent's bosses. The agent is going to grab me and put me in jail. This he will do, even though you try [to] help me out. The agent would not mind you if you tried to protect me. You are talking all right, Kip, but I cannot help it. I am not going. . . . So you [might] as well give up and go back home before you get in trouble. Do not try to force me. I am still going around traveling. I am not doing any harm to anything. I am not stealing any horses from nobody, so you better leave me alone. You can take some of the women who volunteer to go, to the agency with you. But the ones who do not want to go can stay here with me. If I go with you, white men would abuse me. Put me in dark place in jail. . . ." So Kip left us. After they had gone and we were on the trail, the sun eclipsed, and it got dark right away. Wottolen said to his people, "Do not be scared. It will not hurt us. I asked for help so we can hide away from Kip."[21]

As the woman Lucy mentioned in her statement to Captain Falck, five women—as well as two children—turned themselves in. Fourteen men of this group, including Yellow Wolf, were subsequently held in the guardhouse at Fort Lapwai in August, while the women and children (except for Joseph's daughter) were allowed to live with relatives at Kamiah, Idaho, until escorted by soldiers to the Indian Territory that fall. Captain Falck assured Yellow Wolf, "We will also take good care of other Indians coming from Canada."[22] Some of the people indeed had meantime proceeded to the area of Salmon River to retrieve caches of food and materials left there in 1877. As indicated, Wottolen and his son, of White Bird's band of Lamtamas, refused to surrender despite the entreaties of Kipkip Pahliwhkin, a former friend from the agency. Along with a Bannock man who had come south with them, and partly screened by the onset of the eclipse mentioned by Black Eagle, they headed toward White Bird Creek. But fearing more warfare they soon turned back. They wintered on the Spokane River and returned to Canada via Sand Point and Tobacco Plains in northern Idaho Territory to reside once more with the Lakotas, but later returned to the Spokan country before finally moving to the Middle Clearwater near Spalding.[23]

Presumably, by July 1879, Wottolen was back in White Bird's shrunken camp adjoining lodges of the Hunkpapa, Oglala, Minneconjou, and Sans Arc Lakotas, along with the Yanktonais and others along Mushroom Creek near Wood Mountain, where newsman John F. Finerty viewed the assemblage. Yet the migrations by other Nez Perces continued. In 1879 Nimiipuu Phillip Williams went south afoot, along with a dozen other people. One of them reportedly died in a fight with whites, and the others were pursued by bloodhounds. When they reached the Flatheads, their clothing was in rags, and some of the people stayed with that tribe. Near modern-day Stites, along the Clearwater, the other returnees took some horses, only to turn them loose as they approached Lapwai.[24]

It appears that despite the episodes with Wottolen's party in the summer of 1878, many other returnees managed to successfully elude settlers and soldiers in making their way back to Lapwai or to other reservations. Occasionally contacts occurred,

however. On the evening of April 24, 1879, W. L. Lincoln, agent
for the Gros Ventre and Assiniboines at Fort Belknap arrived at
Fort Benton with two Nimiipuu men and one woman "who came
across the line and surrendered" at the agency. These people
claimed to be related to Joseph (the men said they were his broth-
ers) and requested to be sent to join him. On June 13, Captain
Edward Moale, commanding at Fort Benton, received a Nez
Perce family that traveled from near Fort Macleod, North-West
Territories. These people, consisting of Pa-Kow-La-Sin-Lickty
("Five Fish Strung on a Stick," according to Moale), two women
and two children, reached Fort Benton on June 13. In addition, a
Nimiipuu boy captured by the Assiniboines and taken by Major
Ilges to Fort Benton and held there since November 1878, likewise asked to join Joseph's people. Similarly, in May 1879, the
agent for the Flatheads reported having two Nez Perce women at
hand who also expressed a desire to join Joseph's people. Subsequently, in July nine of these people (two men, three women, and
four children) were sent from Fort Benton to Fort Leavenworth,
Missouri, at an expenditure of $484.30 (paid by the Bureau of
Indian Affairs), and turned over to the agent for the Ponca Indians. Meantime, during the first part of 1879 at least seven more
tribesmen who had left Canada surrendered to, or were captured
by, the army command at Camp Howard, Idaho.[25]

As indicated, most of the Nez Perces who returned from
Canada to families and friends at Lapwai or vicinity did so
between 1878 and 1880, with the prevalence of returnees coming
back in 1878 and 1879. Many people lived for years among neighboring tribes until they felt it safe to go home; some doubtless
remained in those new communities, likely intermarrying into the
host tribes, and it is likewise probable that many who did so
stayed with those people except for occasional visits to the Lapwai
agency and reservation. Following the surrender at Bear's Paw,
the people with Joseph, numbering about 440, had been sent to
Fort Leavenworth, Kansas, and then, during the summer of 1878,
on to the Indian Territory; some who were arrested by military
authorities in Montana and Idaho during the weeks and months

following the war likewise were shipped south. Eventually, Joseph's people, as they were called, occupied a small portion of the Quapaw Reservation in what is today extreme northeastern Oklahoma, where many of them succumbed to disease within months. In 1879, the survivors transferred to a tract adjoining the Ponca Reservation farther west and took up ranching and farming. The people termed it "Eeikish Pah," meaning "the Hot Place." Through the years, Joseph worked vigorously on his people's behalf to promote their return to the Northwest, but it was not until 1885 that his objective was realized. In May of that year, 268 Nimiipuu—all who were left—entrained home, 118 going to Lapwai and the remaining 150 journeyed north to the Colville Reservation in Washington Territory to avoid legal prosecution as well as physical harm by whites still angry over the 1877 outbreak.[26] The arrival of Joseph in the Northwest was the signal that opened the way for many of the Nez Perces who had earlier left Canada to reside with other tribes, now to proceed home—no longer fugitives in their own land.

Joseph, leader of the Wallowa band and of the Nimiipuu who surrendered at
Bear's Paw, sat in Crow attire for photographer John H. Fouch at the Tongue
River Cantonment soon after the Nez Perces' surrender in October 1877. Federal
troops conducted Joseph and his people into exile in Kansas and the Indian Territory, where they remained until 1885. The United States government hoped to
entice the Nez Perce refugees in Canada to join their kin, a prospect that failed.
Courtesy James S. Brust.

Sitting Bull, Hunkpapa Lakota, whose people helped establish precedent for sanctuary for Indians of the United States in Canada, as emulated by the Nez Perces in October 1877. The arrival of Nimiipuu refugees fresh from the fighting at Bear's Paw directly influenced Sitting Bull's own rejection of terms for returning to the United States. Courtesy Little Bighorn Battlefield National Monument.

Colonel Nelson A. Miles, Fifth Infantry, whose campaigning in 1876 and 1877 in the Yellowstone River country directly influenced the withdrawal into Canada of Sitting Bull's Teton Sioux, as well as those Nez Perce escapees from the Battle of Bear's Paw Mountains. Miles continued to probe the border country for Sioux and Nez Perces who crossed the line in pursuit of game, and in 1878 he initiated the unsuccessful diplomatic endeavor to induce White Bird and his followers to return to the United States and surrender. Courtesy Paul L. Hedren.

General William T. Sherman, commander of the U.S. Army, endorsed the respective yet separate diplomatic missions to Fort Walsh to persuade Sitting Bull and White Bird to return and surrender. Sherman subsequently evinced concern over Miles's proposed movements toward the Canadian boundary in 1878, and worried that his activist subordinate (and nephew by marriage) might further complicate relations between the two countries. Author's collection.

Lieutenant General Philip H. Sheridan commanded the Military Division of the Missouri, headquartered in Chicago, during and after the Nez Perce War. Over Miles's objection and promises to the Indians, Sheridan ordered Joseph's people to Fort Leavenworth, Kansas, where they spent the winter of 1877–78 before eventually moving to the Indian Territory. Courtesy U.S. National Archives.

Brigadier General Alfred H. Terry, who as Miles's superior oversaw operations in the Great Sioux War and parts of the Nez Perce War. Terry's 1877 trip to Fort Walsh and his diplomatic attempt to coax Sitting Bull's return to the United States failed, largely because of the Lakota leader's dismay at seeing worn and wounded Nez Perce refugees from Bear's Paw streaming into his camps in Canada. Courtesy U.S. National Archives.

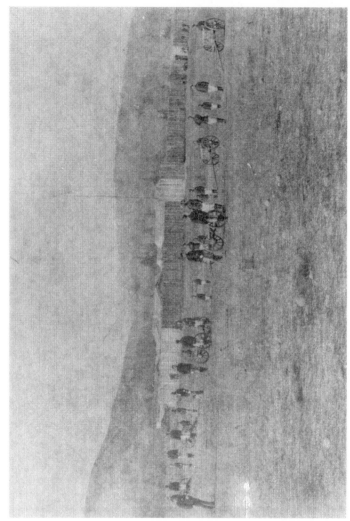

Fort Walsh, North-West Territories, ca. late 1870s. Erected in 1875, the North-West Mounted Police post became a significant monitor of Indian activity in the region during the late 1870s and early 1880s. In 1877 it hosted General Terry's unsuccessful effort to induce Sitting Bull to return to the United States and surrender; in 1878 the fort factored in similar failed negotiations to persuade White Bird and his Nez Perces to return south of the boundary. Glenbow Archives NA-98-13.

The North-West Mounted Police detachment station at the north side of Wood Mountain, Canada. It was here that Sitting Bull appeared in the spring of 1877 and where he acceded to strictures imposed by Inspector James M. Walsh. Glenbow Archives NA-354-9.

Nez Perce Chief White Bird, his wife (Kate?), and No Hunter (Hunts No More), brother of Looking Glass, apparently taken in Canada in ca. 1878–79. White Bird steadfastly repudiated overtures for his return to the United States, finally dying a violent death in Canada in 1892. Glenbow Archives NA-5501-8.

Hunkpapa Sioux Chief Gall's camp at Poplar Creek, Montana Territory, in 1881, as photographed by David F. Barry. These people had come over from Canada in the fall of 1880, and this view of their hide tepees likely matched the appearance of Lakota villages in Canada during the period of refuge there from 1877 to 1881. Courtesy Paul Harbaugh.

Superintendent James Morrow Walsh of the North-West Mounted Police established working relationships with first the Lakotas and later the Nez Perces.
Walsh's work with Sitting Bull significantly realized amicable relations with his
people; his efforts with White Bird and his followers, while on a much smaller
scale, proved just as important. Glenbow Archives NA-1771-1.

These Nez Perce tepees along the Yellowstone River in 1871 likely approximated in appearance those fashioned by the people in Canada a few months after their recuperative stay with the Sioux following their arrival in October 1877. Courtesy U.S. National Archives.

Peopeo Tholekt (Bird Alighting), of the Alpowai band of Nimiipuu, survived the attack by troops on Looking Glass's village in June 1877, and accompanied that chief throughout the ensuing warfare. He escaped the attack at Bear's Paw and with others made his way into Canada to refuge among the Lakotas. In the early summer of 1878, Peopeo Tholekt joined Wottolen's large group, which included Black Eagle, Yellow Wolf, and Joseph's daughter, in returning to the homeland. Courtesy National Park Service, Nez Perce National Historical Park.

In July 1878, First Lieutenant George W. Baird, Fifth Infantry, and Miles's regimental adjutant, led the fruitless mission to induce White Bird to return to the United States and surrender. Baird resorted to vagaries and untruths in his meeting with the Nez Perces, and failed to entice the tribesmen to join Joseph in exile. In after years, he served with the Pay Department, retiring as a brigadier general in 1903. Author's collection.

Yellow Bull, a member of White Bird's Lamtamas, did not cross into Canada, but surrendered with Joseph and the majority of Nez Perces who were sent to Fort Leavenworth and later the Indian Territory. In 1878, he joined Lieutenant Baird's party and journeyed to Fort Walsh to try and induce White Bird and his followers to yield. Courtesy National Park Service, Nez Perce National Historical Park.

James F. Macleod served as commissioner of the North-West Mounted Police during the eminence of the Lakotas and Nez Perces in Canada. His able leadership brought a maintained peace with these refugee wards for the several years of their presence. Later, as Supreme Court justice of the North-West Territories, Macleod played a significant role in the trial, conviction, and eventual death sentence commutation of Nez Percee Sam for the murder of White Bird. Glenbow Archives NA-23-2.

The Reverend John Maclean, Methodist missionary at Fort Macleod, came to believe that Nez Percee Sam's murder of White Bird lay grounded in cultural beliefs that affected his actions. Maclean and others championed a clemency petition for Sam, and in the end his life was spared by the Canadian government. Glenbow Archives NA-1297-1.

Convicted of slaying White Bird, Nez Percee Sam was condemned to death at the Stony Mountain Penitentiary, near Winnipeg, Manitoba. His sentence was eventually commuted to life, and he died in prison in 1893. In this picture, Nez Percee Sam appears with law enforcement personnel and other Indian convicts on arrival at Stony Mountain on June 8, 1892. Standing at rear is Sheriff Duncan J. D. Campbell; center, left to right, Constable Jarvis L. Back, Middle Bull, Bear Shin Bone, and unidentified constable; bottom, left to right, T. McQueen, Medicine Pipe Stem, and Nez Percee Sam (concealing his handcuffs beneath a blanket). Glenbow Archives NB-9-13.

CHAPTER 6

MISSION TO WHITE BIRD

Despite hemorrhaging among the Nez Perce base in Canada in 1878 and 1879, White Bird remained adamant about his own decision to stay put on Dominion soil, perhaps—as his tribesman Wottolen explained—because he feared that, as a chief, he would be hanged if he returned below the line.[1] White Bird had never wavered in his own determination to achieve Canadian sanctuary for the Nimiipuu, regardless of the views of others of his colleagues, from the time of the councils in the earliest weeks of the warfare through Bear's Paw and after, when he alone among the Nez Perce chieftains realized that objective. Yet there appear to have been mixed messages circulating on both sides of the line as to his willingness to consider, at least, yielding with his people to United States authorities under appropriate conditions.

Part of that confusing perception stemmed from widely disseminated reports (previously cited herein) that the Nimiipuu were mistreated by the Tetons in the weeks and months following their arrival at Wood Mountain. It is certain that such a schism between the tribesmen and their benefactors was what American administrators wanted to hear, and the reports, some of them likely exaggerated and generated by Nez Perces friendly to the

United States, might have been motivated simply by a desire on the part of their carriers to gratify army officials. It remained for the enterprising Colonel Nelson A. Miles to determine the credibility of the reported situation. Late in January 1878, Miles commissioned a scout named Christopher Gilson to go forth and ascertain the temperament of the Crows and other tribes in the area of the Musselshell and Missouri, to pinpoint the location of the Lakotas in that region if below the Missouri, and to go among the Nez Perces—if he found them—and try to find Joseph's daughter as he had earlier promised the chief he would do. During his trip, Gilson carried dispatches from Fort Benton to Fort Walsh, and used the opportunity to seek out the Nez Perce camp. His arrival there preceded by several weeks the beginning of the large-scale departure of the Nimiipuu from Canada. He located Joseph's daughter, and presented her with a photograph of her father. Gilson remained among the tribesmen for several days, and according to Miles "ascertained that the Nez Perces were anxious to give up every thing they had and return to their tribe." The scout then brought the information back to Miles at Fort Keogh, where he arrived early in April.

On April 4, Miles wired Gilson's report to department headquarters at Saint Paul. It read,

> Nez Perces all poor—have nothing. White Bird told me if I could bring one Nez Perce from Joseph so they could rely on his telling the truth, that they would all come and give themselves up. They are anxious to come back and begged me to bring some one of their tribe to see them so they could return. Joseph's daughter is well and wants to see her father.

Miles forwarded the message, affixing his belief that "the importance of detaching what remains of the Nez Perces from [the] hostile Sioux is such that I request that one or two Nez Perces selected by Joseph be sent to these Headquarters for the above purpose." Later, Miles elaborated on the opportunity as he saw it: "There existed a short time ago unfriendly feeling between the hostile Sioux and Nez Perces, and I desired to take advantage of it. The presence of a few Nez Perces I consider more dangerous in the Sioux camp than four times their number of those Indians owing to their superior intelligence and knowledge of the settled country."[2]

In late March, in a missive to Major Ilges at Fort Benton, forwarded to Miles at Fort Keogh, Mounted Police Assistant Commissioner Irvine reported on a visit to the police post known as Eastend, sixty miles from Fort Walsh, at the eastern terminus of the Cypress Hills, from which point he monitored the Sioux camps. He noted at this time that although the Nez Perces remained with Sitting Bull's people, rumors derived from mixed-bloods suggested that they intended to cross the line and surrender to the Americans. Irvine told Ilges, "I will not allow them to move south until I communicate with you." By early June the pervasive belief remained that White Bird's people wanted to submit to U.S. authorities. "Nez Perce anxious to return to join Chief Joseph," Macleod wired Secretary of State Scott.[3]

But it was Gilson's visit to the Nez Perce camp and his report thereof that proved to be the impetus of a formal undertaking initiated by Miles and concurred in by Sheridan and Sherman to induce White Bird to bring his people back to the United States. Despite similarities, such proceedings evoked the failed mission to Sitting Bull. By late April, three Nez Perce prisoners—Yellow Bull, Husis Kute, and Estoweaz—had been identified to travel north into Canada as representatives from Joseph's people in exile. At Sheridan's direction through Brigadier General John Pope, commanding the Department of the Missouri, Benjamin Clark, a noted scout and guide who had served Sheridan in campaigns on the southern plains, accompanied them to Chicago. Clark was subsequently directed instead to go with them as far as Bismarck and return south with Little Chief's Northern Cheyennes, then en route to the Indian Territory. But eventually Clark went the whole distance with the Nez Perce trio. (Although he could not speak Nez Perce, he communicated well with Yellow Bull using sign language.) The three prisoners, with Clark, departed Camp Joseph at Fort Leavenworth on Monday, April 29, and were bound up the Missouri. From Bismarck they would travel upstream to Fort Benton, then north via ambulance to Fort Walsh to consult with White Bird. Their principal purpose was to dispel rumors that Joseph's people had been ill treated and to report on their condition in Kansas, and for that reason the tribesmen would travel without military escort.[4]

The three representatives from Joseph were not randomly selected. All were well-respected men of influence among the Nimiipuu and would provide an air of validity in convincing White Bird's people to yield. Yellow Bull (Chuslum Moxmox) belonged to White Bird's own Lamtama band—he was in fact that chief's brother-in-law—and had fought in most of the contests of the recent war. Thirty-eight-year-old Husis Kute (Bald Head) was actually a Palouse whose small band had lived along the Snake River and had historically affiliated with the Nimiipuu. As a youth, he had served the Americans during campaigns against the Spokans in the 1850s, and he always claimed that a close call with a cannonball had taken off some of his hair. In the early stages of the warfare of 1877, Husis Kute had aligned with Looking Glass in that chief's advocacy of going to live with the Crows. At Bear's Paw, he had accidentally killed a number of Nez Perces, believing them to be enemy scouts. A spiritual leader, he was known as a preacher among the people. Estoweaz, whose name was translated variously as "Prying Open," "Heavy Weapon," and "Light in the Mountain," belonged to Joseph's Wallowa band. Considered a brave warrior, Estoweaz had been wounded years earlier in combat with the Assiniboines, an injury that had left him with a decided limp. At White Bird Canyon in June 1877, a bullet had grazed his side, but the injury was not serious. He was known among his fellows "for his truthfulness."[5]

Clark, Yellow Bull, Husis Kute, and Estoweaz were en route from Bismarck to Fort Buford on May 7, when General Terry telegraphed Miles, telling him to arrange with British authorities their passage across the line. Miles was also "to give Ben Clark instructions in accordance with your own views as to the best

methods to achieve the objects to be attained." Terry instructed
his colonel that if the Nez Perces indeed submitted, they were to
be taken to Fort Buford, near the Yellowstone's confluence with
the Missouri River, before being delivered to their people at Fort
Leavenworth. Miles had intended to send Gilson, who had
brought the request from the Nez Perce camp. But he had
departed Fort Keogh, and Miles turned to an officer close to him
to accompany Clark and the Indians into Canada. (Christopher
Gilson shortly returned to Fort Keogh, and Miles sent him to Fort
Walsh to be on hand as an interpreter during any proceedings
with the Nimiipuu.) On May 24, the colonel directed First Lieutenant George Baird to go to Fort Buford, join the Nez Perce party,
and proceed upriver to Fort Benton and secure the necessary
transportation to continue to Fort Walsh. Once there, Miles told
him, "you will communicate to the Commanding Officer of the
Canadian forces the object of your mission, which is—with the
consent of the Canadian authorities—to return the Nez Perces [sic]
Indians to their tribe [at Fort Leavenworth] should they desire so
to do, in accordance with the instructions of the Department Commander. You can give the Nez Perces Indians assurance of safety
and protection on this side of the line, provided they return to
their tribe. . . . You will convey the Indians to Buford, to await further orders from the Department Commander for their transportation to Leavenworth."[6]

First Lieutenant George William Baird knew intimately all
administrative aspects of the District of the Yellowstone. As regimental adjutant of the Fifth Infantry, Baird created most of the
orders signed by the Fort Keogh commander, and, moreover, was
well versed with Miles's predilections regarding the Nez Perce
situation as they might apply within the context of departmental,
divisional, and army policy. Baird, moreover, held Miles's confidence in his judgment in interfacing with Mounted Police officials. A Yale-educated native of Connecticut, Baird had enlisted
in the state's artillery during the Civil War, but transferred to the
Veteran Reserve Corps until appointed colonel of the Thirty-sec-
ond U.S. Colored Infantry in 1864. Mustered out the following

year, he applied and was granted a second lieutenant's commission with the Nineteenth U.S. Infantry, and within months transferred to the Thirty-seventh Infantry. Promoted first lieutenant, he transferred once more, joining the Fifth U.S. Infantry under Miles in 1869, and becoming adjutant of the regiment two years later (a position he would hold until 1879). A brave and dedicated officer, he had served his colonel well during the so-called Red River War against Southern Cheyennes, Southern Arapahos, Kiowas, and Comanches in 1874–75, and in the Great Sioux War of the Northern Plains in 1876–77. Baird went with Miles in pursuit of the Nez Perces in September 1877, and at the climactic engagement near the Bear's Paw Mountains he performed meritorious service while receiving wounds to his left arm and left ear (for which duty he later garnered a Medal of Honor [1894]). Miles termed his junior "an ornament to the profession, and his exemplary course a model for other officers." So it was that Baird stood properly equipped to represent Miles in any deliberations with Canadian officials as well as in any direct dealings with White Bird and his followers.[7]

On May 24, Miles prepared papers for Baird introducing that officer to Commissioner Macleod and enclosing the following statement: "It is understood that the few Nez Perces Indians who have taken refuge on British soil are desirous of returning peaceably to our territory, and the United States authorities have taken these means of assuring them protection and safety while returning to, and remaining with, their people. Should they return, it is ordered by the Department Commander that they be brought to Fort Buford, there to await further orders for their transfer to their own people at Leavenworth." Baird proceeded to Fort Buford and then upriver with Clark, Yellow Bull, Husis Kute, and Estoweaz, reaching Fort Benton on June 9 and there encountering Commissioner Macleod, to whom he delivered Miles's communication. Baird's party continued north, arriving at Fort Walsh on Sunday, June 16. Five days later, after waiting for Macleod to reach the post, he provided that officer with a copy of General Terry's directions to Miles—under which authority he had brought his party into Canada—and a copy of Miles's directions regarding the discharge of his mission. "From both of the enclosures," Baird told Macleod, "it is evident that I am not commissioned to use any solicitation to induce the Nez Perces to return to the United States territory, and am authorized to receive them only on condition that they 'come over and surrender,' in which event I am to afford them safe conduct to Fort Buford, D.T., there to await further instructions from General Terry's Headquarters relative to their transfer to their own people at Fort Leavenworth, Ks."[8]

Mounted Police officials now faced the task of presenting the American offer to White Bird and the Nez Perces. While there appeared no problem in escorting the three men from Joseph's camp to meet their relatives, such was not the case with Baird, Clark, and Gilson. Both Macleod and Assistant Commissioner Irvine had informed Baird that he would not be permitted to visit the Nez Perce camps, and the lieutenant pressed for allowing Ben Clark and Gilson to accompany the police detachment that would escort the tribesmen forward: "If it is deemed wise for one and not both to go, I judge that Interpreter Clark, in whom the three Indians repose entire confidence, and whom they have expected from the first to have accompany them, should be selected." Macleod responded, however, that such a visit was deemed "inadvisable" and that only Assistant Commissioner Irvine and a small escort would accompany Yellow Bull, Husis Kute, and Estoweaz forward to meet their people in the camps: "If we could assure that Clark and Gilson would meet none but Nez Perces, their visit might possibly be of use, but there is sure to be some Sioux about, and I am satisfied the presence of these two men would have a very bad effect." So it was that Irvine alone escorted the three tribesmen to White Bird's lodges.[9]

According to Duncan MacDonald, reporting for *The New North-West* out of Deer Lodge, Montana, Irvine's party encountered him while he was en route to interview White Bird. Irvine engaged the newsman as an interpreter and the group proceeded forward. They found the Nimiipuu camped near three hundred lodges of Oglala Lakotas at the Sandy Hills (Great Sand Hills), some seventy miles above Fort Walsh. MacDonald counted 65 warriors, approx-imately 45 women, and about 6 children, for a total of some 116 people. Speaking of the Nez Perces, MacDonald wrote: "I never saw Indians so badly frightened as were these." Once at the camp, they dismounted and found White Bird's lodge and shook hands with him. "His warriors thought we had come to arrest their chief . . . and they continued to arrive and crowd themselves into the lodge until we were packed so closely there was not room to move. . . . Then seeing the Indians were still somewhat uneasy, we concluded we had best retire without mentioning at the present our mission to the chief." According to Macleod, the negotiations between Irvine and the Nez Perces proved delicate: "These Indians were camped with a large Band of Sioux, whose influence was used to prevent them [from] consenting to return to the American side." The task of convincing White Bird to meet Baird was not easy, wrote MacDonald. "The Sioux told White Bird if he went with us to Fort Walsh he would be arrested. . . . But White Bird finally concluded to go with us and see the American officer."[10]

It was more than a week before the Lamtama chief and seven of his men appeared at Fort Walsh. (It is likely that during the interim Yellow Bull and his companions were able to provide White Bird with a more realistic picture of conditions of Nimiipuu existence at Fort Leavenworth than Baird would have preferred.) Lieutenant Baird met the party at the post and "received the Nez Perces kindly." On Monday morning, July 1, Commissioner Macleod, Irvine, and Baird opened the meeting with White Bird and his party in Irvine's office at Fort Walsh. Because of its singu-lar importance relative to the history of the Nez Perces in Canada, and especially for its context for the future course of White Bird's people, the transcript of the exchange follows in its entirety:[11]

> *Col. Macleod* [addressing White Bird]:—I am glad to meet you here, and to have heard good reports of you from the officers here. Since you crossed into this country, my officer here (Major Irvine) told me that you wanted to return, so I sent word to the American authorities stating that you desired to return. The

American Government have sent three Nez Perces to tell you how the American Government have treated them since the fight with General [Colonel] Miles [at Bear's Paw]. This officer (Mr. Baird) is here now to hear what you have to say, and I should be glad to hear what you have to say in the matter. I think it would be good for you to go back, as the only thing you have to rely on for support here is the buffalo, and there are so many Indians here that, in a few years, there will be none of them left. I understand that the American Government intends placing you on a Reservation and treating you well. We will now listen to what you have to say.

White Bird:—I want to know which way Joseph is going?

Mr. Baird:—I would rather hear all you have to say and will reply.

White Bird:—Would you rather I should speak, or retire and hold council with others?

Mr. Baird:—I would rather you would do just as you please.

White Bird:—I would rather hear you speak. I want to know what you are going to do with Joseph. I am glad Joseph is all right.

Mr. Baird:—I am very glad to see you, and will be glad to hear what you have to say. I know you are brave men, and I like to hear brave men talk, because I know they will tell me the truth. I know your young men were brought up as soldiers; I was brought up as one, and was taught that when men wanted to fight I was to fight them; and when they wanted to shake hands I was to shake hands with them. The American authorities were told that the Nez Perces on this side of the line would like to return to the other side. They were told also that these Nez Perces would like to see their friends who are with Joseph, and sent me to see you. The Great Father [President Rutherford B. Hayes] told General Miles to send those three men up with me, and this gentleman (Mr. Ben Clark) was sent to bring them.

When I came here with them, the Queen's officers took them to the Nez Perces' camp to tell you how they were treated with Joseph. White Bird and the Nez Perces have had a chance to talk with them and to learn how they were treated at our hands.[12] Now, if you, on this side of the line, wish to go to Joseph, you will be treated just as well and have the same protection as Joseph and his people. Joseph and his Indians will be put on a good Reservation, and have an opportunity to live comfortably. The Great Father sent one of his greatest chiefs to look for a Reservation for them [apparently in reference to seeking a site in the Indian Territory], and this gentleman (Mr. Clark) went with him. The Great Father wrote to General Miles to ask him what he thought about sending Joseph back to his old home. General Miles told him he thought they ought to go back to their old home and be protected there. If you here go back to Joseph, you will be with him, and it may be at your old home. Joseph and the Nez Perces have a great many friends among the Americans, and they tell the Great Father that they ought to go back to their old home. If you want to go back with me, I will take you down, and you will go to the same Reservation as Joseph. The Americans are your friends, and want you to go back to your old home, and if you don't, you will go to some other good Reservation. The Queen's officers have treated you kindly, but they have just told you they cannot give you anything to live on, they can only give you protection; but the Americans will give you a good Reservation if you will go back with me. If you want to ask me any questions, you may do so.

White Bird:—If the Chiefs and the President have made arrangements, I don't want to interfere.

Mr. Baird:—I don't understand what you mean by interfere.

White Bird:—If the Indians and the Government have made treaties already, it is not my business to interfere; for my part, I want no more fighting. All the Indians in the country know that they have made peace, and are well satisfied that there is no fighting going on. My Indians are well satisfied, and are glad to hear there are to be no more fights between the Americans and Nez Perces. My heart feels very strong. I want Joseph to come back to our own country. I am glad of the way Joseph was treated. I see how the hearts of both Governments are towards the Indians. I am so happy. My heart is open. I would like to see Joseph, and see him back in his own country.

Mr. Baird:—In that letter that General Miles wrote, he asked to have Joseph remain where he was till you here joined him. I know that Joseph would like to see White Bird and his people, and the quickest way for them is to go where Joseph is. In the letter I brought with me from the Great Chief [the President], he said, you should first go down where Joseph is, and the opportunity is offered you to go where Joseph is. The Queen's officers tell you you can go if you wish, and I tell you I will take you there safely.

White Bird:—I see these three men, and it is just like seeing Joseph. Joseph's heart has reached my camp, as mine has reached his. Major Irvine came and told me I was wanted here, and I came to have a council in his room, and I hope what you have written now will reach Joseph. It was my plan, when I reached here and saw the officers, to send word to Joseph.

Mr. Baird:—The word you sent before to Joseph is the reason these men came over. I don't think it will do any good to tell Joseph any more. He has been told you would come over, and he would be glad to have you come. You can talk among yourselves, and make up your minds if you will come. I can tell Joseph what you said, but, if you want to have Joseph know, you had better go yourselves. The Great Chief did not send me here to hear what you had to say,—I knew that before,—but to take you down, if you wanted to go, because you said you wanted to go. I have the means of taking you down. If you come with me, I will give you rations and transportation, but, if you wait to hear what Joseph says, you may not have the opportunity to go. I came up on purpose to make the arrangements for taking your wives and little children down, but if you wait to go by yourselves, you may not have the means. The Great Father sent over to give you the opportunity to go, so if you want to go, you ought to make up your minds at once. You can ask me any more questions if you would like to. When you have heard my answer, and what the Queen's officer will say to you, I want you to go together in council and decide whether you will go or not.

After this brief exchange, the meeting ended. All but the Nez Perces and MacDonald left the room. The Indians deliberated among themselves and White Bird made ready for resuming the discussion on the morrow. MacDonald reported, "White Bird then asked the Nez Perces from Ft. Leavenworth what Joseph had said. They replied: 'Joseph told us to tell you that you might do as you thought best. If you conclude to go to him he will be glad to see you—if not, well and good.'"[13]

On Tuesday morning the parties reconvened:

Col. Macleod:—What have you to say in reply to what was told you yesterday?

White Bird:—These three men were sent from Leavenworth to tell how they were treated. I wish that you (Col. Macleod) and Major Irvine would hear what Chief Joseph told the three men when they left.

Yellow Bull:—Now, I am going to tell what my Chief told me. I will commence from the time we surrendered at the Bear Paw Mountains. General Miles told Joseph he wished us to surrender when we were fighting. Joseph said, "All right; I don't want to have any more of my Indians killed, so I surrender." Miles and Joseph agreed to make peace right there. General Miles said that he wished never to fight the Indians again, but would live in peace with them. Now, the Government and the Indians under Joseph feel like brothers. Joseph was very glad to hear

General Miles speak that way. General Miles said to Joseph, "I am going to take you all to Tongue River; I have plenty of provisions there, and am going to feed you well. I want you to stop there all winter, and when the spring opens I shall take you back to your own country." General Miles then told us it was better we should surrender and live in peace in our own country, and Joseph answered, "Yes." Joseph wishes to be taken back to his own country, because General Miles promised him. For my part, I know all the Indians at Leavenworth want to go back to their own country. All Joseph's people know how he feels.

Bald Head [Husis Kute] (Preacher):—I was there when we surrendered, and have heard what Yellow Bull said; I heard what General Miles said and what Joseph said. General Miles wished us to surrender, and wished very much we would not fight any more. Joseph said, "All right; I am glad," and shook hands. General Miles said to Joseph, "Are you wide awake now; do you see better now than before we fought?" Joseph said, "Yes; I see plainer now, but we were both blind before, and now the country is like daylight, but before, it was dark." They were both glad. General Miles said we were to go to Tongue River and stop there all winter, and promised to feed us. Joseph said, "I am glad to hear it." Joseph thinks to-day that, because General Miles promised him he would go back to his own country, he will go, he and his people. Joseph does not want to go further south, because it is not healthy; his people die even at Leavenworth. Joseph surrendered just to save his people, so why should he go further south and let his people perish?

Estoweaz:—These two men have explained what occurred between General Miles and Joseph. I was there myself and heard the conversation, because we watch our Chief, and if he tells us to do anything, we do it. When General Miles proposed that Joseph should surrender, we were all glad to surrender; even the children wished to surrender when General Miles sent a man to ask us.

Mr. Baird:—I have heard what these three men have said to you this morning. They have told you what took place between General Miles and Joseph. When General Miles took the Nez Perces to Tongue River, he got orders from the Great Father to take them where the food was plenty. The Great Father has a great many soldiers at Tongue River, and he did not know whether there would be enough for them and the Nez Perces all winter. He wanted them to be comfortable, so he told General Miles to put them where there would be food enough for all winter. So General Miles went himself to put them on the cars, so that they would go safely to where they are now, at Fort Leavenworth. I told you yesterday that General Miles had asked to have the Nez Perces go back to their old home. I told you also that the friends of the Nez Perces (the Americans) wanted them to go back. If White Bird and the Nez Perces, who are here, will go over and join Joseph, there is a very good prospect that they will go back; but if White Bird and his people stay here, there is not a good prospect that Joseph and his people will go back, and I will tell you why: the Great Father may say, "White Bird and his people are living with my enemies, the Sioux, and as long as they live with my enemies I don't want Joseph and his people to go back to their old home." The best thing you here can do to bring about their returning to their old home, is to go over and join him. I tell you again I do not think there is any prospect of Joseph's going back if you stay here, but I think there is a good prospect if you go over with me and join Joseph.

White Bird:—I am glad we are all here to hear Council. You have explained before what the Government wished them to do. Now we know what the Government think[s] about it. We are all glad to hear it. I am glad the other Chiefs surrendered. When they surrendered it shewed they did not want to fight any more. I feel very happy to hear the conversation between General Miles and Joseph. I understand that Chief Joseph and his people don't want to go to the country south of Leavenworth, because it is unhealthy. I hear that is a very bad country for them. For my part, I want Joseph to come back to our part of the country. I don't wish to stop with the Sioux. If Joseph comes back to our part of the country, to a good Reservation, I will join him. I don't like the Sioux, and don't want to stop [stay] with them. I don't care for the Sioux; I just camp there to pass the time. My heart is very good, there is not a bit of bad in it. I have no ill-feeling towards the Government, I am not on the war path just now, and I am not going to fight with the American Government, and am not camped with the Sioux just for that purpose. I know what the police have told me, that I have to behave. I have been told I could sleep well as long as I behave myself. I have kept the advice the Mounted Police have given me.

Col. Macleod [apparently to Yellow Bull, Husis Kute, and Estoweaz]:—I heard you, a few minutes ago, saying that you had seen General Miles and Joseph shake hands, and was glad to hear, at the time, that you had made peace. White Bird and the Nez Perces here, on this side, were not there to shake hands. [Apparently turning to White Bird's party:] Some of them told Major Irvine that they wanted to shake hands with the Americans, and to go back to the other side and join their friends there. The President, as soon as he heard this, was glad, as is shown by his sending an officer all the way here to extend the hand of friendship and to offer you protection if you would return; and not only protection, but to take, transport and feed you on your road to where Joseph is. I think this is a very kind and generous offer on behalf of the President, and if you do not accept it now it may never occur again. I told you, yesterday, that the only thing you could rely on in this country for support was the buffalo. We have a large number of Indians in this country, and we have to make provision for them, so Indians from the other side can expect nothing here but protection from their enemies. I want you to think well over this. Let what I have said influence you in this matter. You are not deciding for to-day and for yourselves, but for years to come and for your wives and children. These three men shew that you can trust and have confidence in the American Government; they tell you they have been well treated down there, and there is no reason to doubt but that you will be treated as they have been. If you take my advice you will go there and be happy too.

The statements of either side were seemingly given with neither reflection nor discussion among the members, and the meetings on Tuesday morning thus appear to have been relatively brief. Following Macleod's remarks, the assembly adjourned— the parties to resume their talk in the afternoon, when the opposing commentaries grew longer:

White Bird:—Since we talked this morning with you, we went out and had a Council, and, for my part, I do not want to go. I am going to ask you one question. I have a brother here. I would like to send a man down, providing you would promise he would return to his camp. If you promise he would return, I would send him down to see Joseph.

Colonel Macleod:—Who are you addressing?

White Bird:—Both, (Colonel Macleod and Mr. Baird.)

Mr. Baird:—What do you want to have him go for?

White Bird:—I want to send him down and find out how my Indians are going to be treated.

Mr. Baird:—I speak first to White Bird. You said, yesterday, that it was just the same as if Joseph was here; that your heart had gone to Joseph, and Joseph's heart had come to you. The men you have seen have come from Joseph to you, and they have told you all that anyone can tell you. If it would do any good to have any men go over and bring them back again, I would take them. I don't think it would do any good to have them go in that way, because they [your people] have seen men from there. I speak now to White Bird and all the Indians. White Bird says he does not want to go back with me; if there are any here who do wish to go back with me, they can do so. Colonel Macleod has told you, and I tell you, that those who go will do better than those who stay.

Colonel Macleod:—White Bird has said he does not want to return. I would like to hear what the rest of you have to say. Each one of you has to judge for yourself, and if you wish to go you can go, each man must make up his own mind for himself whether he is to go or to stay. You will never have so good a chance to return to Joseph and your friends as you have now. A great many bad men through the country have been telling you lies. Don't believe them; don't let those lies influence you. What we and my officers tell you is the truth. If the Queen heard that I told you a lie, she would punish me for it, and, knowing that what we tell you is the truth, let each one of you think well of the offer the Americans have made you. Your great desire appears to get back to your own. From what Mr. Baird says, it appears probable that Joseph will be sent back, and, from what this officer (Mr. Baird) says, the best way to get this done is to [*sic*] for you to go back. From what this officer (Mr. Baird) says, it appears improbable that they will be sent to their old homes unless you join together. From letters I have received from the Governor and officials at Ottawa, I understand that the American authorities are paying great attention to the Indians, and there is a determined intention that you will be well treated. I am convinced that the Indian can look to the American Government with great confidence of good treatment. Think well before you decide not to go; and my advice to you is to accept the kind and generous offer they have made you. The journey will be easy; you will be well fed, and, at the end of it, you will join your own people.

Mr. Baird:—I want to tell you one thing more. Perhaps some of you think you can go back one at a time, just as you please, and have it all right. I want to tell you it will not be all right getting back one at a time, slipping over the line. It will be all right with those who go back with me and join Joseph. Those who slip back, one at a time, can be arrested as hostile Indians. They can be considered so, because they did fight, and have never made peace. I stand here, to-day, and offer you the only terms of peace the United States Government have made to you since the war. It is good for you, and a great deal better for you than it is for us or the Queen's officers, to make peace. The United States Government is great, and the Queen's Government is great, and they think well of the Nez Perces, and that is the reason they make you this offer. You have to consider, not that you are doing a good thing for me, but that you are doing a good thing for yourselves, your wives and children.[14]

White Bird:—My country is over here. Joseph is in the wrong direction, and why should I go to him?

Mr. Baird:—I told you this morning why I thought you ought to do that. I will say it again for you. I want you all to understand. I think you ought to go because if you go now you have a good chance to go to your old home, but if you don't, you will not have a good chance of going, or Joseph either. If you go over with me, you make peace with the United States, and the United States can give you favors; if you don't go over with me, my Government cannot consider you as friends, and can't give you favors; and those are the reasons why I said you ought to go with me—for your own good.

White Bird:—These men (three Nez Perces) were sent by the Government to find out how we feel towards the Government. I want to go back to my country but will not go down to Leavenworth.[15]

Mr. Baird:—Are there any others who want to say anything to me or the Queen's officers? (A long pause.)

Col. Macleod:—Do any of you want to say anything? When White Bird spoke, he spoke for himself; now I want to hear from the others whether they will accept the kind offer of the American Government. Now I want to hear from the others. White Bird spoke for himself as he said.

White Bird:—You know what I said.

Col. Macleod:—Yes, you spoke for yourself; now I want to hear the others.

White Bird:—What I said, I said for all my people.

Col. Macleod:—Do you all agree to it? What I want to know is, whether you agree with White Bird. White Bird has refused the offer the American Government has made; now I want to know whether you refuse also?

No Hunter:—My brothers, I am listening to you talking.[16] Since I first saw the white man I never had any bad feeling towards him. When the white and red men first met together, as far back as I can remember, they never had any trouble. The white man thinks the red man kind, and the red man thinks the white man kind. My father has told me I liked the white man. I have seen my father give a horse to show his friendship for them. I remember when the Cayus [Cayuse] Indians and the Government fought. I remember when my father travelled many miles to keep his people quiet when the Government and the Cayus were fighting. When I saw that, I said to myself: I am going to follow my father's plan. The people, during the war, obeyed my father when he told them not to fight. Now, I have been listening to you talking all the time, and it seems both parties, white men and Indians, don't want any more trouble. As near as I can learn, our Indians and the Government don't want to fight against one another; and now it seems there is a misunderstanding because White Bird does not want to surrender, and the Government does not want to send him back to his own country. I heard White Bird say he was glad to have peace, and I thought so myself. White Bird has told you he is going to move away from the Sioux camp; he does not want to remain with them. Now I see there is nothing to prevent my going to see

Joseph. White Bird has said that it is very likely Joseph is going to move away from his country, and he (White Bird) is going to move away from the Sioux. I would like it. I have learned that the Government wishes Joseph and his Band to go to one place, and I feel in my heart I would like to see him. I would like to go with you and see my relations and come back here. What is going to prevent me from going? I would like to go down and see my relations and come back here. I understand that Mr. Baird and Col. Macleod say that if I go it is no use for me to go alone. I suppose if I go alone it will not cause a war between the American Government and White Bird's Band here. I know the feelings of the United States and Canadian Governments, and they want to treat the Indians kindly, so why can't I go down? For my part, I know we are not going to bother either Governments [sic] long. I like to travel. I would like to go to Leavenworth to see the Indians, not for a bad purpose, but for a good one. Now I ask that question. White Bird does not want to surrender, and that does not look well. I can't understand. Both parties have their doubts. The Government won't promise to send them back to their own country; and this party won't surrender, and I don't understand it. You have seen and shaken hands with White Bird and his men, and it won't take me long to go down and come back again. I want to do what is good, and will not commit any more depredations.

Mr. Baird:—It is several weeks ago since the Great Chief wrote the letter I brought up here. The Great Chief thought that, because the Nez Perces had sent word to the effect that they wanted to come over. When he wrote the letter he told me what to do when you came over, but he did not suppose you would refuse to come over. He did not tell me to bring any over and send them back, because he did not suppose any of you would want to; because my Great Chief did not tell me you might come over and return. I will not tell you so, for I might be telling you a lie. I take great pains to tell you the truth, and I tell you we want you to come over and be friends. I will not tell you you can return, because the Great Chief did not say so. I don't wish to tell you you can, because you may not be able to. The reason the letter was written was because you wanted to surrender, and we supposed you did want to.

Several Indians:—Who is the man that came here and said we wanted to surrender?

Major Irvine:—Henry; the young man who speaks English. He came and spoke to me in the camp.[17]

Mr. Gilson:—One of them told me if Joseph came over he would go. That one did (pointing to an Indian).

Major Irvine:—I saw in the papers that three Nez Perces were coming up, and I told them so.

No Hunter:—Henry ran away, because his father is in Idaho. We did not know he wanted to go.

Mr. Baird:—Where is Joseph's daughter?

No Hunter:—Henry knew he was lying, so he ran away and took Joseph's daughter with him.

White Bird:—I did not know a word about it. I was in another camp when they ran off.

Col. Macleod:—Have you made up your minds to accept the offer? Give an answer. If you want to talk it over you may do so to-night.

White Bird:—We like to see you (to Mr. Baird).

Mr. Baird:—I am glad to have seen you, but I would not have come had I thought you did not want to make friends with my Government.

White Bird:—I would like to send a man down to where Joseph is.

Col. Macleod:—You have three men straight from Joseph; won't you believe them?

White Bird:—Suppose you won't promise that this man will return, he will not go. I would like to send him, although I have seen men from there.

Col. Macleod:—I do not want to force any of you to go, but am advising you for your good. You have a splendid chance. Mr. Baird offers to take you down. These men have told you how they were treated, and I have no doubt you will be treated in the same way. Don't be influenced by what anyone tells you; go according to your own hearts. After a little while you will be glad if you go. You have only to look at those three men to see how happy they are.

No Hunter:—I would like to go and come back.

Col. Macleod:—Mr. Baird has come up here and has no instructions as to that. Your friends have come from there, and your going alone could do no good.

Mr. Baird (to No Hunter):—Do you believe that these three men have been telling you lies? Is there any man down there who will tell you truth better than these men? It is because you have seen them and I have no letter, is the reason I will not promise you shall come back.

No Hunter:—Will you give me time to think?

Mr. Baird:—This (Col. Macleod) is the Chief of all the Queen's officers here. He says I can tell you some of his officers and men will go with you to your camp, and if any of you wish to come back from camp with the Queen's officers you can go down with me—any of you and your families. I shall wait here till the Queen's officers come back from your camp, and will hear what you have to say. It will be the same then as now; those who wish to go can go, and those who wish to stay can do so.

With that, the session adjourned. Baird did not have to wait long for an answer, however. That evening, after the Indians had deliberated among themselves, the assembly reconvened for the final decision:

White Bird:—We will not go.

Col. Macleod:—Have any of the others anything to say?

No Hunter:—I will not go.

Col. Macleod:—Do the others agree to the same thing?

No Hunter:—Our Chief does not want to go, and we will not go either.

In its entirety, the council transcript, with its linguistic twists and turns, is somewhat difficult to comprehend. Condensed, the concepts become more simplified. Throughout, Baird exhibited a disturbing psychology in playing on White Bird's emotions connecting him to Joseph and his surrendered followers. At first blush, he violated the proviso in his instructions against alluring the Indians by insinuating that the prospect of White Bird's people returning to their homeland rested entirely with the fate of Joseph's people at Fort Leavenworth; that is, when and if Joseph ever returned home, White Bird's followers, having surrendered and been sent to join Joseph, would themselves be permitted to return. The linkage was an untruth likely contrived to work on the people's strong sense of family, friends, and community, and in fact represented but a remote possibility. (Nor did Baird mention that even as he spoke preparations ensued for moving Joseph's people from Fort Leavenworth south to the Quapaw Reservation in extreme northeastern Indian Territory, where many would subsequently perish from disease.)

At the outset of the meeting, Commissioner Macleod advised the Indians to take the American offer and go back, as the declining buffalo herds would not sustain them for long. Baird told them that Miles had advocated sending Joseph's people home in the spring, but that limited food resources at Fort Keogh necessitated sending them to Fort Leavenworth;[18] if White Bird and his followers agreed, they could join Joseph, "and it may be at your old home" (meaning in the possible rather than permissive sense). Joining Joseph was thus the "quickest way" to return to their home country. Yellow Bull, Husis Kute, and Estoweaz all acknowledged the good treatment they had received with Joseph, yet registered concerns about going farther south. Baird then suggested that White Bird's continued association with the enemy Lakotas would influence the decision whether to move Joseph back home, eliciting from the Lamtama attempts to ward off that onus with such statements as "I don't like the Sioux," and "I don't care for the Sioux."

At Tuesday afternoon's meeting, the Nez Perce chief professed his disinclination to go—seemingly casting aside the reports of Yellow Bull, Husis Kute, and Estoweaz—and he told Baird he wanted to send his own man down to determine how his people would be treated. The lieutenant responded that that information was already at hand from the three tribesmen. Baird discouraged the people from going back singly or in small groups, as they might be arrested as hostile Indians. He and Macleod advised acceptance of the U.S. offer by others of the Nez Perces who felt compelled to go, telling them that "the journey will be easy," and that "you will be well fed, and, at the end of it, you will join your own people." One of the few Nimiipuu present, No Hunter, said he wanted to go (perhaps as the emissary White Bird wanted to send), but made it clear that he wanted to return into Canada. When the question arose as to the source of the supposed impetus among White Bird's people for surrendering and going home, some identified a young man named Henry, who had apparently gone south with Wottolen's group in May, as having passed false information to that effect. At the final session on the evening of July 2, White Bird spoke for all his people when he told the assembled officers, "We will not go." With that response, Baird's mission ended. According to MacDonald, White Bird "thought the soldiers had told him falsehoods regarding the country and climate to which they would be taken. . . . He could not see the necessity of going to Fort Leavenworth and thence to Idaho. It was a shorter journey from where he was than from Fort Leavenworth, and he will wait until the return of Joseph before leaving the British possessions."[19]

Years later, MacDonald recalled a variant account of part of the proceedings. According to Lucullus V. McWhorter, who interviewed him, MacDonald recalled seeing Lieutenant Baird, whose left ear still bore evidence of having been grazed by a Nez Perce bullet at Bear's Paw. According to MacDonald's recounting of the events for McWhorter, White Bird asked the lieutenant, "Where is Chief Joseph? In Idaho?" Baird told him that he was "in the East," and if he surrendered "you will see Joseph and likely go back to Idaho, but if you do not surrender, Joseph is likely never to see Idaho." MacDonald then offered a stirring rendition of what happened next:

White Bird was slow of speech and deliberate in what he was saying. He had been talking sitting down, but now he raised to his feet, [and] he fixed his gaze on the two British officers, and pointing at them for a moment, spoke through the interpreter, "You, Queen's officers, I want you to listen well and hear my promises to this United States officer." Then turning dramatically to Captain [sic] Baird, he shook his finger at him with outstretched hand for a moment, and spoke in measured tones, "I want you to understand what I am saying. You go back and bring Chief Joseph to Idaho. I will know, I will hear of it. Do this, and I am promising to surrender. I will come to Idaho if I have to go afoot. . . ." Captain Baird answered, "[I] will not say that." "Then I will stay and die in Canada," replied White Bird.[20]

Whatever the closing scene, White Bird evidently rethought the proposition, for within days of the adjournment of the Fort Walsh meeting the chief sent baffling word by one of Macleod's scouts that "if he is sent to his old home he would like to go," but with a Mounted Police escort, because he remained "distrustful of the Americans." Neither occurred, and in the following months the Canadian government attempted to clarify evident confusion over the origin of Lieutenant Baird's visit based on the Nimiipuu expressed inquiry regarding their reported desire to surrender (they apparently believed that Baird had come to Fort Walsh to negotiate with them). Despite reports, messages, and remarks made by them that contributed to the American determination to pursue the surrender of White Bird and his people, both Irvine and Walsh formally disavowed responsibility for conveying data upon which the United States government acted in formulating the Baird mission.[21]

In any event, following the unsuccessful effort to bring White Bird and the remaining Nez Perces back to the United States, Baird and his party (now including the son of one of the Indians), departed south on July 3; the lieutenant returned to Fort Keogh on the 11th and Clark went on to Fort Abraham Lincoln to accompany the Northern Cheyennes south. Yellow Bull, Husis Kute, Estoweaz, and the youth went on to Fort Leavenworth, joining Joseph and the Nimiipuu people there in the move to the Indian Territory, where they stayed until their 1885 return to the Northwest. At Fort Keogh, Baird immediately telegraphed a summary report to the adjutant general, Division of the Missouri, in Chicago. In it, the lieutenant made clear that the Indians "disclaimed all wish for war and expressed desire to return. Had been told would be sent to Indian Territory, would not return unless could go to old home in Idaho. If I had [had] authority to promise that, think could have brought in entire band, twenty-five lodges." The document clarified further that the original stimulus for the mission had been based on faulty information. Baird reported: "They said that those who had previously expressed wish to return did not represent the band, and that they, to number of twenty men with their families, also Joseph's daughter, had [previously] started west to get home that way." He concluded by predicting that "if Joseph's band is sent to Idaho, many of White Bird's band will join it there and some will probably [go there] at any rate, unless prevented or arrested on arrival. . . . Colonels Macleod and Irvine [sic] manifested great desire to have Nez Perces come over and surrender and used strong efforts to that end."[22]

Baird's comment that White Bird's Indians "had been told [that they] would be sent to Indian Territory" is not borne out in the

Canadian transcript of the proceedings. Other than two allu-
sions—one to unhealthy lands "further south," and another to
"country south of Leavenworth," there appears no specific mention of the Indian Territory and the imminent relocation of
Joseph's people to those tracts. And with good reason, for any
such reference removing the tribesmen south from Leavenworth
to unapproved lands would likely have nullified further discus-
sions and certainly doomed Baird's mission. While it is possible
that White Bird's Nez Perces made note of the Indian Territory
option in informal comments to Baird and the Canadian officers
present preceding or following the sessions, it is possible, too, that
Baird used the reference to help rationalize the negligible results
of his conference with those people. In the end, Baird's mission
seems to have germinated from scant unsubstantiated reports
generated by a few Nez Perces who individually expressed their
desire to return and who did indeed go forth below the line in the
late spring and early summer of 1878. The rumors nonetheless res-
onated not only among American army officials, but among select
Mounted Police authorities as well; together they created an
atmosphere that misled both sides to anticipate results that, for
White Bird and the majority of his followers, at least, could not
and would not be sanctioned.

CHAPTER 7

CANADIAN STALWARTS

Chief White Bird's insistence on Joseph's return to the Northwest as preliminary to his own departure from Canada drove his decision to remain in the Queen's country in the months and years following Lieutenant Baird's attempt to convince those Nimiipuu to return to the United States and join their kinsmen at Fort Leavenworth. In subsequent interviews with Duncan MacDonald, the Lamtama leader repeatedly alluded to the prospect of going south. "I came over here simply as to an asylum, and am waiting Joseph's return to Idaho. . . . If the [United States] Government sends him back to his home in Idaho, I will at once go back and make peace." And, in regard to the recent forced relocation of Joseph's people from Kansas to the Indian Territory, White Bird declared, "If Joseph is moved to the Indian Territory I will not surrender, because it is against my will and Joseph's will to go to that place." "The United States recognizes Indians as nations and not as slaves," he said. "Why does she want to coop us up in a bad climate that will cause us to die in a short time?" While adamant in his position, he was realistic in the face of growing game shortages north of the line: "I don't want to fight. I want justice from the Americans, and if I cannot get it I am going to remain in the North and do the best I can for subsistence."[1]

That, in essence, is the course White Bird followed for the next several years. He, his family, and some immediate followers stayed in Canada. Although largely undocumented, it is likely that attrition from his ranks continued, with small groups of people continuing to pull away and make their way directly to Lapwai or intermittently to the welcoming hearths of neighboring friendly tribes or even of former enemy peoples. One such instance occurred early in the summer of 1879, when a group of Canadian Nez Perces appeared in Montana within forty miles of the Flathead Indian Reservation. Informed of their presence, Agent Peter Ronan sent word that if they entered the reservation they would be arrested and held as prisoners. The Indians had been inspired by an elderly chief, Eagle from the Light, who had left Idaho before the war to live with friends on the Flathead Reservation and now welcomed his brethren to do the same. The party was headed by Looking Glass's brother, No Hunter, who had spoken prominently during the conference with Lieutenant Baird and the Mounted Police the previous year, and who requested Ronan to contact authorities in Washington regarding their situation.

These Nez Perces desired "to get a home either on the Jocko [Flathead] Reservation or somewhere in this northern country where they could cultivate the soil and live in peace." Commissioner of Indian Affairs Ezra A. Hayt answered in late October, telling Ronan that the tribesmen might enter the reservation only "as prisoners of war, and trust to the clemency of the Government." Thereafter, No Hunter, joined by Eagle from the Light and Red Mountain—another Nimiipuu living among the Flatheads—met with Ronan at the St. Ignatius Mission, where the Reverend Joseph M. Cataldo, S.J., interpreted. No Hunter agreed to the conditions, but hedged on committing his followers and instead offered to explain the terms to them and return with their decision the next spring. "We want a home here," he told Ronan. "Your [Flathead] Indians are willing that we can come upon their lands or live somewhere here as neighbors. . . . Give us a home among our friends where our children will grow up and follow the white man's road." After the council, No Hunter led these Nez Perces back into Canada.[2]

Thereafter, the documentary trail of most of the Nimiipuu still living north of the international boundary for the most part becomes murky. Because these people were never recognized as Canadian Indians—that is, part of any existing treaties—they were scarcely referenced in official reports or correspondence except, perhaps, incidentally, and mostly then whenever individuals brought notice for having perpetrated crimes, and so on. (In 1879, for example, Indian Commissioner Edgar Dewdney cited "some Nez Perces" having come upon [and reported?] some Stoney [Assiniboine] Indians butchering cattle presumably killed by the Stoneys.[3]) Rarely, brief mentions of the Nez Perces appeared in area papers.[4]

At the time of the departure south of the group with No Hunter in the summer of 1879 (although only to return that fall), White Bird's immediate following seems to have dwindled to ten or twelve lodges numbering probably fewer than one hundred people, some of them doubtless represented in No Hunter's group. Over the following year, as the subsistence situation among the Lakotas worsened, the Nez Perces drew farther away from them and coalesced more and more in the area of Fort Macleod, not far from the Piegan Reserve, where by now their presence had become acknowledged. Although there is record of the people continuing to hunt and to trade horses below the border in 1880, it is likely that more individuals and family groups drifted away to forge new associations with Canadian or American tribes. White Bird and his family, among others—perhaps influenced by the southwestern Alberta mountains' similarity to those in eastern Oregon—located approximately fifty miles southwest of Fort Macleod, near a quarry along the banks of Pincher Creek and west of the community of Pincher Creek, near the edge of the Piegan Reserve. There, within view of the foothills in an area between the Piegan lands and the Mounted Police station, the tribesmen raised cabins of poplar and pine logs. They lived at what was locally termed the "Nez Percy camp," evidently down the hill close to a

wagon ford of the creek near a place called High Bush, and existed
on whatever game resources they might acquire in the vicinity
while drawing occasional employment from local establishments.
Along the cliff banks near High Bush, the people reportedly exca-
vated bread ovens. Reportedly, too, in the summer White Bird
kept his two wives segregated in different tepees, alternately visiting them. In 1880, at least two Nimiipuu men whose names were
recorded only as Dexter and Dick worked for a freighter around
Fort Macleod. In a dispute over wages, they sued Thomas Ban-
bury before Lieutenant Colonel Macleod and the case was settled.
Two Nez Perce women, sisters named Sarah and Kate, meantime
had jobs in the growing Pincher Creek community. An early resident described the two as having apparently been scarred from
injuries received in some action, perhaps in the Nez Perce War.
Sarah was "a handsome woman" who "used to ride around on
horseback selling berries for which she asked 25 cents."[5]

A settler named G. W. Morden recalled the Nez Perces in the
community bartering fish, venison, mountain sheep meat, blue-
berries, and gooseberries for sugar, tea, and flour. He termed the
people "the finest type of Indians I have ever seen [—] lithe, keen
fellows six feet and over in height with aquiline noses and strong
features. They were splendid hunters and perfect horsemen."
Morden remembered that these people denoted Americans by the
sobriquet "Boston man" versus "King George man" for the Canadians. In one instance, the Fort Macleod newspaper commented
on their fishing proclivities: "Some fine trout were recently
brought in by the Nez Perce Indians. Some of them must have
weighed as much as ten or fifteen pounds." For the most part,
however, the Nez Perces at Pincher Creek maintained a low profile and evidently worked diligently when afforded the opportunity. Occasionally the records reflected crimes committed by these
people (or suspected to have been committed by them), as well as
incidents of public drunkenness. In January 1883, Nez Perces
were implicated in the killing of cattle near Pincher Creek. The
Mounted Police sent a detachment from Fort Macleod to investi-
gate, but the results proved inconclusive. Superintendent Crozier

nevertheless instructed his men "to watch these Indians closely, and if such is the case they will no doubt be detected." In the autumn of 1888, a Nez Perce identified as Fish Hawk was convicted of drunk and disorderly conduct and sentenced to one month of hard labor; thirty-four days later, Fish Hawk repeated the offense, was again found guilty, and received the same penalty. And in September 1894, two individuals known as Nez Perce Jack and Nez Perce Pete were charged with receiving stolen property and theft, respectively (of property worth less than $10). Each received a sentence of "1 month imprisonment with hard labour."[6]

Not all of the Nimiipuu who left White Bird's nucleus moved south and west. A few individuals seem to have migrated north to the area around Fort Battleford, accompanying some Nakota-Assiniboine (Stoney) bands from the area of the Cypress Hills and Fort Walsh, when those people took up new reserves away from the international boundary in June 1882. Three years later, when the North-West Rebellion erupted, in which the Métis in what is now Saskatchewan (aided by various Indian groups) sought government representation and self-determination within the Dominion government, at least two Nez Perces who then lived among the Stoneys took part and were killed in the ensuing conflict. According to a remembrance by an employee on the Cree reserve,

> One of these [Nez Perces] disappeared early in the disturbance and it was said in the camp that he had gone into the barracks [at Fort Battleford]. It appears that he had put in a good deal of his time among the police, doing little chores for them in return for his food, and this intimacy was given as reason for such deduction. However, after all was over, his body was found in the bush on the south side of the [Battle] river, and nothing is known as to how he met his end.

Further, this man, fighting with the rebels and recognized only as Nez Perce Jack, was shot and killed by Private Harry H. Nash of the Battleford Home Guards positioned across Battle River while

Jack harrassed a water detail near Fort Battleford. On May 2, 1885, the other Nez Perce, identified as Hole in the Nose, died at Cut Knife Hill, forty miles west of Battleford, fighting with the rebels, when a coalition of fifteen hundred Crees and Assiniboines led by Chief Poundmaker successfully withstood an assault by forces under Colonel William Otter. Hole in the Nose was shot as the Indians advanced preparing to charge the government artillery complement. Otter's troops eventually withdrew after a hard day of fighting.[7]

Most of the Nez Perces who remained in Canada managed to avoid entanglement in the Métis crisis. As indicated, there is scarcely any mention of the people in area tabloids; the dearth of press notice is perhaps indicative of how generally law abiding and low profile they had become, but it is also likely a reflection of just how few of them still remained in Canada—or remained there together. Of those still there, White Bird, the only major Nimiipuu leader to cross the line in 1877, seems to have kept largely to himself and his family. After Joseph and his followers returned to the Northwest in 1885, White Bird, who had vowed to return there after Joseph did, changed his mind, deciding to stay in his cabin in his adopted land. By then in his early sixties at least, the chief whose tribal leadership status was largely unknown to area whites seems to have increasingly ministered to those of his followers who stayed nearby. White Bird was a shaman, or medicine man, and during his expatriation he seems to have indulged this proclivity on behalf of the Nez Perces in the Pincher Creek community.

Yellow Wolf, who had returned to Lapwai in 1878, told a story he evidently learned later about White Bird in Canada, and how a tall white man known to the Nimiipuu as Owl Eyes happened to meet White Bird while working as a cowboy near the line. The encounter, grounded in the reputed mysticism of the aging chief, proved tragic for the cowboy. When he saw White Bird, Owl Eyes spoke to him in Nez Perce, addressing him three times by his name of Peopeo Hihi. But each time the chief denied that he was that person, finally saying "My name Chow-kes-kus." Again, four

times more White Bird denied his identity. As Yellow Wolf
recounted:

The fifth time White Bird was mad and said to Owl Eyes: "You
are no good son of bitch! I will kill you right here!" Owl Eyes
stepped away. He kept his mouth shut, said nothing. Always
when White Bird came to that place, the Canadian soldiers
wearing red coats [Mounted Police] gave him food. They were
friends, and liked White Bird. After Owl Eyes left him, White
Bird was sitting out alone. A soldier came out and called to him,
"Come over here!" White Bird came, and the soldier took him
to the dinner-room. He saw Owl Eyes there sitting at the table.
The soldier gave White Bird a seat beside Owl Eyes. Owl Eyes
said again, "You are Peopeo Hihi!" This was repeated and Owl
Eyes got mad. He kept quiet for a time. Then he drew his hand
back like this, across his own breast, and struck White Bird in
the face [demonstrating a backhanded blow]. The food was red
with blood that gushed from his nose. Blood was on the table-
cloth. A soldier hurried there and spoke sharply to Owl Eyes:
"Hold on! You do not have to do that to him!"
    White Bird got up from his chair. He stepped out from the
room all bloody. The soldier followed him and helped him
wash the blood from his face. The blood flowed for quite a
while. When [it] stopped, the soldier said to him, "Better come
now and eat!" But White Bird replied, "No! I do not feel like eating." White Bird then went home to his tepee. It came middle
of afternoon, when Owl Eyes felt an itching on his wrist. It was
like a mosquito bite. It began to swell, and soon his arm was
growing big. He then found that was a medicine man's work.
He had more than one doctor to come, but they could not help
him. Nothing they could do was any good. Owl Eyes thought,
"I better go to the Indian doctor about this!" He said to a soldier,
"Go see this Indian I struck. He must be a medicine man. I offer
him this one hundred dollars if he will fix up my hand and
arm." The soldier went and showed Peopeo Hihi the one hundred dollars, and said, "You are needed over there right away!"

Peopeo Hihi made reply: "No! I will not go! He is mad at me and might shoot me!" Peopeo Hihi did not go. That evening before sleep-time, Owl Eyes was dead. *Chow-kes-kus*, the man-goat knows! He was protecting Peopeo Hihi. When Owl Eyes struck, he had his horn standing out from Peopeo Hihi's breast. The wrist of Owl Eyes had struck the point of that horn. The man-goat's power is strong medicine. Peopeo Hihi had this power. His medicine man's [*sic*—medicine's?] name was *Chow-kes-kus*.[8]

Although Yellow Wolf's account was certainly hearsay, it exuded the mystical quality about White Bird that seems to have focused the chief's last years and provides an entrée to what finally happened to him at Pincher Creek. One of White Bird's neighbors in the community was a Nimiipuu man named Charlie Ilamnieenimhoosoos, also known, according to Yellow Wolf, as Hasenahmahkikt. This individual—who was commonly identified among area white residents as "Nez Percee Sam," but was apparently known among his people as Left Hand—presumably had been born in the United States and had come into Canada as a youth following the Bear's Paw action in 1877. Twenty-six years old in 1892, Sam stood nearly five feet ten inches tall and was married to two women with whom he had several children. He had lived at Pincher Creek for some years where he and his wives earned money by fishing and making and selling articles of clothing.[9]

There exist several accounts of this man's motivation for killing White Bird. One version—again offered by Yellow Wolf—stated that when Sam's son became mortally ill the father asked the youth, "Who are you?" and he responded, "Peopeo Hihhih"— interpreted by Sam to mean that the power of White Bird was killing his son. Subsequently, the second son fell deathly ill, and when the father asked, "Who are you?" the youth likewise responded with the medicine man's name before he succumbed. Thereupon, acting in accordance with tribal custom, Sam determined to kill White Bird. Another account, however, suggests only that the two boys' lives had been threatened by the magical force of the Lamtama chief. Other reports described other scenarios—one of Piegan origin stated that one of the youths entered White Bird's cabin and distressed him by running around and causing a commotion, whereupon the man aimed his pipe at the boy and he collapsed dead. Regardless of how one or another of the sons purportedly perished, the death or deaths, or the imminent threats of such, convinced Sam that White Bird, through his "evil influence," was intent on destroying his family.[10]

Exactly how White Bird died emerged in the transcript of the court proceedings of Monday, May 30, 1892, as recorded at Pincher Creek by then-Justice James F. Macleod of the Supreme Court of the North-West Territories. Six sworn jurors heard the testimony, and Charles F. P. Conybeare prosecuted on behalf of the Crown. The case was followed closely in the Canadian press. On the evening of March 6, 1892, the chief had left his cabin to go to the stream. He never returned. White Bird's two wives, Kate and Wyanatotampip, recalled hearing shouting and other vocal sounds in the distance, as of one afraid and suffering. Kate left the cabin and saw Sam carrying an axe, moving quickly past with his two sons. (According to Kate, Sam admitted to the killing: "Sam hallooed to me 'I killed your husband up above there,'" and she related to Wyanatotampip what Sam had said when she returned inside.) Sam shortly had one of the sons hide the axe, then Sam destroyed his clothing in a bonfire set near his home. The next morning a Nimiipuu man named Billy came upon White Bird's body and notified the Mounted Police. Kate also saw the body, located "about 15 yards from my home." She related that "when I saw Sam he was coming from where the body was." Sergeant James Davis investigated and found a single set of tracks leading from the corpse to within a few yards of Sam's house, at which place he arrested the Nez Perce man for the murder. Aided by members of a coroner's jury, Davis made a thorough search of the crime scene and turned up the still-bloody axe in a woodpile. The sergeant also located in Sam's house a pair of moccasins that precisely matched the footprints leading from the dead man's body; he later uncovered pieces of scorched clothing from the scene of the bonfire. Sam's wife nobly maintained that she, not her husband, had killed the Lamtama, and both were incarcerated to await trial for the deed (she was apparently later released in Justice Macleod's care). As for the relationship between White Bird and Sam, Kate told the court that "White Bird tried to be good friends with Sam, but Sam would not [reciprocate]. I did not hear any threats made by Sam." Wyanatotampip recalled that "Sam and White Bird were not good friends for the last four years."

The Nez Perce man, Billy, testified that he had seen the bonfire burning when he returned to his home after dark. He found White Bird's body next morning when he went after horses. "The body was lying on its side, and chopped all up," he stated. "It was just beyond White Bird's house about 70 feet off. It was laying in a hollow there." Billy identified the moccasin tracks in the mud (it had snowed during the night) as those of a man and pointed them out to Sergeant Davis. Davis recounted that Sam at first refused to be arrested, but acceded after the sergeant placed his hand on his revolver. Apparently a map of the crime scene was prepared, showing the location of White Bird's body thirty paces away from his house. Davis saw no signs of a struggle. Blood from the axe was analyzed by Dr. William S. Smith, who collected it at the scene and who concluded, "[I]t is the blood of some mammal of which man is the principal order." Dr. Smith also concluded that White Bird had been struck by the axe four times—three of them in the face—and that he had died from a severe brain injury. At the scene, he said, he had fitted the axe to the wounds. At the outset of the trial, the court refused to accept the guilty plea of Mrs. Sam (whose name was Sarah) and entered instead a plea of "not guilty" on her behalf. Later, her two sons—Pete, "an intelligent looking boy of about 12 years of age," and Jack—gave confusing testimony regarding their mother's involvement. They were very much distressed, the youngest "crying in a very pitiful manner."

When Sam addressed the jury, he told them of his innocence, and that White Bird "and I were always friends and I used to share every thing I get at the stores with him." Then he referred to the Lamtama chief's malevolence: "Four years ago he diseased one of my boys and he has diseased others in the camp." The interpreter, Sam Pablo, was unable to properly convey what Sam meant by his remarks. Wrote Justice Macleod. "At last I made out that Sam was accusing White Bird of having had an evil influence over his son and the others. That, in fact, he was 'Bad Medicine' to them. What among the Crees I think is called a 'Windigo.'" The trial amounted to a full-fledged prosecution. Nez Percee Sam had no attorney for his defense, and there was no available counsel in the area who might be assigned, and in the end the jury convicted him of murder. On June 4, Macleod sentenced Sam to die and remanded him to prison to await execution. The convicted man's commitment papers stated that he was "to be imprisoned in Manitoba penitentiary until sixteenth day of July next" and then taken to the place of execution and there hanged.[11]

Press coverage of the death of White Bird and its aftermath started slowly, but expanded significantly following the trial. In 1892, the chief was not well known outside his community.[12] The crime itself drew brief notice in papers in the immediate area, with both *The Macleod Gazette* and *The Lethbridge News* carrying identical copy: "There has been a murder case at Pincher Creek. Two Nez Percee [*sic*] Indians got into a dispute, and one man chopped the other to pieces with an axe. The murderer was arrested."[13] A column in the former tabloid on March 17 presented for the first time a specific motive for the crime, although particulars yet remained unclear:

> The story is somewhat as follows: Nez Percee Sam lived with his family on the outskirts of the village of Pincher Creek. Close by or with him lived another old Indian. Sam and his boys had been in the habit of stealing wood and rails, and the old man had remonstrated with him, saying that if it continued, they would not be allowed to remain where they were. The evening of the killing, there had been a repetition of the stealing, and the old man had again remonstrated. Sam sent his two boys out to thrash the old man, and they went at him with a hatchet. When they saw the blood, they were afraid, and ran back to the house. Sam

then went out with an axe and finished the job, splitting the old man's head open from top to bottom. Sam and his two boys were arrested and brought to Macleod, where they now are.[14]

Although court testimony clarified the events connected with the killing, this element of motive never appeared during the recorded proceedings. In the weeks after the trial, however, Justice Macleod began to second-guess the outcome, largely because of the issue over motive: "The only thing that I can possibly have any doubt about is as to what occurred at the time of the killing. It is just possible," he speculated in a letter to the Minister of Justice in Ottawa,

> that Sam & White Bird met and had a row and in the heat of passion Sam may have delivered the blows which caused White Bird's death. It is significant, however, that Sam in his statement said nothing about a row between them. There is no doubt but that there was bad blood between them on account of White Bird finding fault with Sam's children for stealing fencing from a neighboring ranchman. This did not appear in the evidence and I think the crown prosecutor made a mistake in not bringing it out, as he told me afterwards that he could have established the fact.

Macleod also commented on Mrs. Sam's attempt to take the blame for the crime: "It is a very remarkable and touching thing [about] Sam's wife trying to take the whole weight of the crime upon herself in order to shield her husband." He mentioned that while Sam was jailed at Fort Macleod awaiting trial, she stayed at his home, in one instance relating to the justice's housekeeper "that Sam had nothing to do with the killing." The wife stated that "she had done it, and had cut out the dead man's heart with a knife." "This of course," wrote Macleod, "was utterly untrue."[15]

Between the time of the sentencing and the scheduled execution of Nez Percee Sam, the case regarding the death of White Bird became something of a media sensation across central and western

Canada. There occurred initial confusion over the scheduled date of execution; one paper, *The Manitoba Daily Free Press* announced that Sam was to die on June 16 rather than on July 16. Sentiment rose quickly, especially in Winnipeg, where the district attorney general wired the Defense Ministry of his concern that Sam had not been appropriately defended. "Strong feeling here for Reprieve until full investigation," he reported. The prisoner, along with three other Native convicts accompanied by Sheriff Duncan J. D. Campbell and an escort of Mounted Police, arrived at Stony Mountain as news about the killing and trial quickly circulated. Based on a misconstrued view that Sam had punished the medicine man for having mystically slain his children, one reader took issue with the court's verdict. Wrongly treated by White Bird, concluded citizen J. G. Moore of Winnipeg, "they died, and I should think any of our M.D.'s would think it more than probable that the diagnosis of the father was right. . . .'Blood for blood,'—not a strange idea to be found in an Indian's breast. I feel that this man should not die without an effort being made to save his life." Moore pointed out that "several white men have been convicted of murder in the province of Manitoba within the past ten years, but not one died upon the gallows. . . . I hope public sentiment will not allow this man to die on the scaffold. To do so would be to commit as grave a crime as Nez Percee Sam is convicted of."[16]

As the days leading to the execution passed, public interest mounted in the case. Some raised jurisdictional questions regarding whether existing statutes would permit the hanging of Sam in a judicial division beyond that where the crime had occurred and where sentence had been administered. *The Lethbridge News*, close to the scene, questioned the legitimacy of Mr. Moore's statement regarding White Bird's killing of Sam's children: "He has four children alive now, and the statement concerning the bewitched sons was generally understood to refer to two boys present, and who gave evidence at the trial, and if Sam had any other sons that died, nothing is known about them by the public." The paper pointed out that the "bewitching," however, was not the direct cause of the crime: "The direct cause appears to have been in connection with

certain fence rails owned by Charles G. Geddes. Sam was understood to say he would kill White Bird if he told Geddes. White Bird
did tell Geddes and Sam killed him." The editor condemned the
vengeance murder as "more atrocious when it is remembered that
White Bird was a feeble old man and the prisoner Sam in the prime
of manhood."[17]

Yet a movement for Nez Percee Sam's life had begun. Sparked
by the press coverage, the Reverend John Maclean, Methodist
missionary at Fort Macleod, persuaded that Sam had acted in
defense of his family, welcomed the help of fellow missionary, the
Reverend John McDougall, and others to the cause. Because Sam's
scheduled execution was just weeks away, they and other clergy-
men recruited to the cause had to act quickly. In Winnipeg, the
place where most of the sympathy originated, the Reverend
Arthur W. Goulding, Protestant chaplain of the Stony Mountain
Penitentiary, helped marshal favorable sentiment. Goulding
attended Sam as he awaited retribution, even baptizing him
before the other prisoners, and he came to believe that the Nimiipuu had reacted to the dictates of his Native religion. When the
annual Manitoba and North-West Methodist Church conference
convened in Winnipeg, the Reverends Maclean and McDougall
moved that Sam's sentence be commuted to life imprisonment.
The attendees agreed, voting a resolution asking clemency for
Sam, and a petition bearing in excess of seven hundred signatures
was dispatched to Ottawa along with a plea for commutation
from the Reverend Alfred Andrews, President of the Methodist
Conference. Throughout the region, as well as in eastern Canada,
many newspapers took notice of "Nez Percee Sam" and the fact
that he had had no counsel at his trial, and editorially called for
lifting the death decree.[18]

In the area of Pincher Creek and Fort Macleod the calls for
leniency were mostly unappreciated. The *Macleod Gazette* reacted
strongly. "To see a lot of christian [sic] ministers, headed by two
missionaries, begging for this man's life on these grounds is silly
in the extreme. The men who propose such things should have
long ears and eat grass. Where the Winnipeg people have been

mislead [sic] is in supposing that Nez Percie [sic] Sam's children died from the mal-practice of the Medicine man. They did nothing of the sort, but are as lively and frisky as ever." "The jury was made up of men who live on the spot, and who were the best judges of what Sam deserved. . . . We can see no reason why this Indian should not suffer the consequences of his crime." Ultimately, in the face of excerpted court testimony, the *Free Press* backed away from its call for leniency, stating that "there is nothing to commend Nez Percee Sam to the mercy of the crown, other than the ignorance of an uncivilized Indian in any instance."[19]

Papers respecting Sam's case, including the petition for clemency, lay in the hands of the Dominion's Minister of Justice, Sir John Thompson. Sam reposed in the prison as execution day drew nigh. A correspondent touring the facility described a massive brick edifice fixed with iron grates and thick oak doors. Cells for 102 convicts were arranged in three tiers, or decks, and in early July 1892, 75 occupants resided there. Except for Sam, the only man slated for execution, all of the prisoners passed their days performing labor; because of his condemnation, Sam was spared that assignment and passed his days walking on the grounds. For breakfast Sam, like the others, consumed cold meat "without bone," bread, coffee, and sugar. For dinner they received a larger portion of the same meat, besides bread, potatoes, and soup or tea, while for supper the men devoured bread, tea, and sugar. "Of bread," related the visitor, "it will be noticed there is no restriction; every convict can have as much as he wants." Sam was described as "taking his constitutional" as a squad of prisoners hauled firewood nearby. The visitor exchanged small talk with Sam, commenting that the Indian "has not much English." "He fully realizes his doom, that before another nine suns go down he is to die the death. He does not know how old he is, but he looks only about 25."[20]

But Sam did not die at the appointed time of execution. On the evening of July 8, Warden George L. Foster received telegraphic notification from the Ministry of Justice that on July 7 Governor General Lord Stanley of Preston had laid before the Privy Council a petition favoring the commutation of Sam's sentence to life imprisonment. The reversal no doubt stemmed from the outpouring on Sam's behalf from the Methodists and others who believed that his Native beliefs had been ignored or subordinated during the trial proceedings and that he had not received a modicum of defense. Certainly the opinion of Justice Macleod, who himself acknowledged the lack of an established motive for the crime, went a long way to influence the decision. And his own request to Minister Thompson "that the Royal clemency may be extended to this unfortunate man" likely sealed the matter. Yet Sam did not live long in prison. Doubtless depressed, he purportedly starved himself. Likely infected in the incommodious facility at Stony Mountain, he finally succumbed less than fifteen months later, on October 1, 1893.[21]

By the time of the White Bird's murder in March 1892, the chief had been away from his Idaho home for nearly fifteen years, an estrangement that had compounded with the departure of many of his followers during the late 1870s and early 1880s. Just as White Bird lost personal touch with his extended family and friends to the south, they likewise came to retain inexact recollections of the aging chief, and particularly of the events surrounding his death. While there was consensus that White Bird had been killed with an axe, the perpetrator of the deed was variously identified among the Nimiipuu in Idaho and Washington as Hasenahmahkikt (known in Canada among whites as Nez Percee Sam), Laamnimhoosis or Lammisuim Husis (aka Charley Ilamnieenimhoosoos, or Shriveled Head), and Robert Moses. One account stated that Shriveled Head "blamed White Bird for the bringing on of the war. They got into a quarrel and he killed White Bird with an ax or hatchet." Another stated that White Bird "and another Nez Perce got into a quarrel over some stock and White Bird was killed." Some believed that the murder had occurred near Fort Macleod, while others said Fort Walsh was the place. Such were the uncertainties regarding White Bird's demise years later, when the people in Idaho and Washington told their thoughts of the long-departed leader.[22]

A nephew of White Bird whose family went into Canada with the chief and whose mother died there was later given his uncle's name out of respect for him. The young man and his father, Buffalo Head, eventually returned south. Following his brother's murder, Buffalo Head held a memorial feast during which the chief's name was bestowed on the youth. Years later, the younger White Bird remembered that Chief White Bird "was buried by the side of my mother, across the line. . . . Up some canyon near Fort McCloud [*sic*] is the burial place. Five or six [Nez Perces?], all told, are buried there. White Bird was killed after we left, but [we] have been told he was buried there." Evidently, the grave went unmarked, and later the site was used for agriculture; the exact place of White Bird's interment remains unknown, although it was likely in the area of the Nimiipuu community at Pincher Creek.[23]

In the aftermath of the slaying, and of the sensation surrounding the trial of Nez Percee Sam, some of the Nimiipuu residents of the community near the stone quarry near Pincher Creek moved away. According to one historian, a schism appeared within the group and at least two families departed, relocating down the creek in the river bottom on the adjacent Piegan Reserve. Over ensuing years, the others who remained near the rock quarry eventually died or moved away to other areas, a few perhaps returning to Lapwai or going to Colville. White Bird's wives, Kate and Wyanatotampip, returned to Idaho, occupying an allotment at Lapwai in the name of their husband. Nez Percee Sam's two boys, who had testified at their father's trial, proved rebellious young men. Two years after their father died, Pete Sam and Jack Sam, as they were called by whites, were arrested for breaking into the residence of a J. Schofield and stealing clothes, and each received a month in jail. In 1895, they were described by a North-West Mounted Police inspector as being aged "18 and 14 respectively. The eldest had to leave here some three years ago, and returned last summer. Since then he has had one term of imprisonment and is now in some more mischief. The youngest, in the last two years, has had three terms of imprisonment. Both are thoroughly bad, and a nuisance, and are likely to get worse, if not placed out of harm's way."[24]

Sam's widow, Sarah, continued making and selling moccasins and other articles of clothing. In 1895, she was considered "a hard working woman, doing washing, etc. Her family consists of 2 boys of 18 and 14 years and 2 girls of 11 and 8 years. The boys have bad characters, the mother and girls good ones." In that year, the Mounted Police inspector responsible for the appropriate subdivision of the Macleod District where Sam's widow lived asked if "it may be found possible to dispose of the Indians mentioned [Sam's family] by placing [them] on a Reserve." In November, the recommendation was approved—attaching the family to the Piegans, but not allowing them treaty money earmarked only for those people. The Department of Indian Affairs further advised that the two boys be enrolled in the St. Joseph's Indian Industrial School at Dunbow, but that prospect failed when they ran off. Meantime, Sam's widow continued working and served as a charwoman at a nearby church. She was well known in the community, where one local merchant portrayed her in 1898 as "the only remaining Nez Perce woman" there. Sarah died from tuberculosis in 1899 and her daughters were temporarily cared for by area residents; eventually they were conveyed to Lapwai to live with relatives.[25]

With the passage of time the Canadian Nez Perce presence subsided, any remaining Nimiipuu either dispersing for parts unknown or merging through intermarriage with the Piegans, the Métis, other Canadian Natives, and area whites. As a political body possessing self identity, the Nez Perces in Canada ceased to exist, although genealogical research might determine others of the people and their descendants now living north of the international boundary. For example, those people who associated closely with the Piegans named one young man Warrior in recognition of his brave deeds in the 1877 war. His lineage, at least, carried forward when Warrior married a Piegan, Woman Never Holds—evidently in the mid-1890s. As a Piegan, she received annuity payments in accordance with treaties. Among their children were

Sam, Joe, Bob, and Lucy. Of these, Joe became a noted cowboy who in 1940 competed in the Calgary Stampede. Sam Warrior died in 1926 as the result of an accidental goring by a bull. Lucy married a Piegan, William David; they had a son, Billy David, and two daughters, June and Emily. Lucy later married Jack Buffalo, and that union yielded a daughter, Cindy. Sam's children were Josephine, Henry, Pete, and Edward. Today, Faye Morning Bull, daughter of Edward and Eleanor Warrior, and granddaughter of Sam, lives in Brocket, not far from Pincher Creek. She; her siblings, Spencer, Sam, Irene, Trynie, and Roxanne; and numerous children, grandchildren, nieces, and nephews all evince the vitality of the Warrior family tradition, and thus one strain of the historic Nez Perce lineage, that remains in Canada today.[26]

Through the efforts of Shirley Crowshoe, Piegan from Brocket, W. Otis Halfmoon, Nez Perce from Lapwai, and others, after more than a century the Canadian descendants of Chief White Bird's followers ultimately joined their American counterparts in observing, sharing, and celebrating their familial relationships and rich cultural past. The reunion took place in Brocket on Thursday and Friday, October 5–6, 1995, with nearly two hundred Nez Perces in attendance from the Lapwai, Colville, Umatilla, and Piegan Reservations (approximately seventy were descendants of the Canadian White Bird band). In a historic confluence lasting two days, the families traded songs and stories, and became reacquainted through such traditions as pipe ceremonies, giveaways, powwows, feather games, and a revitalizing Seven Drum Ceremony led by Nimiipuu elder Horace Axtell from Lapwai. Homage to the 1877 dead, as well as the dead of all wars, was paid in an Empty Saddle Ceremony and a reading of names of the warriors of 1877. Josephine Warrior Crowshoe, daughter of Sam Warrior, told the assemblage that her name was "Far Away Nez Perce Woman" and that she was indeed one of them. On Saturday, October 7, the Americans journeyed south into Montana to a powwow hosted by the Gros Ventres and Assiniboines. The heartwarming union between the Canadian and American Nez Perce descendants has since carried forward, with many of the people

exchanging visits to their respective locales. One poignant journey involved some of the Canadian descendants visiting the Wallowa country of eastern Oregon where Joseph and his followers
had lived before the war in 1877, as well as the grave of the chief
at Nespelem, Washington. At the latter place, Faye Morning Bull
and her family placed a Canadian coin to symbolize a homecom-
ing of sorts.[27]

There are likely more descendants of the Nimiipuu in Canada,
perhaps among other tribes living in the area of southeastern
Alberta or scattered elsewhere throughout the western provinces.
Possibly, they, too, either sense or will rediscover their heritage
and help to further close the circle started in October 1877, when
Lamtama chief White Bird and nearly three hundred expatriated
people straggled north from Bear's Paw and settled tenuously
with Sitting Bull's Lakotas near Wood Mountain on the frigid
plains of the North-West Territories. Although most of these
tribesmen eventually found their way back to the United States, it
is clear that many others stayed, forged new lives, and merged
into other cultural mainstreams. Either way, it was a troubled
sanctuary. Forced by circumstances, those who remained ultimately invested their future in their adopted land, and, as their
kinsmen in Idaho and Washington, the Canadian Nez Perces survived under conditions no less threatening and just as uncertain.
That both groups today have sought and claimed their common
heritage is a measure of their strength and unity after so long a
time. That either group succeeded in making its way despite ever-
compounding hardships testifies, moreover, to the resilience of
the human spirit that they as a people continue to exemplify so
well.

List of Identified Warriors Escaping the Bear's Paw Battle Who Were Killed by Enemy Tribes and Whites

Adapted from compilation by Many Wounds and Black Eagle. Source: Box 11, Folder 79; and from compilation of Many Wounds and Wottolen, November, 1926. Source: Box 10, Folder 62, McWhorter Collection, WSU.

Ahk-tai-lah-ken (Fatal Throat Wound). Killed by Crows, Cheyennes, or Blackfeet.

Hass-we-ya-tsi-ken (Speaking Water). Responsible tribe not named (possibly Assiniboines).

He-mene Hai-hai-ih. Killed by the Blackfeet.

Im-nie-wa-nah. Killed by white men near Helena.

Johnal-kom-kon. Killed by the Northern Cheyennes, or the Hal-lu-teen.

Ka-wis-kute (Kills Himself). Killed by the Gros Ventres.

Laka-tsits-ka-nen. Killed by Crows, Cheyennes, or Blackfeet.

Mol-mol-ken. Killed by Crows, Cheyennes, or Blackfeet.

Pe-tom-ya-nou Hai-hai (White Hawk). Killed by Gros Ventres or Northern Cheyennes or Sioux.

Pit-pe-lu-lin (or Pit-pee-lu-hen) (Muscular Leg). Killed by the Northern Cheyennes or Gros Ventres or Sioux.

Red Spy. Killed by the Gros Ventres.

So-tah-wa. Responsible tribe not named.

Sodana. Killed by Crows, Cheyennes, or Blackfeet.

Ta-wish-to-kai-tat. Killed by Crows, Cheyennes, (Blackfeet.

Te-neh-nat (Subject to Death). Responsible tribe not named
(possibly Assiniboines).

Te-we-yan-nah. Killed by the Crows.

Tip-suci. Killed by Gros Ventres or Northern Cheyennes or
Sioux.

Tip-yah-la-na Kaps-kaps (Strong Eagle). Killed by the Northern
Cheyennes or Gros Ventres or Sioux.

Wa-moas-ka-ia. Killed by Gros Ventres or Northern Cheyennes
or Sioux.

Wai-nat-ta-can. Killed by the Gros Ventres.

We-ya-ta-na-to-lah-ka-wit. Killed by the Blackfeet.

Weh-sie-lat-kath (Come Out from Water). Killed by white men
near Helena.

White Hawk. Responsible tribe not named.

White Owl. Killed by the Blackfeet.

Wot-yet-mas-ta-mal-we-yon (Black Eagle Law Giver). Killed by
Northern Cheyennes.

APPENDIX B

Nez Perces Escaping from Bear's Paw Who Were Later Captured

Source: Box 11, Folder 79, McWhorter Collection, WSU.

He-kah-kus Sou-yeen, or He-kah Koo-sou-yun, later known as Luke Wilson.

To-wus. Place of capture not named. Died in captivity.

Tak-yah-nin. Place of capture not named. Died in Kamiah, Idaho.

Wosno Mox-mox. Place of capture not named.

Yellow Wolf. Surrendered at Lapwai Agency, 1878. Sent to Indian Territory. Returned in 1885 with Chief Joseph and lived at Nespelem, Washington.

E-lah-weh-mah (About Sleep). A boy 12 years old, held one year by the Gros Ventres and escaped to Sitting Bull's camp in Canada. Later sent to the Indian Territory. Died in Nespelem.

APPENDIX C

KNOWN NEZ PERCES WHO ESCAPED TO CANADA IN 1877 AND WHO REMAINED THERE OR RETURNED TO THE UNITED STATES IN SUBSEQUENT YEARS

Source: List compiled by W. Otis Halfmoon in "Nez Perce in Canada" File, library and archives, Nez Perce National Historical Park, Spalding, Idaho. Based on materials in Box 11, Folder 79, McWhorter Collection, WSU, including "Nez Perces Who Escaped to Canada and Never Were Captured," compiled by Many Wounds and Black Eagle, 1928.

Women

Tah-ton-mi
He-Yume-te-yat-kikt
Peopeo Tholekt's mother
Kap-Kap-on-mi (Joseph's daughter)
Wet-a-ton-mi
Penah-weh-non-mi
Yiyik Wasumwah (Yellow Wolf's mother)
Niktseewhy (She also had two children)
Ipnatsubah-lew-lus-son-mi (Anything Burning and Making Its
    Noise)
Heyoom Telebinmi (Rising Sun Against the Bear)

Tommi Yohomi
Whepwheponmi
Pellutsoo (She also had two children)
Weyadooldipat (Flock of Animals Running to the Hillside)
Tuk'not (Julia Hines)
Hattie Carl Jackson (She was born in Canada)

Men

Chief White Bird (Killed in Canada in 1892)
Wottolen (Died in 1928)
Ip-non-to-tsa-konon (Died in Canada)
La-am-nish-nim-Hu-sis (Died in Montana)
We-yah-wa-tsts-kon
Rainbow, Sr. (First cousin to Rainbow who was killed at Big
    Hole. Senior was maternal grandfather of Many Wounds)
Tip-yahla-nah Tsiah-ka-ai-kan
Mel-mel-s-ta-li-ka-ya
He-yuum-ti-ka-likth
Tsu-lim-ta-ka-hats-wel (Died in Canada)
Ka-lah-tass (Died in Canada)
Tok-ka-lik-si-mai (Brother of Chief Looking Glass, never
    returned to Idaho and died later in Montana)
Wa-too-ainy
Red Bird
As-ha-was
Jackson Sundown (Young brother of As-ha-was; father was Kol-
    kolh-ke-qu-tol-lekt)
Sis-to-is (Died in Canada)
He-ma-kaaun (Died in Montana)
Two Moons
Lil-kim-kan (Died in Montana)
Te-nat-ta-Kaweyun
Too-nah-hon
Helu-lat-kati

Wela-toli-ka-kats
Husis-pa-Ow-yiin
Charles Stevens
John Dog (Wounded in forehead at Big Hole)
Red Cloud
Wolf Head (Killed by railroad train near Lewiston, Idaho)
Wis-lah-naka
Mes-ka-ya-a
Wa-youh-Temaniin
Yet-mah-hn-kuts
He-kah-Koo-sou-yeen (Luke Andrews)
Wat-yet-mas Yah-oun-ya-oun
John Miller
Peter Gould
John Red Wolf
Jim Williams
Charles McConville
Yotsh
Wa-an-ne-Hai-hai-ih
We-yah-tana-tola-ka-wit (Killed by Blackfeet)
He-min Hai-hai-ih (Killed by Blackfeet)
Ela-a-ta-hat
We-yah-ta-na To-lat-pat
Te-me-mue-nin (A member of White Bird's band also known as
    Puyahnaptah and Arthur Simon)
Paka-tam-ki-kai-kith
John Walker
Phillip Evens
Nik-yel-lil-me-hom
Red Earth
White Bull
Black Elk (Died later near Pendleton, Oregon)
Watai-watai-how-lis
Nusnu Kohat Mox Mox
Lape-yah-lute
Wai-lim-lau-sie

To-wus

Tam-yah-nin

William Jones

Ha-hots Toi-nu-kuns (No Tail Grizzly, died on the Flathead
    Reservation trying to reach Lapwai)

Its-spil-ia-Es-klaked (Became lost in Montana trying to reach
    Lapwai)

Hasenahmakikt (Left Hand, the man known to whites as Nez
    Percee Sam, who killed White Bird)

Yellow Wolf

Koolkool-sni-niin

Peopeo Ta-mal-we-ot

Ku-yel-kiskis (also known as Aka He-lah-tot)

Black Eagle

Daniel Jefferson

Peopeo Tholekt

Sy-ya-kin Illp-pillp

Kow wish-chute

Bad Young Grizzler Bear

Ip-sus-nute

Moolmool-kin

Ah-tai-leh ken

Rattle Blanket

Yoom-tin-I-liken

Espowyes

Ealahweemah

Samuel Tilden

Welehewoot

Iskiloom

Henry Tabadour

Tipyahlahna-kikt

Gehwahaikt

Ooyekun

Tomamo

Wewass Pahkalatkeikt

Kootskoots Tsomyowhet

Ipnamatwekin
Wahseenwes Sawhohtsoht
Seeloo Wahyakt
Pauh Wahyakt (also known as Pa-yoo Wa-hyakt)
Weyooseeka Tsakown
Kowtoliks
Putum Soklahtomah
Tahmiteahkun

NOTES

Chapter 1

1. This greatly abridged account of the causes and course of the Nez Perce War is drawn from Greene, *Nez Perce Summer*. For the Nez Perce people, see Walker, "Nez Perce"; Josephy, *The Nez Perce Indians and the Opening of the Northwest*; and Haines, *The Nez Perces*. For Nimiipuu viewpoint, see also McWhorter, *Hear Me, My Chiefs!* and *Yellow Wolf*.

2. Greene, *Nez Perce Summer*, 106–107, citing McWhorter, *Hear Me, My Chiefs!* 334–36; McWhorter, *Yellow Wolf,* 104–105; MacDonald, "The Nez Perces," 245; and Yellow Bull account in Curtis, *The North American Indian,* vol. 8, 166; Yellow Bull Account, ca. 1912. Camp Interview Notes. Walter M. Camp Manuscripts, Lilly Library, Indiana University, Bloomington.

3. Greene, *Nez Perce Summer*, 117–19, citing MacDonald, "Nez Perces," 252–53, 255; Yellow Bull account in Curtis, *North American Indian,* vol. 8, 166; McWhorter, *Hear Me, My Chiefs!* 357–58; and Haines, *Nez Perces,* 248–49.

4. Greene, *Nez Perce Summer*, 133, 143.

5. Greene, *Nez Perce Summer,* 177–78, 201, 436–37n88, 439n119; Marquis, *Memoirs of a White Crow Indian,* 128; Haines, *Nez Perces,* 263.

6. Greene, *Nez Perce Summer,* 213–14.

7. Greene, *Nez Perce Summer,* 213–14, 219–20, 224, 229, 231–32. The quotation is from McWhorter, *Yellow Wolf,* 194. See also ibid., 187–88, 194.

8. Greene, *Nez Perce Summer,* 242–43, citing McWhorter, *Hear Me, My Chiefs!* 473–74; McWhorter, *Yellow Wolf,* 203.

9. This account of the establishment and marking of the boundary is condensed from that in LaDow, *The Medicine Line,* 2, 5, 6–11.

10. LaDow, *The Medicine Line,* 3–5, 40–42.

11. LaDow, *The Medicine Line,* 23, 41–42. Quotations in ibid., citing Robert P. Higheagle Manuscript, Walter Stanley Campbell Collection, University of Oklahoma, box 104, folder 21, 41; McCrady, *Living with Strangers,* 3–4, 11–15.

12. For overviews of United States policy respecting the Northern Plains tribes and the warfare that resulted, see Fritz, *The Movement for Indian Assimilation*; Wooster, *The Military and United States Indian Policy*; Utley, *Frontiersmen in Blue, Frontier Regulars*, and *The Indian Frontier of the American West*; and Hutton, *Phil Sheridan and His Army*.

13. Surtees, "Canadian Indian Policies," 89–91; Stonechild, "Indian-White Relations in Canada," 277–79. See also St. Germain, *Indian Treaty-Making Policy*, passim.

14. St. Germain, *Indian Treaty-Making Policy*, 24, 45; Frank W. Anderson, *Fort Walsh and the Cypress Hills*, 35; LaDow, *Medicine Line*, 55, 57–58 (quotation is in ibid., 58); Sharp, *Whoop-Up Country: The Canadian-American West*, 33–54; 78–106. A succinct statement of the reason for the effectiveness of the Mounted Police with Indians, including American Indians, in the North-West Territories, appears in Jennings, "The Plains Indians and the Law," 58: "In contrast to the maze of laws and jurisdictions on the American frontier, particularly after 1849 when the control of Indian affairs was taken away from the Army, the Mounted Police came armed with the simplicity of the 'Queen's Law' which was impressed on the Indians almost in terms of holy commandments. These laws were easy for the Indians to understand and were swiftly enforced."

15. "Report of Major General E. Selby Smyth," November 27, 1875, xl–xliii (quotation, xl), in "North West Mounted Police, Reports, 1875–1878"; Turner, *The North-West Mounted Police, 1873–1893*, 37–42. The other two police posts were Fort Saskatchewan and Fort Calgary.

16. 5 Parliament, 5 session, *Annual Report of the Department of the Interior for the Year ended 30th June 1877*, xvii; Howard, *The Canadian Sioux*, 25–31; Meyer, "The Canadian Sioux," 13–28. (Abridged version in Nichols and Adams, eds., *The American Indian*, 168–82.) For background on the Santees, including their uprising in Minnesota in 1862, see Meyer, *History of the Santee Sioux*.

17. Lieutenant Colonel H. Richardson to Assistant Commissioner A. G. Irvine, N.W.M.P., Fort Macleod, May 26, 1876. Appendix E, "North West Mounted Police, Reports, 1875–1878," 24 (first quotation); Dufferin to Thornton, May 27, 1876, quoted in Pennanen, "Sitting Bull," 123–24 (second quotation). The Canadian government had received confidential report of the overall strategy and location of the campaign, too: "It is supposed that one body will move westward from Bismarck [Fort Abraham Lincoln, Dakota Territory]; another has, it is stated, moved east from Fort Shaw, and a third moves north from some southern point [Fort Fetterman, Wyoming Territory]." Ibid. See also Irvine to Richardson, July 1, 1876, in ibid. These materials, as well as others bearing on the presence of Lakotas in Canada, are reprinted in "Papers Relating to the Sioux Indians of the United States Who Have Taken Refuge in Canadian Territory." Governor General's Office, Governor General's Numbered Files. RG 7, G 21, vol. 323, file 2001–1, prints 1875–1879, 1–2 (hereafter cited as "Papers Relating to the Sioux Indians").

18. Irvine to Secretary of State R. W. Scott, September 19, 1876; Solomon statement, August 18, 1876; Inspector L. N. Crozier to Irvine, August 18, 1876, all in appendix E, "North West Mounted Police, Reports, 1875–1878," 24–27; Frederick White to Secretary of State Scott, December 30, 1876, in appendix D of ibid., 21–22.

19. For particulars of the post–Little Bighorn campaign, see Greene, *Yellowstone Command*.

Chapter 2

1. Inspector Lief N. Crozier to Assistant Commissioner Acheson G. Irvine, August 18, 1876; Major Guido Ilges, Seventh U.S. Infantry, to Walsh, September 25, 1876; Walsh to Secretary of State Richard W. Scott, September 29, 1876, all in "Papers Relating to the Sioux Indians," 4–5, 6–7, 9, 10. Canadian officials worried that such a scenario would derail the amicable relations they had previously forged with Washington, D.C., particularly in relation to matters involving trade. Canadian and British objectives in their relations with the United States are succinctly delineated in Manzione, *"I Am Looking to the North for My Life,"* 37–41.

2. Macleod, "James Morrow Walsh" and "James Farquharson Macleod." An undocumented biography of Walsh appears in Ian Anderson, *Above the Medicine Line with James Morrow Walsh*.

3. Frederick White to Secretary of State R. W. Scott, December 31, 1877, in "North West Mounted Police, Reports, 1875–1878," appendix D, 20; Walsh to Commissioner James F. Macleod, December 31, 1876, in "Papers Relating to the Sioux Indians," 9–11 (including Walsh quotation); Macleod to Secretary of State, March 27, 1877, in ibid., 9; Irvine to Scott, May 23, 1877, in ibid., 15–16; Harry H. Anderson, "A Sioux Pictorial Account of General Terry's Council at Fort Walsh," 105; Sharp, *Whoop-Up Country*, 250–53. There existed fears in the Canadian government that the few hundred Mounted Police available would be "entirely inadequate to restrain the Sioux refugees from making their present encampment [at Wood Mountain] a base for raids upon the posts and settlements of the Missouri river. . . . Whether any effectual restraint can be imposed on their hostile movements south of the international line is doubtful." U.S. Consul James W. Taylor to Acting Secretary of State J. L. Cadwalader, March 8, 1877. NA Microfilm Publication T24, "Despatches from United States Consuls in Winnipeg, 1869–1906," vol. 5, April 6, 1875, to December 31, 1881, roll 5.

4. Walsh to Irvine, March 15, 1877, in "North West Mounted Police, Reports, 1875–1878," appendix E, 31–32 (also in "Papers Relating to the Sioux Indians," 12–13); Sharp, *Whoop-Up Country*, 252–53. These Indians rationalized the legitimacy of their British heritage: "From childhood they were instructed by their fathers that properly they were children of the British; they were living with

strangers but their house was to the north; that in their tribes can be seen the medals of their White Father [the King] given to their fathers for fighting the Americans; . . . that they always intended moving to the country of their fathers." Ibid., 13. See also Anderson, "A Sioux Pictorial Account of General Terry's Council at Fort Walsh," 105. Four Horns's status is described in Utley, *Lance and the Shield,* 80.

5. White to Scott, December 31, 1877, in "North West Mounted Police, Reports, 1875–1878," appendix D, 20; Macleod to Scott, March 27, 1877, in ibid., appendix E, 27; Irvine to Scott, May 25, 1877, in ibid., 33; Irvine to Scott, May 23, 1877, in "Papers Relating to the Sioux Indians," 16–17; Earl of Dufferin to Secretary of State for the Colonies, June 18, 1877, in ibid., 20; Macleod to Governor-General Alexander Mackenzie, May 30, 1877, in "North West Mounted Police, Reports, 1875–1878," appendix E, 34–35 (also in "Papers Relating to the Sioux Indians," 18; Anderson, "A Sioux Pictorial Account of General Terry's Council at Fort Walsh," 105. A report as early as February 1877 had Sitting Bull at Wood Mountain with "1000 horses and mules captured from the United States troops." Taylor to Cadwalader, March 8, 1877. NA Microfilm Publication T24, "Despatches from United States Consuls in Winnipeg, 1869–1906," vol. 5, April 6, 1875, to December 31, 1881, roll 5. News of Sitting Bull's arrival in Canada reached Fort Walsh on May 7, 1877. Joyner, "Hegira of Sitting Bull," 7–8. To be precise, Sitting Bull crossed into Canada on April 30. McCrady, *Living with Strangers,* 73. Numbers were estimated by Trader Jean Légaré, the *Manitoba Free Press,* July 16, 1877, and American Consul James Taylor in Winnipeg (*Toronto Globe,* August 9, 1877), as cited in Pennanen, "Sitting Bull," 125. In actuality, many of Sitting Bull's people, having lost their tepees in the flooding of the Missouri, had been crowded into existing lodges so that the true number of Lakota tepees present on Canadian soil was closer to three hundred. "Papers Relating to the Sioux Indians," 29. There were also around 200 lodges of Tetons under a chief named Bear Spirit who had crossed into Canada in 1876 to stay clear of the fighting in the United States. Ibid., 30. Historian Kingsley M. Bray suggested that as of May, 1877, following Sitting Bull's arrival, the Lakotas in Canada consisted of 185 lodges of Hunkpapas, 45 lodges of Sans Arcs, 35 lodges of Minneconjous, 20 lodges of Blackfoot Sioux, and 15 lodges of Oglalas "and other stragglers." "We Belong to the North," 30n1. More Sioux fled north from the Great Sioux Reservation during the fall of 1877 and the winter of 1877–78. Ibid., 31, 33, 34, 39, 40–41, 42; *Chicago Times,* October 1, 1877. A news correspondent enumerated Sitting Bull's direct followers in October at "one thousand three hundred and forty souls." *Chicago Times,* October 21, 1877. Walsh's personal role in the various Lakota arrivals is detailed in a convoluted third-person letter to his daughter, Cora, dated May 21, 1890, although it is possible that this missive was written by one of Walsh's fellow officers, as at least one Glenbow archivist has argued. Copy in the Glenbow Archives, Calgary, Alberta. Copy provided by Utley (hereafter

cited as Walsh to Cora, May 21, 1890). See also Utley, *Lance and the Shield*, 186, and discussion of the arrival of the Sioux in Manzione, *"I Am Looking to the North for My Life,"* 43–50.

6. Macleod to Mackenzie, May 30, 1877, in "Papers Relating to the Sioux Indians," 18–19 (also contained in NA Microfilm Publication M50, "Notes from the British Legation in the United States to the Department of State, 1791–1906, roll 102). See also Sharp, *Whoop-Up Country*, 254–57.

7. W. A. Hirnsworth, Clerk of Privy Council, June 1, 1877, in NA Microfilm Publication M50, "Notes from the British Legation in the United States to the Department of State, 1791–1906, roll 102 (quotation). Quotation about Sitting Bull in Irvine to Scott, June 6, 1877, and transcript of council of June 2, 1877, in "North West Mounted Police, Reports, 1875–1878," appendix E, 35–41 (also in "Papers Relating to the Sioux Indians," 23–27). Somewhat conversely, another contemporary, J. J. Healy, described Sitting Bull physically as "a short, thick-set man, about 45 years of age, and weighs, probably, 175 pounds. He is undoubtedly a full blooded Indian, and not a remarkably intelligent looking one at that. He is minus one toe, having at some time or other had his feet frozen." *Benton Record*, October 26, 1877. British authorities had long been aware of the capricious nature of U.S. treatment of its Indian population. Earlier, Edward Thornton, minister for Great Britain at the Washington legation, had forwarded copies of the Fort Laramie Treaty of 1868 along with missives verifying the Americans' overall poor performance in their conventions with the tribes. Manzione, *"I Am Looking to the North for My Life,"* 38. The "benign discouragement" description is in ibid., 51.

8. Sherman to Secretary of War George W. McCrary, July 16, 1877, in "Papers Relating to the Sioux Indians," 36–37.

9. Fred White to Irvine, August 14, 1877 (quotation); The Earl of Carnarvon to the Earl of Dufferin, datelined "Downing Street," August 2, 1877, in "Papers Relating to the Sioux Indians," 31–32. See also Earl of Carnarvon to Earl of Dufferin, August 9, 1877, in ibid., 32; and Sharp, *Whoop-Up Country*, 257–58.

10. Francis R. Plunkett to the Earl of Derby, July 24, 1877, in "Papers Relating to the Sioux Indians," 32–33 (Evarts quotations); Plunkett to Evarts, June 20, 1877, in NA Microfilm Publication M50, "Notes from the British Legation in the United States to the Department of State, 1791–1906," roll 102 (quotation). A standing irritant to United States officials must have been the realization that "the Canadian authorities consider United States horses, mules, and arms in their [the Lakotas'] possession, not as stolen property but as spoils of war." Taylor to Assistant Secretary of State F. W. Seward, July 24, 1877. NA Microfilm Publication T24, "Despatches from United States Consuls in Winnipeg, 1869–1906," vol. 5, April 6, 1875, to December 31, 1881, roll 5; Sharp, *Whoop-Up Country*, 258–59; Joyner, "Hegira of Sitting Bull," 9. The evolving diplomacy involving Canada, Great Britain, and the United States emanating from the "Sitting Bull

Crisis" is detailed at length in Manzione, *"I Am Looking to the North for My Life,"* 53–59.

11. Mills's trip to Washington was unauthorized by Great Britain and provoked consternation among British diplomats on the scene since it violated Great Britain's protocol respecting its handling of Canada's foreign affairs. His visit, nonetheless, proved a major influence, and the commission to Sitting Bull derived directly as well as chronologically from Mills's attendance at the capital. See Plunkett to Deputy-Governor W. R. Richards, August 11, 1877; David Mills, "Memorandum," August 23, 1877; Earl of Carnarvon to the Earl of Dufferin, September 6, 1877, and September 7, 1877; excerpt from *New York Herald,* August 10, 1877, all in "Papers Relating to the Sioux Indians," 33–34, 41–44, 57–58, 59; Joyner, "Hegira of Sitting Bull," 10; Sharp, *Whoop-Up Country,* 260–63. See, particularly, Manzione, *"I Am Looking to the North for My Life,"* 60–73; and Pennanen, "Sitting Bull," 127–28.

12. *Report of the Sitting Bull Commission,* 3–4, including quotations; *New York Herald,* October 25, 1877; Joyner, "Hegira of Sitting Bull," 11, and quoting the *National Republican,* August 15, 1877. A manuscript copy of the commission report is in National Archives Microfilm Publication M666, roll 283, 4163 AGO 1876 (hereafter cited as Sioux War Papers).

13. Scott to Macleod, August 13, 1877, and August 15, 1877; Plunkett to Mills, August 16, 1877; *Washington National Republican,* August 15, 1877, all in "Papers Relating to the Sioux Indians," 34–35. McNeil's background is in Heitman, *Historical Register and Dictionary,* vol. 1, 679.

14. Taylor to Acting Secretary of State F. W. Seward, September 4, 1877. NA Microfilm Publication T24, "Despatches from United States Consuls in Winnipeg, 1869–1906, vol. 5, April 6, 1875, to December 31, 1881, roll 5 (first quotation); Mills to Macleod, August 24, 1877 (second and third quotations); Deputy Minister of the Interior E. A. Meredith to Macleod, August 28, 1877, in "Papers Relating to the Sioux Indians," 44, 46; Sharp, *Whoop-Up Country,* 270–71. In correspondence with Mills on October 17 following the commission's meeting with the Lakotas, Macleod related, "I communicated to the Commissioners the substance of my [earlier] interview with the Sioux, as far as it related to their position as refugees from the other side, but *I was careful not to inform them of the last paragraph of your letter of the 24th of August* [emphasis added]." Macleod to Mills, October 27, 1877, in "Papers Relating to the Sioux Indians," 78–79. An account of the preliminaries to the Terry Commission is in Turner, "Sitting Bull Tests the Mettle of the Redcoats," 71–72.

15. Plunkett to Deputy-Governor W. B. Richards, August 25, 1877; Plunkett to Richards, August 30, 1877, in "Papers Relating to the Sioux Indians," 46–49, 51–52; *National Republican,* August 30, 1876, reprinted in ibid., 53–54; Manzione, *"I Am Looking to the North for My Life,"* 76. As for expenses, it was considered likely that the War Department's nominated commissioner—General Terry—would

provide expenses for the commission out of monies advanced by the department for that purpose. Congress was expected to eventually reimburse members for their out-of-pocket costs. Ibid., 48. The *National Republican* of August 24, 1877, alluded to a "Sitting Bull Epidemic" as affecting those tapped. The prospect of "traveling a thousand or two miles, and paying one's expenses, to wait upon Hon. Sitting Bull, seems to act as a nausea upon those invited to serve on the Commission"; "It may not be surprising that the sickness of the gentlemen will form a sort of epidemic among those who are called upon to act." Ibid., 50. For Walker's background, see Heitman, *Historical Register and Dictionary*, vol. 1, 995. For exchanges regarding Sitting Bull's whereabouts, including his rumored presence south of the boundary, see Telegram, W. R. Richards to Plunkett, September 5, 1877; and Plunkett to Seward, September 5, 1887, in NA Microfilm Publication M50, "Notes from the British Legation in the United States to the Department of State, 1791–1906," roll 102.

16. Miles to Sitting Bull, August 19, 1877, and September 1, 1877, datelined "HdQrs Yellowstone Command, Cantonment at Tongue River, M.T." National Archives (hereafter NA), Record Group (hereafter RG) 393, Part 3, Entry 886. Letters Sent, Yellowstone Command, August 2, 1877–September 4, 1877 (ledger), 57, 93–94 (quotations); Greene, *Nez Perce Summer*, 250, 252. It is clear that Miles's presence had an effect on the disinclination of the Sioux to consider proposals for their return. As correspondent Charles Diehl of the *Chicago Times* noted in the paper's September 24, 1877, edition, "The story that American troops under Gen. Miles are ready to fall upon the Sioux the moment they recross the frontier with the commissioners has done its work, and it is believed nothing they can offer Sitting Bull will induce him to leave his present quarters."

17. Terry to McCrary, September 11, 1877, and Terry to the Governor-General, September 12, 1877, in *Report of the Sitting Bull Indian Commission*, 4, 5, 6; Richards to Plunkett, September 3, 1877 (quotation); Plunkett to Richards, September 8, 1877, and September 12, 1877, all in "Papers Relating to the Sioux Indians," 54, 55, 56; *Chicago Times*, September 6, 1877; *Chicago Times*, September 16, 1877; Turner, *North-West Mounted Police*, vol. 1, 362–63. The Canadians also feared that too large an assembly of Americans beside the commissioners might "excite the suspicions of the Indians." Plunkett to the Earl of Derby, October 9, 1877, in ibid., 74–75.

18. Originally, Company K, Seventh Cavalry, was to conduct Terry's party to the line; on orders from Department of Dakota headquarters, Miles replaced this unit with the Second Cavalry battalion under Tyler. Greene, *Nez Perce Summer*, 248, 252. For the attack on the Nez Perces at Bear's Paw and the subsequent battle, see ibid., 271–324.

19. *New York Herald*, October 10, 1877; *Chicago Times*, October 22, 1877; *Report of the Sitting Bull Indian Commission*, 5–6; Macleod to Scott, ca. October 14, 1877, in "Papers Relating to the Sioux Indians," 73. Some telegraphic correspondence

between Secretary of State Scott and Commissioner Macleod respecting the commission was apparently conducted in coded format. Macleod to Scott, October 31, 1877. Ibid., 76–77. "During the presence of the Commission, [Fort] Benton looked as though it was having a revival of the freighting season. The town was full of strangers and the streets were blockaded with teams." *Benton Record*, October 26, 1877. The Terry party had started from Fort Benton and had camped at "the 28-mile springs" on the night of October 4. *Benton Record*, October 5, 1877. Apparently, early plans called for the American commissioners to travel directly to "the Sioux lodges" rather than meet the leaders at Fort Walsh. Note from Plunkett(?) attached to Telegram, W. B. Richard to Plunkett, September 3, 1877, in NA Microfilm Publication M50, "Notes from the British Legation in the United States to the Department of State, 1791–1906, roll 102. On September 17, Plunkett notified Seward that "Colonel Macleod has . . . been informed that it would facilitate communications if Sitting Bull, other Chiefs, and Headmen would meet Commissioners at Fort Walsh." Ibid.

20. The direct text of Walsh's report to Macleod appeared in the *New York Herald*, October 22, 1877, although a slightly different rendition appeared in the *Chicago Times*, October 23, 1877. See also Manzione, *"I Am Looking to the North for My Life,"* 99–100; and McCrady, *Living with Strangers*, 77–78. A backup plan, should the Indians not agree to go to Fort Walsh, had the commission being escorted to their village by a detachment of Mounted Police. *Chicago Times*, September 16, 1877. Sitting Bull's loss of his son is mentioned in both newspaper accounts dated October 22, 1877. See also Utley, *Lance and the Shield*, 193, 372.

21. Walsh to Cora, May 21, 1890.

22. *New York Herald*, October 22, 1877 (quotation). See also Utley, *Lance and the Shield*, 192–93.

23. Macleod to Mills, October 27, 1877, in "Papers Relating to the Sioux Indians," 77. Macleod reported that on arrival at Fort Walsh the Lakotas refused to enter the place, "Sitting Bull saying that he had never been in a fort, and that he would rather camp outside. However, upon my giving him my word that there were no Americans inside, and getting all our men outside the gate to shake hands, he at last consented." Ibid.

24. From the courier, Jerome Stillson learned, "To all their [Nez Perces'] pleadings for the assistance of the Sioux warriors, Sitting Bull lent an indifferent ear. 'You may smoke and eat here,' he responded. 'You are welcome. But this is your fight, not mine. You must not expect that any of my warriors will go across the border to help you.'" *New York Herald*, October 17, 1877. Charles Diehl wrote, "The courier reports that about fifty Nez Perces Indians have crossed the line and joined the Sioux under Sitting Bull. These include those who escaped at the opening of the fight in the Bear Paw mountains, and some who were absent from Joseph's camp when the fight commenced. Among the number are some wounded, who got by Gen. Miles' pickets during the engagement. In this num-

ber is reported to be the war chief, White Bird, who succeeded in escaping."
Chicago Times, October 17, 1877. On the other hand, there was some hope among
the Americans that the reported attack on the Nez Perces would influence Sitting
Bull "with a more favorable idea of the power of the United States army than he
had before." *New York Herald,* October 16, 1877.

25. *Chicago Times,* October 22, 1877. Diehl noted, "[W]e crossed the forty-ninth
parallel at 3:20 o'clock," and that "a troop of the mounted police, resplendent in
red coats and white corduroys, helmets, and lances, were drawn up a short distance north of the boundary. . . . The spectacle presented by the Canadians was
very gorgeous for those lonely plains." Ibid. Private William F. Zimmer, a Second
Cavalry enlisted man who accompanied Captain Tyler's three-company battalion escort, stated that only Company H accompanied Terry's people to the line,
then moved back one and one-half miles to "a sheet of water called Wild Horse
Lake." Furthermore, "twelve [Seventh] infantrymen went along with Terry &
party and they were disarmed before crossing to the British soil." The Second
Cavalry battalion was instructed to remain at Wild Horse Lake until the com-
mission's return. Zimmer, *Frontier Soldier,* 134–35. Through a prearrangement,
Captain Corbin served as an ad hoc reporter for the *Washington Post* and the
Columbus, Ohio, *Dispatch,* to the ultimate chagrin of Stillson and Diehl. Diehl,
The Staff Correspondent, 125–27.

26. Ibid., 128 (quotation); Macleod to Mills, October 27, 1877, in "Papers Relat-
ing to the Sioux Indians," 77–78; *New York Herald,* October 22, 1877; Greene, *Nez
Perce Summer,* 340.; Turner, *North-West Mounted Police,* vol. 1, 363–64; *Benton
Record,* October 26, 1877; *Chicago Times,* October 22, 1877 (quotation). The other
Canadian officers were Captain Crozier, Captain McIllree, Captain Allen, Cap-
tain Frechette, and Doctors Kittson and Nevitt. *Benton Record,* October 26, 1877.
Another acting newsman accompanying the commission was a minister named
Cowlick (pseudonym?) of Cheyenne, Wyoming, who represented the *Cheyenne
Daily Leader. Benton Record,* October 26, 1877. Others of the assemblage at Fort
Walsh included British-born John Howard, who was a scout with Colonel
Miles's command; Catholic Abbot Martin Marty; and a number of U.S. Army
veterans, apparently already in Canada, including one who had served during
the War with Mexico. Turner, *North-West Mounted Police,* 365. It is clear that Sitting Bull continued to be unsure of the purpose of the coming meeting and even
feared that the whole business might be but a ruse to turn him over to the Americans to be killed. *Chicago Times,* October 22, 1877.

27. Charles Diehl described Sitting Bull on this occasion as follows: "He is the
contradiction of all twaddle which has been published about him. Dark and
swarthy, his straight black hair falling down upon his shoulders, his beardless
face and strongly marked countenance all betoken the pure-blooded savage. He
stands five feet ten inches in his moccasins, and is splendidly proportioned. A
few wrinkles can be seen on his face, but not enough to create an appearance of

age. The one peculiarity of his face is in his almost Roman features, which heighten the air of intelligence and adds to the almost judicial gravity of his countenance. The one drawback to his really fine bearing are [sic] a pair of bowed legs, a peculiarity possessed by nearly every Indian horseman. . . . Sitting Bull wore a fox cap ornament with the tail of a badger, which hung over the left side of his head; a heavy navy blue blanket was wrapped closely about his shoulders and neck. He wore no ornaments in his ears or hair, and no paint was discernible on his face. . . . [Beneath the blanket he wore] a blue calico shirt which was worn over his leggings. His leggings were made of dark blue cloth, with a dark stripe extending down the side, and around his neck was tied a red-banded handkerchief." Spotted Eagle also impressed Diehl. "He was bared to the waist, and the tremendous physique of the savage was displayed in a splendid manner. In his moccasins he measures six feet and two inches. Across his left shoulder was thrown a belt filled with Winchester rifle cartridges, and in his left hand he held a tomahawk, at the head of which were fixed three large knife blades. His arms and neck were covered with white paint, indicative of mourning for those who had been killed in battle." *Chicago Times,* October 22, 1877.

28. *Report of the Sitting Bull Commission,* 6–11. This report, from which the selected entries were derived, also appears in *Report of the Secretary of the Interior, 1877,* 719–28. Variant transcripts of the proceedings, wherein the gist remains the same despite considerable word differences, appear in Macleod to Mills, October 17, 1877, in "Papers Relating to the Sioux Indians," 79–80; *Benton Record,* October 26, 1877; *Chicago Times,* October 22, 1877; *Chicago Times,* October 23, 1877 (quotation by Diehl); and *New York Herald,* October 22 and 23 (quotation by Stillson), 1877; unidentified newspapers containing articles, "A Picturesque Powwow," ca. October 1877, and "Conference at Fort Walsh," etc., in James Morrow Walsh Scrapbook #11. Glenbow Archives, Calgary. John J. Healy, chronicler for the *Benton Record,* stated that The Crow kissed all of the Canadian officials. He further noted that "to allow a squaw to speak in council is one of the worst insults that an Indian can offer." October 26, 1877. Correspondent Stillson afterwards interviewed Sitting Bull at length about the Little Bighorn battle for a column that ran in the *New York Herald* on November 16, 1877. (It is excerpted in Graham, comp. and ed., *The Custer Myth,* 65–73.) Routine documents affecting the commission also appear in NA, "Notes to Foreign Legations in the United States from the Department of State, 1834–1906. Great Britain, July 28, 1875–February 26, 1879," in File Microcopies of Records in the National Archives: no. 99, roll 46, 446, 450, 451. See also Utley, *Lance and the Shield,* 192, 194, 195–98; Diehl, *Staff Correspondent,* 129–30; Manzione, "*I Am Looking to the North for My Life,*" 74–107; Robert Vaughn, *Then and Now,* 346–51; Turner, *North-West Mounted Police,* vol. 1, 367–72; Cecil E. Denny, *The Law Marches West,* 124–27 (Denny wrote that among the Sioux attendees at Fort Walsh was the Hunkpapa warrior Rain In the Face); Sharp, *Whoop-Up Country,* 273–76; and Stanley Vestal, *Sitting Bull: Champion of the Sioux,* 214–20.

29. "Interview between Lieut.-Col. J.F. Macleod, C.M.G., Commissioner N.W.M.P., and Sitting Bull and other Chiefs of the Sioux Nation," Fort Walsh, October 17, 1877, in "Papers Relating to the Sioux Indians," 81–82; Macleod to Terry and Lawrence, October 17, 1876, in "Papers Relating to the Sioux Indians," 81 (also in *New York Herald*, October 25, 1877); Macleod to Mills, describing the meeting, October 27, 1877, in "North West Mounted Police, Reports, 1875–1878," appendix E, 45–47 (also in ibid., 78). See also telegram, October 23, 1877, no sender indicated, though apparently from Terry, to the secretaries of War and the Interior, conveying the substance of Macleod's post-council meeting with the Lakotas, in Sioux War Papers. The reference to the wall being broken down "and the Americans may be permitted to cross" was apparently given as a watered-down version of Interior Minister Mills's tough admonishment in his message to Macleod of August 24. Beyond quoted utterances contained in the official documents bearing on the council, Lakota viewpoint seems almost nonexistent, although Sitting Bull, according to another source, purportedly told the Canadians: "I came to you, in the first place, because I was being hard driven by the Americans. They broke their treaties with my people, and when I rose up and fought, not against them, but for our rights, . . . they pursued me like a dog, and would have hung me to a tree. They are not just. They drive us into war, and then seek to punish us for fighting. That is not honest." Quoted in Maclean, *Canadian Savage Folk*, 113–14. (The chief's purported complaints notwithstanding, in fact, he never subscribed to the Fort Laramie Treaty of 1868, the accord he referenced.) Furthermore, two interrelated Lakota drawings rendered soon afterwards made their way through the mail to Boston, and then to "Curley Hair" at the Cheyenne River Agency in Dakota Territory. They indicated that a mixed-blood Canadian named Howling Wolf served as intermediary between the sides during the meeting. The graphics represented that, besides Sitting Bull and the other leaders mentioned at the onset of the council, at least twenty-eight other Sioux men attended, and further figuratively registered General Terry's disappointment at its conclusion. Names of those indicated as present: Spotted Eagle, Strike the Ree, Boot, Travois, Elk Pipe, Black Bear, two individuals named Roman Nose, One Arrow, High Lodge, Big Man, One Eye, Kills the White Man, Ghost Face, War Bonnet, Two Lance, Eagle Shield, The Elk, Hollow Bear, Sitting Bull, Black Moon, Yellow Bull, Bull Bear, Bugler, and Many Dogs. Three individuals were listed as unknown. See Second Lieutenant Ralph W. Hoyt, Eleventh Infantry, to Post Adjutant, Cheyenne Agency, D.T., November 20, 1877. Sioux War Papers, roll 283. For further analysis and explication of this interesting document, see Anderson, "Sioux Pictorial Account of General Terry's Council at Fort Walsh," 93–116.

30. Word of the council's outcome reached the American troops waiting at the line on October 18. Private Zimmer recorded "that the chiefs don't want to have anything to do with the United States, and from this [time] out they are a-going to live with the queen." *Frontier Soldier*, 136.

31. *Report of the Sitting Bull Indian Commission,* 11; Sheridan to E. D. Townsend, October 22, 1877, and October 24, 1877, in Sioux War Papers, roll 283; *New York Herald,* October 22, 1877 (quotation); *New York Herald,* October 25, 1877 (quotation); entry from *Ottawa Free Press,* December 2, 1877, reprinted in "Papers Relating to the Sioux Indians," 86; Mills to Macleod, December 6, 1877, in ibid., 85–86 (quotation); *Benton Record,* October 26, 1877. Second Lieutenant Lovell H. Jerome commanded an escort of ten enlisted men on the mackinaw trip to Fort Buford, each man outfitted with Springfield rifle, prairie belt, and ammunition. *Army and Navy Journal,* November 24, 1877. An aside to the Terry Commission's trip concerned the seeming discovery in Sitting Bull's camp of a soldier of Company I, Seventh Cavalry, who had been taken prisoner by the Sioux at the Little Bighorn in June 1876. On the downriver trip from Fort Benton, Terry's interpreter, Baptiste Shane, told of having seen the man, Corporal Martin Ryan, months before while in the camp. Back in Saint Paul, Terry had reportedly confirmed Ryan's presence in the battle. He then notified Canadian authorities, who dispatched Assistant Commissioner Irvine to search the Lakota camps for Ryan, who was not found. Sitting Bull, Spotted Eagle, and other chiefs declared that no prisoners had been taken in the battle, and the matter was dropped. Correspondence relating the incident is in "Papers Relating to the Sioux Indians," 97–99. See also, *Chicago Inter Ocean,* November 30, 1877. A check of rosters of troops at the Little Bighorn disclosed no man named Martin Ryan present, although a Corporal Daniel Ryan, of Company C, was indeed killed with Custer's battalion. Two other men named Ryan, in companies B and M, respectively, fought at the Little Bighorn and survived. Hammer, *Biographies of the 7th Cavalry June 25th 1876,* 70, 78, 222.

32. *Report of the Sitting Bull Commission,* 11–12 (including quotations); *Benton Record,* October 26, 1877; Jackson, *A Century of Dishonor,* 180 (quotation regarding Interior Department entry). The *New York Herald* doubtless expressed the sentiment of most U.S. officials, stating, "[W]e wish the Great Mother joy with her new subjects." The *New York Times* reported that the Indians' "refusal to accept the terms presented by the Commission relieves this Government of all responsibility for them, and leaves them [in the] charge of the Dominion authorities." See also Manzione, *"I Am Looking to the North for My Life,"* 108–109, for reaction to the Terry Commission results, including the quotations of the above newspapers.

33. *Benton Record,* October 26, 1877. "It is to be hoped," the *Chicago Times* editorialized, "Mr. Hayes is by this time cured of all sentimental nonsense about sending olive-branches to savages before they have been thrashed. The time to negotiate with wild beasts of the Sitting Bull variety is when they are conquered. The only propositions for peace that these brutes appreciate are those which go from the muzzles of rifles and Gatling guns."

34. Pennanen, "Sitting Bull," 129–30.

Chapter 3

1. Greene, *Nez Perce Summer,* 312–18. The time of Joseph's surrender is confirmed in Second Lieutenant Charles E. S. Wood to Major Edwin C. Mason, Chief of Staff, "Headquarters Department of the Columbia—In the field. Miles [*sic*] Camp on Eagle Creek, M.T.," October 6, 1877. NA, RG 393, Part 3. Entry 107. District of the Clearwater, Letters Sent (box unnumbered).

2. Greene, *Nez Perce Summer,* 241–43.

3. Ibid., 266, citing McWhorter, *Yellow Wolf,* 205; McWhorter, *Hear Me, My Chiefs!* 478–81; Joseph (Heinmot Tooyalakekt), "An Indian's View of Indian Affairs," 428; and Garcia, *Tough Trip through Paradise,* 293. The initial army attack at Bear's Paw is detailed in Greene, *Nez Perce Summer,* 272–78.

4. "Narrative of Mrs. Shot-in-Head [Mrs. Wounded Head]," box 8, folder 43, Lucullus V. McWhorter Collection (Cage 55). Washington State University Library, Pullman (WSU); "Mrs. Shot-in-Head's Sequel to Former Narrative," box 7, folder 38. Ibid; see also untitled note in box 10, folder 62. Ibid. See also McWhorter, *Hear Me, My Chiefs!* 508–509.

5. Arthur account in Walter M. Camp Papers, Camp Mss. Field Notes, Walter Mason Camp Unclassified Envelope 127 (typed transcription prepared by Hammer, 560–61). Little Bighorn Battlefield National Monument, Crow Agency, Montana.

6. "Black Eagle's Narrative of the Last Fight," box 10, folder 62, McWhorter Collection, WSU; "The Remaining Fragment of Black Eagle's Story," box 10, folder 59. Ibid.

7. "Statement by Samuel Tilden," box 10, folder 62, McWhorter Collection, WSU.

8. Greene, *Nez Perce Summer,* 272, 279–80; Statement of Second Cavalryman John Lewis, in the Walter Mason Camp Papers, Western History Department, Denver Public Library, box 8, folder 1.

9. Greene, *Nez Perce Summer,* 280–81.

10. Account of Ealahweemah, in McWhorter, *Hear Me, My Chiefs!* 483–84.

11. Garcia, *Tough Trip through Paradise,* 293–94.

12. Dorrity, "Mrs. James Dorrity's Story," 80. Elements of another Nimiipuu statement, this by Peopeo Hihhih, a child in 1877, indicates that he indeed might have been with one of the groups that fled early from the Bear's Paw fighting on September 30 (although *he* believed he fled with the Nez Perce accompanying Chief White Bird's escape in the night of October 5–6 following Joseph's surrender). His account is as follows: "It was morning and we children were playing. We had hardwood sticks, throwing mud balls. I looked up and saw a spotted horse, a Cheyenne Indian wearing a war bonnet come to the bluff above me. He was closely followed by the troops. Some of the children ran back to the camps, some hurried to the gulch. I was with these last. Bullets were flying. We had to

get away! I had no moccasins. I jumped in the creek and swam across, maybe. When I got away I had only a shirt as clothing. Cold, wet, I was freezing! Some were on horses, and one woman showed pity for me. She took me up behind her. . . . After we left the battle-camp that night [?], we traveled slow. In the evening the men killed two buffalo bulls. We made camp in a gulch, built fire and roasted meat and ate. We could hear the cannon at the battle ground. Father [Buffalo Head] overtook us there. He wrapped my feet in his skin leggins." "Story of Peo-peo Hih-hih, 'White Bird,'" box 8, folder 43, McWhorter Collection, WSU.

13. Camp Papers, Little Bighorn Battlefield National Monument, BYU-719.

14. Letter, McWhorter to Many Wounds, and reply, both undated. Box 11, folder 79, McWhorter Collection, WSU; "Black Eagle's Narrative"; Note from Black Eagle, "Length of Time Reaching Canada," box 10, folder 62, ibid.; "Narrative of Mrs. Shot-in-Head."

15. "Narrative of Mrs. Shot-in-Head"; "Mrs. Shot-in-Head's Sequel to Former Narrative"; McWhorter, *Hear Me, My Chiefs!* 509. Wounded Head's statement, using practically the same language, is in ibid., 510.

16. In one of the most ridiculous insinuations of the journalistic history of the Nez Perce War, a reporter for the *New York World*, purportedly citing two Indians who had brought word to the Mounted Police at Fort Walsh, allowed that Joseph's surrender was but a sham designed to yield the decrepit and feeble of his followers while the spirited who yet remained made their way north into Canada. According to this unnamed correspondent, Joseph "acquiesced and handed over to Miles about 150 warriors, a number of squaws and some fifty dead, . . . [some of which] bodies having been brought to the scene for theatrical effect." Thus, "Joseph and the old and rheumatic warriors of the nation, with the oldest of the squaws, are prisoners, while nearly three hundred braves, now on the Cottonwood [in Canada], are as free to create trouble as ever they were. Joseph's surrender in this way was due partly to his illness—he is on his last legs with lung complaint—and partly to his unwillingness to cope longer with the soldiers unassisted by the Sioux and other tribes who have a common cause with him." The piece by the *World* writer appeared in the *Idaho Statesman*, November 13, 1877.

17. For background on White Bird, see Painter, *White Bird*, 8 and passim; Mrs. Ollokot's account in McWhorter, *Hear Me, My Chiefs!* 510–11 (quotation, 510). Another account placed White Bird's age in 1877 at 45. Camp Mss Field Notes, Walter Mason Camp Unclassified Envelope 127, 565. Hammer, Little Bighorn Battlefield National Monument transcriptions. According to this source, White Bird "originally lived on White Bird Creek, but when the whites began to settle in the neighborhood he took his family and went up and dwelt on Rapid River 5 or 6 miles from its mouth on Little Salmon, about where Pollock is now. His tribe [band], however, remained around White Bird Creek and Salmon River." Ibid. The statement regarding Looking Glass's collusion with White Bird regarding leaving is in MacDonald, "The Nez Perces," 270–71. Inner politics affecting gov-

ernance within the non-treaty Nez Perce body in 1877 is addressed in an undated note by Lucullus V. McWhorter, ca. 1930s, and note of V. O. McWhorter, July 23, 1945, in box 10, folder 62, McWhorter Collection, WSU. An unidentified Nez Perce woman who was present stated that "White Bird would not surrender! He said Chief Joseph could do as he pleased." "Incidents of the Last Battle and Surrender." Ibid. See also comments regarding Yellow Bull, himself a Lamtama, in box 10, folder 62, ibid. One source suggested that Joseph's followers surrendered slowly, or intermittently, in order to give others an opportunity to escape in the process. Pinkham, *Hundredth Anniversary of the Nez Perce War of 1877,* unpaginated. William Bent recalled that Joseph had informed Miles (apparently at the time of the surrender) that White Bird did not want to yield and wanted another night to ponder his action. Noyes, *In the Land of the Chinook,* 97.

Several Nez Perce sources state that White Bird's escape occurred earlier than the night of Joseph's surrender. For example, Yellow Bull maintained that White Bird departed during the night of September 30–October 1. "We had a council, at which I was present, and White Bird told Joseph that he would remain and help fight it out. He broke his word, however, for he soon skipped out, without saying anything, taking 103 people with him. He went over the line, into Canada." "Yellow Bull's Story," Camp Collection, Little Bighorn Battlefield National Monument, folder 59. But another account stated that White Bird escaped during the night of October 2. Camp Papers, Little Bighorn Battlefield National Monument, BYU-719. Yet Wottolen, who accompanied White Bird's people from the camp, simply stated that "White Bird did not leave at the commencement of the fight. It is a lie!" "The Last Fight and Surrender," box 10, folder 62, McWhorter Collection, WSU. See also Greene, *Nez Perce Summer,* 489n126. Official army sources are generally nebulous about when White Bird departed, and probably purposefully, since his contingent represented a sizable proportion of the people ensconced at Bear's Paw that managed to get away. Private William F. Zimmer, however, noted in his journal on October 6 that "last night Chief White Bird crawled through our lines with a few followers & made their escape." Zimmer, *Frontier Soldier,* 128.

18. See "Fallacies of History. Did Chief White Bird Violate Surrender Compact?" Box 9, Folder 53, McWhorter Collection, WSU. Moreover, an entry in Private Zimmer's journal for October 5 is perhaps revealing in discussing what followed Joseph's surrender: "White Bird & Looking Glass's people want to hear from their people in the hills [those who got away earlier?] before they surrender, so a few were let go to hold council with them, but leaving their arms." *Frontier Soldier,* 128. This comment suggests an apparent atmosphere of laxity among the troops that added to other conditions that potentially facilitated White Bird's departure.

19. McWhorter, *Hear Me, My Chiefs!* 510–11; "Incidents of the Last Battle and Surrender," box 10, folder 62, McWhorter Collection, WSU. See Yellow Wolf's

comment in McWhorter, *Yellow Wolf*, 229. Yellow Wolf in leaving responded to a request from Joseph to search for his (Yellow Wolf's) mother and Joseph's daughter, both of whom had fled during the opening assault on September 30. Yellow Wolf passed by the pickets near daybreak. "I watched but pretended not seeing them. They did not bother me." He found a horse hidden in a nearby canyon, mounted it, and took the trail of the White Bird party. Later that day at the Milk River mixed-blood camp he received food and new moccasins and kept on, the trail now fading beneath blizzard snows. Surprisingly, that evening he caught up with Nimiipuu who had escaped on September 30, which body included both his mother and Joseph's daughter. He did not return to the Bear's Paw camp. By Yellow Wolf's account, this party seemingly crossed into Canada on October 10. McWhorter, *Yellow Wolf*, 230–33. See also McWhorter, *Hear Me, My Chiefs!* 511–12.

20. Camp Papers, Little Bighorn Battlefield National Monument, BYU-719.

21. "Horses at the Last Battle," box 10, folder 62, McWhorter Collection, WSU.

22. "The Last Fight and Surrender," box 10, folder 62, McWhorter Collection, WSU.

23. MacDonald, "The Nez Perces," 271. Most Nez Perce sources appear inconclusive regarding the exact number of people leaving with White Bird. Wottolen said that "Chief White Bird and about forty-five others, some women, and two or three children" escaped from the Bear's Paw camp. "The Last Fight and Surrender," box 10, folder 62, McWhorter Collection, WSU. In one account, Yellow Bull stated that there were 103 in White Bird's party, and in another he said there were fifty. See Greene, *Nez Perce Summer*, 489n126. Another man, No Feather, who went out with White Bird, reported that "more than 40 people" escaped with the chief. "We slipped out at night quietly and were not fired upon by soldiers." Weptas Nut (No Feather), Interview by Walter M. Camp, February 15, 1915. Camp Interview Notes. MS. 57, box 2. Walter M. Camp Papers. Microfilm. Archives and Manuscripts Division, Harold B. Lee Library, Brigham Young University, Provo, Utah. (See further discussion of the total number of Nimiipuu who made it into Canada, 67–68.) In his piece "The Nez Perces," 271, MacDonald reported that "about two hundred head of horses" accompanied White Bird's people. Most Nez Perce accounts, however, do not mention horses with White Bird's group leaving the Bear's Paw camp, and state that the people traveled by foot. "Horses at the Last Battle," box 10, folder 62, McWhorter Collection, WSU. Indeed, MacDonald wrote later that "White Bird left in the gathering darkness of night, and while the surrender was yet taking place, for Canada. Afoot, they made but slow progress, for there were women and children, and some wounded in the party." MacDonald to McWhorter, December 15, 1929, reproduced in "Fallacies of History. Did Chief White Bird Violate Surrender Compact?" box 9, folder 53, McWhorter Collection, WSU. Significantly, MacDonald here made no statement concerning horses accompanying White Bird's group, and, based on accounts by participants who claim that these people walked all

the way into Canada, it seems likely that they were indeed horseless as they set out to the north.

24. Many Wounds Statement. Box 11, folder 79, McWhorter Collection, WSU; "The Last Fight and Surrender." Box 10, folder 62, ibid.; McWhorter, *Hear Me, My Chiefs!* 511.

25. Genin letter, December 13, 1877, quoted in Linda W. Slaughter, "Leaves from Northwestern History," *Collections of the State Historical Society of North Dakota*, I (1906), 274–76. Quoted and cited in McWhorter, *Hear Me, My Chiefs!* 511n4.

26. Howard to Miles, October 20, 1877, "Camp at Black Rock Crossing of Milk River M.T." NA, RG 393, Part 3. Entry 107. Letters and Telegrams Received by District of the Yellowstone Headquarters, September 1877–April 1878. Box 3. Regarding the numbers of people reported to be with the Lamtama chief, Howard's letter raises more questions than it answers, for while it specifies a figure, it is far below the forty or fifty people that Nez Perce accounts denote and drastically smaller than the number given by Duncan MacDonald. While it is indeed possible that not all the people accompanied White Bird into the "Half-breed Camp," Howard's letter suggests that the total number of Nez Perces were so few as to permit their attack and capture by the number of "halfbreeds" in that camp. In any event, his figure seems to have influenced official reports, and General Howard stated that "White Bird, with his two squaws, and accompanied by about 14 warriors, crept out between the pickets and fled to British Columbia." "Supplementary Report: Non-Treaty Nez Perce Campaign," December 26, 1877, in *Report of the Secretary of War, 1877*, 631.

27. Miles to Terry, October 3, 1877. NA, RG 393, Part 3. Entry 886. Ledger, District of the Yellowstone, "Letter Book, District of the Yellowstone. From Sept. 4th 1877 to Dec. 25th 1877," 83–84.

28. Miles to Walsh, October 9, 1877. Ibid., 92.

29. Johnson, *The Unregimented General*, 207; Account of William Bent, in Noyes, *In the Land of the Chinook*, 98. Maus later claimed to have captured thirteen Nez Perces. Maus, "Memoranda of Active Service of Lieut. Marion P. Maus, 1st Inf'y 1887 and 1886." U.S. Army Military History Institute, Army War College, Carlisle, Pa., Nelson A. Miles Papers, box T-2, folder "Nez Perces Campaign 1877, official reports and letters, clippings." See signed statement by Maus, "Half Breed Camp, Milk River, M.T., Oct. 13, 1877," certifying "that Carlos La Fontaine has taken care of Twelve Nez Perces Indians—Surrendered—by giving them shelter and rations to the possible value of Twenty five (25) Dollars." NA. RG 393, Part 3. Entry 107. Letters and Telegrams Received by District of the Yellowstone Headquarters, September 1877–April 1878. Box 3. Yet Hugh L. Scott, a second lieutenant in 1877, maintained that he and a detachment of six Seventh cavalrymen joined Maus and took part in the capture of forty-five Nez Perces. "Hiring some Red River carts, we loaded them with women and children and

started for Miles's camp on the Missouri near the mouth of the Musselshell." En route, the people experienced great discomfort. "The children would cry all night until we killed some buffalo and wrapped them up in the green hides, and fed them and our men with meat without salt, cooked without utensils." Scott, *Some Memories of a Soldier*, 75–77. Maus later stated that the number of captured was "forty-one or two Indians," thus revising upward his original figure of thirteen. Maus to Scott, June 26, 1902, in ibid., 77–78. See also Scott's reminiscence in unclassified envelope 110, 640, Camp Manuscript Field Notes, Camp Papers, Little Bighorn Battlefield National Monument, in which he stated that the detachments captured "45 or 50 Nez Perces refugees." Given Maus's statement of October 13, cited above, however, the true number of Nez Perces captured was probably twelve.

30. Field Orders No. 10, October 5, 1877, Fort Benton, Montana Territory, as cited in *Army and Navy Journal*, November 24, 1877.

31. Miles to wife, Mary, October 14, 1877, quoted in Johnson, *Unregimented General*, 207; Terry to Colonel Samuel D. Sturgis, October 5, 1877. NA, RG 393, Part 3. Entry 107, box 3; Statement of Moccasin, August 18, 1931. Manuscript Archives, Montana Historical Society, SC 489; Statement of Speak Thunder, August 18, 1931. Manuscript Archives, Montana Historical Society, SC 767; *Benton Record*, October 5, 1877; Major Guido Ilges to Miles, October 7, 1877. NA, RG 393, Part 3. Entry 107, box 3; *Benton Record*, October 12, 1877. In a letter of October 5, 1877, Terry told Miles that the results of the Box Elder Creek skirmish between the Gros Ventres and the Nez Perce refugees "pretty certainly determines that the Nez Perces can find no refuge with the Gros Ventres . . . & I think may incline them to move toward the Sioux." NA, RG 393, Part 3. Entry 107, box 3. Some specifics of this encounter, as well as the enemy tribes' motives, were provided by John J. Healy to the *Benton Record*, appearing in the issue of October 12, 1877: "Mr. George Croft and I left [Fort] Benton on the afternoon of the 3rd instant, arrived at Box Elder creek at 4 o'clock the following day. . . . Here we met Bull's Lodge, a Gros Ventre chief, who told us that the Assinaboins [*sic*] and Gros Ventre, assisted by three white men, had attacked the Nez Perce camp in the Bear Paw Mountains, somewhere in the vicinity of Clear Creek, and that the fight was still going on. A number of Indians who were with Bull's Lodge said they had captured two women and two boys, and killed several warriors. They had one fresh scalp with them, which was evidence enough that they had turned out against the Nez Perces. . . . My impression was, and Mr. Croft agreed with me, that they would not have attacked Joseph [Joseph's people] if the latter had not met with some reverse. We concluded from this that Gen. Miles had used up the hostiles, and that the Gros Ventre and Assinaboins were making a show of friendship for the whites by slaughtering the defeated enemy. . . . We also learned that the action of the two tribes was in a measure brought about through the influence of Major Ilges, who had been untiring in his efforts to induce the Gros

Ventres to join the whites against he Nez Perces, and the Gros Ventres had pledged themselves to follow his instructions and do all in their power to prevent the enemy from crossing the line."

32. Camp Papers, Little Bighorn Battlefield National Monument, BYU-719; McWhorter to Yellow Wolf, January 25, 1935, and response. Box 10, folder 62, McWhorter Collection, WSU.

33. "Mrs. James Dorrity's Story," 81.

34. Scott, *Some Memories of a Soldier,* 76.

35. Zimmer, *Frontier Soldier,* 129; Woodruff, "We have Joseph and all his people," 33 (quotation).

36. *New York Herald,* October 15, 1877 (first Miles quotation); Bent account in Noyes, *Land of the Chinook,* 97; Miles to Terry, October 9, 1877. NA, RG 393, Part 3. Entry 886. District of the Yellowstone, "Letter Book, District of the Yellowstone, from Sept. 4th 1877 to Dec. 25th 1877" (ledger), 96 (quotation); *The New North-West,* March 21, 1879 (quoted in MacDonald, "The Nez Perces," 273).

37. Garcia, *Tough Trip through Paradise,* 295–96; "An After Last Battle Tragedy—Gros Ventres Enmity." Box 11, folder 79, McWhorter Collection, WSU; "Pathetic Incident of After War Tragedies." Box 10, folder 62, McWhorter Collection, WSU. Yellow Wolf stated that those people killed by the Assiniboines and Gros Ventres were never found. Box 10, folder 62, McWhorter Collection, WSU. For more of the killing of Nez Perces by enemy tribes, see McWhorter, *Hear Me, My Chiefs!* 514–15. For lists of those who escaped Bear's Paw only to be killed by enemy tribesmen and whites or subsequently captured, see appendices A and B.

38. "Mrs. Shot-in-Head's Sequel to Former Narrative," box 7, folder 38, McWhorter Collection, WSU; "Refugees Reach Sitting Bull's Camp" (narrative by Peopeo Tholekt), box 11, folder 79, in ibid. See also McWhorter, *Hear Me, My Chiefs!* 513.

39. McWhorter, *Hear Me, My Chiefs!* 513. Walsh later related that Sitting Bull's people got word of the Nez Perces advance along Cow Creek (south of their Bear's Paw camp), and that when he went to the Sioux he "found the Indians in a great state of excitement and the warriors 1000 in number ready to take the field." Later, on news of the army assault at Bear's Paw, the Sioux camp became electrified with excitement and the warriors were bent on going to the Nez Perces' rescue. Walsh and others quickly explained to them "that this could not and must not be or asylum [for them] . . . north of the line would cease and Canada would no more be a place of safety for them. . . . The man who crosses that line from this camp is from the moment he put[s] his foot on U.S. Terr. our enemy." Walsh to Cora, May 21, 1890. While it is indeed possible that Sitting Bull personally intended to lead a relief column in the hopes of helping the tribesmen besieged at Bear's Paw, it did not happen on October 8, when Walsh was present in the Sioux camp. Moreover, the Mounted Police had delivered the Lakotas ample

warning against such action as would jeopardize their own stay in Canada. Some Nez Perce accounts, however, including that provided by Duncan MacDonald, indicate that Sitting Bull's party riding south encountered White Bird's people coming north with word of the surrender, which caused the Sioux to turnabout and conduct the refugees to their camp. *The New North-West,* March 21, 1879 (reprinted in MacDonald, "The Nez Perces," 272–73). And in his 1929 letter to McWhorter, MacDonald related that White Bird's party met Sitting Bull "on the vast plain north of the Milk River." "They saw a long string of mounted Indians coming towards them. The man on [in] the lead was riding a fine, mouse-colored horse, . . . [and he] proved to be Sitting Bull." MacDonald to McWhorter, December 15, 1929. Box 9, folder 53, McWhorter Collection, WSU. Yet this could not have happened. Sitting Bull and his headmen departed the Sioux camp for Fort Walsh on October 8, following the arrival of the first large body of Nez Perces, and did not return to the camp until the 21st, a timeline that is not conducive to any meeting with White Bird because of that chief's arrival after October 8th, nor with an attempt by Sitting Bull to raise the army siege at Bear's Paw because he and his leaders were present at Fort Walsh. For Nez Perce accounts nevertheless describing a Sitting Bull relief effort, see "Mrs. Shot-in-Head's Sequel to Former Narrative," box 7, folder 38, McWhorter Collection, WSU ("Sitting Bull was angry! With his warriors he hurried away—an army mounted and with extra war-horses—to help the Nez Perces. But too late!"); and that of Peopeo Tholekt, which stated that a war party led by Sitting Bull contained "many hundreds of warriors," but when they met the White Bird refugees and learned of Joseph's surrender they turned back. McWhorter, *Hear Me, My Chiefs!* 513. For pictorial depiction of a likely meeting between Lakotas and Nez Perces, possibly with at least one of the "halfbreeds" present, see Thompson, *I Will Tell of My War Story,* 78–79.

40. Walsh's report to Macleod, October 12, 1877, in *New York Herald,* October 22, 1877; Macleod to Mills, October 27, 1877, in "Papers Relating to the Sioux Indians," 77; Manzione, *"I Am Looking to the North for My Life,"* 98–100. Stanley Vestal (Walter S. Campbell) erroneously stated that the Nez Perces appeared on September 28, which would have been even before Miles had struck the Bear's Paw camp. (He had the year as 1878, too, but that is likely a typo.) "As they swarmed down the slope, he [Sitting Bull] saw that many of them were wounded and bloody, some in travois, some tied in their saddles; the tired haggard women were crying, the men looked grim, and babies whined from their cradles slung from saddlehorns." A Nez Perce man, Robert Moses, spoke English to them, saying "We want to be friends with the Sioux." Vestal's account, supposedly derived largely from Sioux and Nez Perce sources, indicates that no relief effort was mounted by Sitting Bull. Vestal, *New Sources of Indian History,* 241–42.

41. Walsh to Cora, May 21, 1890.

42. Black Elk, *The Sixth Grandfather,* 207.

43. Walsh to Cora, May 21, 1890.

44. "Major Walsh's Report," Fort Walsh, October 26, 1877. Clipping in unidentified newspaper in James Morrow Walsh Scrapbook #11, Glenbow Archives. A report in the *Chicago Times,* October 21, 1877, noted that eighty Nez Perces "joined Sitting Bull's forces on the 10th and thirty or forty more are reported about the Three Buttes." Yellow Wolf's recollection of his leaving Bear's Paw on October 6 and meeting a party of Nez Perces late that day, further confirms an arrival of those people among the Sioux in Canada on October 11. McWhorter, *Yellow Wolf,* 231–33. Vestal's account states that the White Bird party arrived on the same day as the first group, which is extremely unlikely. *New Sources of Indian History,* 242.

45. McWhorter, *Yellow Wolf,* 234–36; see also McWhorter, *Hear Me, My Chiefs!* 515.

46. Quoted in Vestal, *New Sources of Indian History,* 242. White Bird told Duncan MacDonald that Sitting Bull told him: "If I had known you were surrounded by soldiers at Bear Paw Mountains, I certainly would have helped you. What a pity that I was not there with my warriors. But now you are here, and as long as you are with me I will not allow the Americans to take even a child from you without fighting for it." White Bird gave the Hunkpapa a gift of seven horses. *The New North-West,* March 21, 1879.

47. "Major Walsh's Report," Fort Walsh, October 26, 1877; Turner, *North-West Mounted Police,* vol. 1, 373–74.

48. Walsh to Cora, May 21, 1890.

49. "Major Walsh's Report," Fort Walsh, October 26, 1877; "Report of Indians that surrendered or were captured through the exertions of the troops of the District of the Yellowstone." December 15, 1881 folder: Fifth Infantry, Ft. Keogh, M.T., box T-2: Fifth Infantry to Aug. 1881. Nelson A. Miles Papers, Manuscripts Division, U.S. Army Military History Institute, Army War College, Carlisle, Pa.; Greene, *Nez Perce Summer,* 266, 315, 464n72, 491nn149–50. Black Eagle first informed Lucullus V. McWhorter that the escapees numbered 220, comprising 140 men and boys and 80 women and children. "Refugee Nez Perces Who Returned to Sitting Bull's Camp the Second Time." Box 11, folder 79, McWhorter Collection. He later provided a "corrected estimate" that accounted for 140 men and boys and 93 or 94 women and girls, for a total of 233 or 234 who "reached the Sioux camp in Canada." "Nez Perces Escaping from the Last Battle Computed by Black Eagle." Box 10, folder 62, McWhorter Collection. A census of the prisoners taken at Saint Paul, Minnesota, in late November 1877, while en route to Fort Leavenworth, totaled 431 people; another subsequently taken at Fort Leavenwoth totaled 418 prisoners—including losses through deaths, and a few births. Pearson, *The Nez Perces in the Indian Territory,* 75.

50. Quoted in *The New North-West,* August 9, 1878. Possibly this or another council is portrayed by a Nez Perce artist tentatively identified as Laamnisnimusus in Thompson, *I Will Tell of My War Story,* 68–70.

51. John Howard to Miles, November 3, 1877. NA, RG 393, Part 3. Entry 107, box 3, 1877; John Howard to Miles, January 10, 1878, in ibid.; *Bozeman Times,* December 27, 1877; *Benton Record,* November 10, 1877; *Benton Record,* December 14, 1877; Peopeo Tholekt and Mrs. Shot-in-Head (Wounded Head) accounts cited in McWhorter, *Hear Me, My Chiefs!* 513–14; Greene, *Nez Perce Summer,* 341. See also Vestal, *New Sources of Indian History,* 243–44.

52. Howard to Miles, "Battlefield of Eagle Creek Near Bear Paw Mountains MT," October 7, 1877. NA, RG 393, Part 3. Entry 107. District of the Clearwater, Letters Sent (box unnumbered).

Chapter 4

1. McWhorter question and Black Eagle response, box 10, folder 59, McWhorter Collection, WSU.

2. McWhorter, *Yellow Wolf,* 234–36.

3. "Wottolen's Dance in the Sioux Camp," box 9, folder 53, McWhorter Collection, WSU. According to Wottolen, Mool-mool-kin, along with four other Nez Perce men, were killed by the Crows in 1878. Ibid. Another of these men was identified by Wottolen as Throw-away Horn. "Wottolen at the Last Battle. The Vengeful Cheyenne," box 10, folder 62, McWhorter Collection, WSU.

4. McWhorter, *Hear Me, My Chiefs!* 515–16; Legare to Walter M. Camp, March 26, 1912 (quotation). Walter Mason Camp Collection, box 1, folder 21. Manuscripts Division, Brigham Young University Library, Provo, Utah (microfilm).

5. Gibbon to Walsh, December 15, 1877, and William Lincoln to Secretary of War George W. McCrary, January 26, 1878. Typescript copies in the archives of Nez Perce National Historical Park, box 10, file 11; *Army and Navy Journal,* January 12, 1878 (quotation). The man with Old George was not identified in the correspondence. Buell to Assistant Adjutant General (AAG), Department of Dakota, December 6, 1877. Sioux War Papers. NA Microfilm Publication M666, roll 283 (quotation).

6. Sheridan to Adjutant General Edward D. Townsend, December 27, 1877, citing an undated telegram from Gibbon to Terry. Nez Perce War Papers. NA Microfilm Publication M666, roll 339; First Lieutenant George W. Baird to Commanding Officer, Fort Custer, February 14, 1878. NA, RG 393, Part 3. Entry 889. Miles wrote to Colonel Gibbon the following about Old George and his situation: "[He] came through with General Howard to get his daughter, who was in the hostile [Nez Perce] camp. He was very useful as an Interpreter at the surrender and after the Nez Perce camp was secured. I sent him to Sitting Bull's camp for his daughter and with a message to those who escaped. He secured his daughter, got as far south as Carroll, where he was foully dealt with by miserable white men; was shot in several places as his unhealed wounds will show and his young

girl used worse. I presume he was left for dead, but succeeded in reaching the Crow camp. His daughter was taken I understand to Fort Benton, where she remained at last accounts. For his good service and to repair, as far as possible, the wrong done, I sent him with two Government ponies to you, hoping that he may yet recover his child. Should he do so please send him back to his home or make such disposition of them as you deem best. . . . If the white men who committed the crime are caught, I would suggest that you report it to Department Head Quarters, as the Department Commander orders the affair investigated." Miles to Gibbon, June 23, 1878. NA, RG 393, Part 3. Entry 889. District of the Yellowstone, Letters Sent. See also *Army and Navy Journal,* January 5, 1878.

7. Howard to Miles, October 20, 1877 (quotation). NA, RG 393, Part 3. Entry 107. Letters and Telegrams Received by District of the Yellowstone Headquarters, September 1877–April 1878, box 3; Vestal, *New Sources of Indian History,* 236–40; Utley, *Lance and the Shield,* 202.

8. Ilges to AAG, District of Montana, Fort Shaw, Montana Territory, November 22, 1877. Sioux War Papers, roll 283; Lieutenant Colonel Daniel Huston, Jr., to AAG, Department of Dakota, December 14, 1877. Sioux War Papers, roll 283; Huston to Miles, January 9, 1878. NA, RG 393, Part 3. Entry 107. Letters and Telegrams Received by District of the Yellowstone Headquarters, September 1877-April 1878, box 3; Miles to AAG, Department of Dakota, January 12, 1878. NA, RG 393, Part 3. Entry 889. District of the Yellowstone, Letters Sent, September 20, 1877 to February 13, 1879 (ledger); Miles to AAG, Department of Dakota, February 9, 1878. NA, RG 393, Part 3. Entry 889. District of the Yellowstone, Letters Sent, February 1878–August 1878 (ledger) (quotation); Evarts to Thornton, February 23, 1878. "Notes to Foreign Legations in the United States from the Department of State, 1834–1906." Great Britain, July 28, 1875–February 26, 1879. File Microcopies of Records in the National Archives: No. 99, roll 46, 535; Utley, *Lance and the Shield,* 200, 202; Pennanen, "Sitting Bull," 30. Rumors abounded about a massive assembly of all the tribes. Reported Commissioner Macleod, "A grand confederation of all the Indians was to be formed hostile to the Whites, every one of whom was to be massacred as the first act of confederation." He, however, believed the report to be "without foundation." "Extract from Commissioner's Report, 1877" (includes 1878), in "North West Mounted Police Reports," appendix D, 21. On the matter of a potential confederation of tribes, see U.S. Consul at Winnipeg James W. Taylor to Seward, Despatches No. 272 and 273, March 21 and 26, 1878; and Taylor to Seward, February 27, 1878. "Despatches from United States Consuls in Winnipeg, 1869–1906," vol. 5, April 6, 1875–December 31, 1881. NA Microfilm Publication T24, roll 5. See also Manzione, *"I Am Looking to the North for My Life,"* 125–28. Regarding Sitting Bull's presence south of the line, Taylor stated that "there is every probability that hunting parties of Indians freely cross and recross the frontier in pursuit of buffalo. It is not probable that Sitting Bull has traveled himself south of the line,

but I have no doubt that his followers pay little regard to its location when engaged in the chase." Taylor reported that Sitting Bull "mainly accompanies his protestations that he will be peaceable and submissive while on Canadian territory by fierce invective against the United States, and an avowal of his future purpose to wage war against Americans." Taylor to Seward, Dispatch No. 265, February 27, 1878. "Despatches from United States Consuls in Winnipeg, 1869–1906," vol. 5, April 6, 1875–December 31, 1881. NA Microfilm Publication T24, roll 5. For related correspondence, see also "Papers Relating to the Sioux Indians," 100–107, 111.

9. Ibid.; *Benton Record,* November 2, 1877; *Benton Record,* November 10, 1877; Gibbon to AAG, Department of Dakota, December 17, 1877. Sioux War Papers, roll 283. Miles believed that the Milk River "half-breeds" had not only helped the Nez Perces in their movement north, but "have given aid and comfort to the hostile Sioux," and were providing them ammunition. Miles to AAG, Department of Dakota, February 19, 1878, in ibid. Scout Howard had learned that the buffalo "are scarce near the Teton camp and they [the people] will soon have to go somewhere else." He told Miles that he wished that "the north side of Milk River was all burnt." "That, I think, would either bring them over here or drive them north." Howard to Miles, October 20, 1877.

10. Secretary of State Scott, Memorandum, February 11, 1878, *Papers Relating to the Foreign Relations of the United States, 1878,* 344–45; Irvine to Scott, February 2, 1878, in ibid., 346; Manzione, *"I Am Looking to the North for My Life,"* 110–11; *Fort Benton Record,* October 26, 1877; "Report of Col. T. H. Ruger," September 23, 1879, in *Report of the Secretary of War, 1879,* 75–77;. Frazer, *Forts of the West,* 79, 83.

11. Greene, *Yellowstone Command,* 225–26; Irvine to Scott, March 2, 1878 (quotation of "no danger"), in Manzione, *"I Am Looking to the North for My Life,"* 114; Irvine to Scott, February 2, 1878. *Papers Relating to the Foreign Relations of the United States,* 346; Utley, *Lance and the Shield,* 204, 375n12; *Fort Benton Record,* February 1, 1878, February 8, 1878, and March 1, 1878. Miles finally toned down his advocacy: "My object was not 'to initiate a war' or any 'measures likely to lead to one,' but to prevent, if possible, a recurrence of one, to preserve the loyalty of the friendly tribes, to prevent the gathering on our territory, at least, of the hostile element." Miles to AAG, Department of Dakota, March 11, 1878. NA, RG 393, Part 3. Entry 886. District of the Yellowstone, "Letter Book, District of the Yellowstone. From Sept. 4th 1877 to Dec. 25th 1877" (ledger). Yet within weeks he proposed demanding that the Canadian authorities immediately arrest Sitting Bull and fourteen other chiefs, including the Nez Perce White Bird, and again advocated moving troops to the border. Miles to AAG, Department of Dakota, April 3, 1878, in ibid.

12. "Extract from Commissioner's Report, 1877," (includes 1878) in "North West Mounted Police Reports," appendix D, 21 (quotation); Manzione, *"I Am Looking to the North for My Life,"* 128. For the Northern Cheyenne breakout from

the Indian Territory, see Monnett, *Tell Them We Are Going Home;* and Hoig, *Perilous Pursuit.* The Bannock breakout is aptly treated in Brimlow, *The Bannock War of 1878.*

13. "Extract from Commissioner's Report, 1877" (includes 1878), in "North West Mounted Police Reports," appendix D, 22.

14. Evarts to Thornton, March 18, 1878, and Evarts to Thornton, April 5, 1878. "Notes to Foreign Legations," roll 46, 535–56, 546; Miles to AAG, Department of Dakota, February 19, 1878, in "Papers Relating to the Sioux Indians," 112; "Report of a Committee of the Honorable the Privy Council, approved by His Excellency the Governor-General in Council, on the 26th March, 1878," in "Papers Relating to the Sioux Indians," 113–14; Irvine to Frederick White, November 10, 1878, in "Papers Relating to the Sioux Indians," 125–26; Manzione, *"I Am Looking to the North for My Life,"* 117–18. The estimate of 580 lodges is from Bray, "We Belong to the North," 45n65. The breakdown of the various groups provided here is in Irvine to Scott, July 14, 1878, in "Papers Relating to the Sioux Indians," 119–20. It is likely that during June or July 1878, the Nez Perces witnessed a Lakota Sun Dance, perhaps near Wood Mountain. A colored pencil drawing bearing elements of one obviously Sioux Sun Dance appears in Thompson, *I Will Tell of My War Story,* 71. See also Brown, ed., *The Sacred Pipe,* 67.

15. Miles to AAG, Department of Dakota, October 14, 1878. NA, RG 393, Part 3. Entry 889. Letter Book, District of the Yellowstone, from August 6, 1878, to August 8, 1879 (quotation). The distancing of certain Sioux Indians from Sitting Bull began as early as July 1878, when several Lakota leaders met with Lieutenant Governor David Laird and would "scarcely acknowledge that they knew him." Laird to Superintendent-General of Indian Affairs, Ottawa, December 5, 1878. 4 Parliament, 1 session, *Sessional Papers,* no. 41, 42.

16. Irvine to White, November 10, 1878, in "Papers Relating to the Sioux Indians," 125–26. On the demise of the borderland herds, see Dobak, "Killing the Canadian Buffalo, 1821–1881."

17. Irvine to Captain Edward Moale, November 24, 1878, in "Papers Relating to the Sioux Indians," 131–32; Seward to Thornton, February 13, 1879, in "Notes to Foreign Legations, Great Britain," roll 46, 691–92; Constable (N.W.M.P.) Gordon Rolph report, February 14, 1879, in ibid., 132; Seward to Thornton, February 13, 1879, in ibid., 133; J. S. Dennis to Irvine, February 26, 1879, in ibid., 134; N.W.M.P. Sub-Inspector W. D. Antrobus to Irvine, February 24, 1879, in ibid., 135; Evarts to Thornton, March 15, 1879, in ibid., 137–38 (second quotation); Irvine to Dennis, March 15, 1879, in ibid., 142–43; Irvine to White, March 15, 1879, in ibid., 143. For Sioux activities in regard to their raiding Piegan ponies near the Bear's Paw Mountains in the fall of 1878, see, Indian Agent John Young to the Commissioner of Indian Affairs, July 28, 1879, in *Report of the Secretary of the Interior, 1879,* 195–96; Walsh to Irvine, January 25, 1879, in "Papers Relating to the Sioux Indians," 129 (first quotation); Greene, *Nez Perce Summer,* 347–48;

Manzione, *"I Am Looking to the North for My Life,"* 129, 131–32; McCrady, *Living with Strangers*, 95–98.

18. Memorandum by MacDonald, February 28, 1879 (quotations), in "Papers Relating to the Sioux Indians," 139–41. For an assessment of the situation regarding buffalo availability in 1879, see the quotation by Macleod cited in Denny, *The Law Marches West*, 135–36.

19. Privy Council report, September 22, 1879, attached to Thornton to Evarts, September 30, 1879; Thornton to Evarts, November 15, 1879. "Notes from the British Legation in the United States to the Department of State, 1791–1906." National Archives Microfilm Publications, Microcopy No. 50, vol. 104, May 1– December 29, 1879. Roll T-104; Turner, "Sitting Bull Tests the Mettle of the Redcoats," 73.

20. Seward to Thornton, August 9, 1879, in *Papers Relating to the Foreign Relations of the United States, 1879*, 504–505; Miles to Macleod, June 26, 1879. NA, RG 393, Part 3. Entry 889. Letter Book, District of the Yellowstone, from August 6, 1878, to August 8, 1879, 218–19 (quotation); Walsh to Macleod, December 16, 1879, in "North-West Mounted Police Force. Commissioner's Report, 1879," 13–14; Utley, *Lance and the Shield*, 204. Lieutenant Tillson carried the following missive from Miles to Commissioner Macleod: "I have the honor to inform you that on the 28th day of March a party of seven 'Nez-Perces' and two 'Sioux' Indians killed a citizen of Custer county of this territory. They committed other depredations and stole some fifty or sixty head of stock. From all the indications, and from reports that have been made to me of their work, I am satisfied they came from and returned to the northwest Territory, and arrived at Wood Mountain the last of April. The bearer Lieut. Tillson will explain the matter to you, and citizen Sterns [or Stearns] will be able to identify the murderers and stolen stock. I have to request that the parties may be arrested and held for the action of your government, or if you are authorized, to return them to such point on the line most convenient to you, in order that they may be arraigned before a proper tribunal." Miles to Macleod, June 26, 1879. During the tour of the Sioux camp looking for horses, Walsh later related, "I caused Johnson [the Nez Perce] . . . to go up and speak to Stearns when he (Stearns) said positively that he was not one of the party who committed the depredations." Quoted in J. C. Atkins to Privy Council, September 9, 1879, in *Papers Relating to the Foreign Relations of the United States, 1879*, 492–93. See also "Report of Superintendent Walsh," December 16, 1879, in "North-West Mounted Police Force. Commissioner's Report, 1879," 13–14; and John H. McIllree to Walter M. Camp, December 7, 1913. Walter M. Camp Papers in Robert S. Ellison Collection, Western History Department, Denver Public Library.

21. Bird to Hayt, April 19, 1879. NA, RG 393, Part 3. Entry 889. "District of the Yellowstone, Letters Sent, Letters Received from Aug. 8th 1879 to May 29, 1881."

22. Terry to AAG, Division of the Missouri, April 2, 1879; Evarts to Thornton, April 19, 1879; and Evarts to Thornton, May 27, 1879 (quotation), in *Papers Relat-*

ing to the Foreign Relations of the United States, 1879, 491, 492, 496–97; "Report of Brig. Gen. Alfred H. Terry," October 1, 1879, in *Report of the Secretary of War, 1879,* 53; Pennanen, "Sitting Bull," 131.

23. Bird to Hayt, June 13, 1879 (quotation); Miles to AAG, Department of Dakota, September (no day specified), 1879. NA, RG 393, Part 3. Entry 889. "District of the Yellowstone, Letters Sent, Letters Received from Aug. 8th 1879 to May 29, 1881," 70–83 (quotations) (Miles's report also appears in *Report of the Secretary of War, 1879,* 68–75); Utley, *Lance and the Shield,* 206–10; Pennanen, "Sitting Bull," 133; Turner, "Sitting Bull Tests the Mettle of the Redcoats," 73–74. Details of Miles's campaign to the line, and of his exchange with Superintendent Walsh, appear in Finerty, *War-Path and Bivouac,* 225–300 (see, particularly, 264–65), and in Haines, ed., "Letters of an Army Captain [Eli L. Huggins] on the Sioux Campaign of 1879–1880," 42–45. See also, Utley, *Frontier Regulars,* 286–87; Turner, *North-West Mounted Police,* vol. 1, 463–67; Manzione, *"I Am Looking to the North for My Life,"* 135–36. Walsh later claimed, probably exaggeratedly, that Sitting Bull determined to attack Miles below the line and that he (Walsh) succeeded in council with other Sioux leaders to stymie that proposition and by so doing purportedly saved Miles's command from annihilation. Walsh to "My dear Cora," May 21, 1890. See Utley, *Lance and the Shield,* 376–77n20.

The Nez Perce Oliver Brisbo's account of the Milk River action suggests that by the fall of 1879, at least (the newspaper referred to the fight as having happened "last summer"), the scout had seemingly developed a negative view of the army's action, as evinced by his tone in the piece. Likewise, the quoted purported comments from Sitting Bull suggest that Brisbo had learned this information from Lakota participants. Partial clipping from *Bismark Tribune,* October 31, 1879, in James Morrow Walsh Scrapbook #11, Glenbow Archives.

24. Finerty, *War-Path and Bivouac,* 268–83, including various quotations. Another correspondent, Stanley Huntley of the *Chicago Tribune,* interviewed Sitting Bull in June 1879. Utley, *Lance and the Shield,* 207–208.

25. Terry's report, October 1, 1879, in *Report of the Secretary of War, 1879,* 63–64 (quotation); "Report of Lieutenant-General Sheridan," October 22, 1879, in *Report of the Secretary of War, 1879,* 43 (quotation); Acting Minister of the Interior, to the Governor-General, August 13, 1879, in *Papers Relating to the Foreign Relations of the United States, 1879,* 509–510.

26. Walsh to Macleod, December 16, 1879, in "North-West Mounted Police Force. Commissioner's Report, 1879," 16; Pennanen, "Sitting Bull," 134–35; Joyner, "Hegira of Sitting Bull," 18. During the winter of 1879–80, as many as 17,000 Canadian Indians—Blackfeet, Bloods, Piegans, Assiniboines, and Crees—came below the line to hunt. "Report of Col. Thos. H. Ruger," September 21, 1880, in *Report of the Secretary of War, 1880,* 77.

27. Titley, "Edgar Dewdney"; George H. Young to the Minister of Customs, October 19, 1879. National Archives of Canada (NAC), Record Group (RG) 10,

vol. 3700, File 16798. Microfilm roll C-10122; Thornton to Marquis of Torne, February 28, 1880, enclosing Evarts to Thornton, February 27, 1880. NAC, RG 10, vol. 3707, File 19485. Microfilm roll C-10124; "Report of the Deputy Superintendent-General of Indian Affairs, 1879"; "Report of Col. N.A. Miles," September 21, 1880, in *Report of the Secretary of War, 1880,* 74–75; Colonel John W. Davidson to Lieutenant Colonel Joseph N.G. Whistler, May 22, 1880. NA, RG 393, Part 3. Entry 890. "Hd Qrs Dist. Yellowstone. Various documents, 1880 (ledger), 122.

28. Nathan S. Porter to Hayt, August 12, 1880, in *Report of the Commissioner of Indian Affairs, 1880,* 235 (quotation); "Report of the Commissioner of Indian Affairs," October 24, 1881, in *Report of the Department of the Interior, 1881,* 179. McCrady, *Living with Strangers,* 100–101. The most precise accounting of the situation regarding the Lakotas, including assorted surrenders into July 1880, is that prepared by Walsh after he had departed the Wood Mountain Mounted Police post. See "Report of Superintendent J. M. Walsh," December 31, 1880. For events and departures of Sioux between July and December, 1880, see "Report of Superintendent L. N. F. Crozier," Decembe, 1880. Both reports in *North-West Mounted Police Force Commissioner's Report, 1880,* 25–29. See also Manzione, *"I Am Looking to the North for My Life,"* 145–47; Pennanen, "Sitting Bull," 135–36; Pakes, "Sitting Bull in Canada," 18–19.

29. Evarts to Thornton, February 5, 1881, in *Papers Relating to the Foreign Relations of the United States, 1881,* 577–78 (quotations); "Report of Superintendent L. N. F. Crozier, Dec., 1880," 32; Turner, "Sitting Bull Tests the Mettle of the Redcoats," 74, 75. After Ilges's attack on the Sioux at Poplar River, Sitting Bull told Crozier, "I went towards the agency against my will because the Great Mother told me to go. . . . I took one step forward & stopped to think before going on again. . . . They [the Americans] are untruthful and I have come back here and here I am going to remain to raise my children." Crozier to Macleod, February 8, 1881. NAC, RG 10, vol. 3653, File 8589–1A. Microfilm roll C-10114.

30. For the final years of the Sioux in Canada and the events immediately culminating in Sitting Bull's surrender at Fort Buford, see Utley, *Lance and the Shield,* 199–233; DeMallie, "The Sioux in Dakota and Montana Territories," 48–54; Turner, *North-West Mounted Police,* vol. 1, passim; Manzione, *"I Am Looking to the North for My Life,"* 140–49; Hedren, *Sitting Bull's Surrender at Fort Buford,* 3–37; Poitevin, *Captain Walter Clifford,* 233–51; Vestal, *Sitting Bull,* 224–33; Pennanen, "Sitting Bull," 136–40; and Turner, "Sitting Bull Tests the Mettle of the Redcoats," 74–76. Details of Jean Louis Légaré's role in convincing Sitting Bull to surrender, as well as of his claim filed for compensation for his expenses in conducting the people to Fort Buford, appear in NAC, RG 10, vol. 7894, File 38001-1-2. Department of Indian Affairs, "Claim of J. Louis Legare Re Sitting Bull." Microfilm roll C-12139 (quotation); and NAC, RG 15, vol. 281, Series D-11-1, File 49185, microfilm roll T-2547. See also the various communications from Walsh, Crozier, Minister David Mills, and others, 1879–81, regarding Sit-

ting Bull in Canada, in NAC, RG 10, vol. 3691, file 13893, microfilm roll C-10121; "Report of Superintendent J. M. Walsh, December 31, 1880," 25–29; "Report of Superintendent L. N. F. Crozier," December, 1880," 32–33; Consul James W. Taylor to Secretary of State James G. Blaine, Despatch 318, May 28, 1881, "Despatches from United States Consuls in Winnipeg, 1869–1906," vol. 5, April 6, 1875–December 31, 1881; and Irvine to Mills, February 1, 1882, 4 Parliament, 4 session, *Sessional Papers*, no. 18. The intermittent surrenders of 1880–81 totaled 2,858 Lakotas. Soldiers accompanied the tribesmen downstream to Fort Yates, where most went on the adjoining Standing Rock Agency; some joined relatives at Cheyenne River Agency, and some earlier had gone to lands near Pine Ridge Agency, although Sitting Bull and his immediate followers were imprisoned at Fort Randall, along the Missouri River in southeastern Dakota Territory. "Report of the Commissioner of Indian Affairs," October 24, 1881, in *Report of the Secretary of the Interior, 1881*, 37–38; Valentine T. McGillycuddy to the Commissioner of Indian Affairs, September 1, 1881, in ibid., 102. Not all the Lakotas surrendered, and some remained in what is present-day Saskatchewan. In 1885 "about eleven lodges" were camped near the One Arrows Reserve, where "the settlers & [Canadian] Indians are much annoyed by their cutting dry wood, begging, &c." Commissioner Dewdney urged the nearest Mounted Police commander "to use his endeavor in getting them to go south [of the line]." Dewdney to Irvine, November 20, 1884. NAC, RG 18, vol. 1021, Series B-1, file 2747. These Lakotas eventually realized a small reserve in 1910. See Papandrea, *They Never Surrendered*, 14–27.

31. McWhorter, *Yellow Wolf*, 52–53. Miles's scout, Joseph Culbertson, saw Steps months before the surrender when he visited Sitting Bull's camp on Porcupine Creek. He recalled: "I met a very small Nez Perce Indian. He went by the name of Stepes [*sic*]. He was a cripple, but a great broncho buster, and the first thing that he wanted me to do was to play a game of poker for money, but I told him that I didn't know how to play poker. . . ." Trout, ed., *Joseph Culbertson's Indian Scout Memoirs*, 41. Steps was listed as a member (son) of White Dog's family while imprisoned at Fort Randall. Greene, *Fort Randall on the Missouri*, 141, 186. Steps's presence at Fort Bennett in 1890 is chronicled in the *New York Herald*, November 24, 1890. See also *Chicago Tribune*, November 21, 1890, for mention of "Stepps-the-Cripple."

Chapter 5

1. Years later, one Mrs. Lelah Stevenson explained in an interview that her great-grandmother had gone into Canada from Bear's Paw and stayed with the Lakotas thereafter, evidently later submitting with the Sioux who returned south. Mrs. Stevenson, proud of her Nimiipuu heritage, reported that her mother

had lived with her Lakota husband in South Dakota. Thompson, *I Will Tell of My War Story*, 23, citing Alvin M. Josephy, Jr., to Thompson, January 7, 1994.

2. Greene, *Nez Perce Summer*, 290, 349–51. The reality was that the federal government could not guarantee the protection of Nez Perces returning from Canada to Idaho, where, it was believed, they would be subjected to murder trials by local courts, or worse, incensed local citizens might try to kill them. *Army and Navy Journal*, January 12, 1878.

3. It is known that some Nimiipuu temporarily ventured south, however. It is possible that Peopeo Tholekt reported on an incident with his friend Koo-sou-yeen during one of these visits below the line, wherein they breakfasted at a Cree or Plains Ojibwa camp along Milk River. After they enjoyed eating frybread, a detachment of American soldiers arrived and the two men fled up a nearby hill and prepared to fight the troops. But the soldiers never approached them, and Peopeo Tholekt and Koo-sou-yeen apparently crossed back into Canada to reach the Sioux village. It is possible, too, that this incident occurred as these men traveled south with Wottolen to reach the home country. "The Adventure of Peo-peo Tholekt and Ko-sou-yeen." Box 11, folder 79. McWhorter Collection, WSU.

4. Miles to AAG, Department of Dakota, January 12, 1878. NA, RG 393, Part 3. Entry 889. District of the Yellowstone, Letters Sent, vol. September 20, 1877, to February 13, 1879 (ledger); Irvine to Scott, February 2, 1878, in "Papers Relating to the Sioux Indians," 106; Miles to AAG, Department of Dakota, April 3, 1878, in NA, RG 393, Part 3. Entry 886. District of the Yellowstone, "Letter Book, District of the Yellowstone. From Sept. 4th 1877 to Dec. 25th 1877." (ledger) (quotation); Irvine to Scott, July 14, 1878, in "Papers Relating to the Sioux Indians," 119–20; Irvine to Scott, August 11, 1878, in "Papers Relating to the Sioux Indians," 121; Macleod to Scott, August 26, 1878, in "Papers Relating to the Sioux Indians," 122; Irvine to White, November 10, 1878, in "Papers Relating to the Sioux Indians," 125–26; Walsh to Irvine, December 30, 1878, in "Papers Relating to the Sioux Indians," 127–28; Walsh to Irvine, January 25, 1879, in "Papers Relating to the Sioux Indians," 129–30; Manzione, *"I Am Looking to the North for My Life,"* 129–31. A sketched portrayal of Sioux or Nez Perce tepees, apparently drawn by the artist Laamnisnimusus, is in Thompson, *I Will Tell of My War Story*, 74.

5. McWhorter, *Yellow Wolf*, 238 (including quotation); McWhorter, *Hear Me, My Chiefs!* 516–17; "Fallacies of History," Box 9, folder 53, McWhorter Collection, WSU; Mark Arthur interview in Walter M. Camp Field Notes, Unclassified Envelope 127. Hammer Collection, box 10, folder 8.

6. *The New North-West*, July 26, 1878. White Bird told MacDonald: "Some of my Indians are deserting me; they do so when I am sound asleep in my bed; they run off at night and if these men commit depredations I am not to blame. You know that I am doing my best to keep them here." *The New North-West*, August 9, 1878.

7. McWhorter, *Hear Me, My Chiefs!* 517n22 (including quotation); "Fallacies of History," 4. Box 9, folder 53. McWhorter Collection, WSU; "Mrs. Shot In-Head. Refugees Returning from Canada." Box 11, folder 79. McWhorter Collection, WSU; "Story of Peo-Peo Hih-Hih. 'White Bird.'" Box 8, folder 43. McWhorter Collection, WSU (quotation); Greene, *Nez Perce Summer,* 342. Soldiers from Camp Baker, Montana, clashed with Indians thought to be Nez Perces on May 20, 1878, near Diamond City. Poitevin, *Captain Walter Clifford,* 142–52.

8. J. H. Jones, "The Rock Creek Massacre," ca. 1904. J. H. Jones Reminiscences. SC 914, Montana Historical Society Archives, Helena, 3–4; Martha E. Plassmann, "Miner's Story," undated. Martha Edgerton Plassman Papers. MC 78. Montana Historical Society Archives, 1; *The New North-West,* July 26, 1878.

9. Vaughn, *Then and Now,* 243–44.

10. *The New North-West,* July 19, 1878.

11. Camille Williams to McWhorter, March 21, 1938. Box 11, folder 79. McWhorter Collection, WSU; "Nez Perces Refugees among the Sheepeaters," Box 11, folder 79. McWhorter Collection, WSU (quotation).

12. Black Eagle's tallies listed twenty-eight people (13 men, 9 women, and 6 children), as follows: Men: Wottolen, Black Eagle, Peopeo Tholekt, Wewass Pahkalatkeikt, Iskeloom, Kootskoots Tsomyowhet, Ipnamatwekin, Wahseenwes Sawhohtsoht, Seeloo Wahyakt, Pauh Wahyakt, Weyooseeka Tsahown, Kowtoliks, and Hemene Moxmox (Yellow Wolf). Women and children: Niktseewhy, with two children; Ipnatsubah Loolussonmi; Yahyow, with two nieces, including Joseph's daughter; Heyoom Telelbinmi; Tommi Yohonmi; Heyoom Yoyikt; Whepwheponmi; Bellutsoo, with two children; and Weyadooldipat. Adapted from McWhorter, *Yellow Wolf,* 239n2. See also, "Names of the Nez Perce Refugees Who Returned with Wot-to-len from Sitting Bull's Camp." Box 10, folder 59. McWhorter Collection, WSU. Another member of the group appears to have been Tomimo (White Man). Miscellaneous questions to Black Eagle, with answers, 169. Box 10, folder 159, McWhorter Papers. Black Eagle was specific about the time of the departure from Sitting Bull's camp: "We . . . left Sitting Bull in May, late part of May." "The Nez Perce Refugees Subsequent to the Sun Eclipse, as Told in Yellow Wolf's Narrative. This Finis is Black Eagle's Telling." Box 10, folder 59. McWhorter Collection, WSU. Peopeo Tholekt maintained that "Wottolen's prime object in this secret return to Idaho was to ascertain if possible the fate of Chief Joseph and those who had surrendered to General [*sic—*Colonel] Miles. It was rumored that the exiles were to be brought to the Nez Perce Reservation, and he then went back to Canada and advised White Bird that it would be safe for him to surrender, but the wiley chieftain would not be convinced." "Additional Information by Peo-peo Thokelt." Box 11, folder 79, McWhorter Collection, WSU.

13. Details of encounters with the Assiniboines (including an exchange between Yellow Wolf and an Assiniboine man) and Lemhis are in McWhorter, *Yellow Wolf,*

239–41, 243–44. The quotation from Yellow Wolf is in ibid., 245. The story of Ta-ton-mi is in a note entitled "To Go with Black Eagle's Story of Last Fight and Return to Idaho." Box 11, folder 79, McWhorter Collection, WSU. For Yellow Wolf's perspectives of these episodes, see McWhorter, *Yellow Wolf,* 249–56.

14. McWhorter, *Yellow Wolf,* 252. The Willow Creek location of this event is suggested in Jones, "Rock Creek Massacre," 3.

15. See *The New North-West,* July 9, 1878, which includes the following statement, slightly different from the above regarding the Rock Creek killings: "Wm Joy had no more than turned to get them something to eat until two pistol shots were fired and Joy lay dead on the floor. Jones immediately run and left Elliott surrounded by five sturdy bucks well armed. Some of them were clad in old coats, pants and boots." See also Greene, *Nez Perce Summer,* 342–43; and Fahey, *The Flathead Indians,* 201. The skirmish with miners on Rock Creek and the escape of one is recounted in Jones, "Rock Creek Massacre," 3–14, with quotations on 13 (the author was subsequently referred to as "Nez Perce" Jones). See also McWhorter, *Yellow Wolf,* 254–55. Plassman, "Miner's Story," 1–4, mentions the killing of the two additional miners at Bear Gulch. A John Spencer (not Spence) later visited Canada seeking the thieves who took his stock. *The New North-West,* July 26, 1878.

16. Report of Flathead Agent Peter Ronan, August 12, 1878, in "Report of the Commissioner of Indian Affairs," November 1, 1878. *Report of the Secretary of the Interior, 1878,* 584–85.

17. Lieutenant Wallace's report appeared in *The New North-West,* August 9, 1878; statement by Major Henry L. Chipman, Third Infantry, *The New North-West,* August 2, 1878.

18. McWhorter, *Yellow Wolf,* 253–54 (Yellow Wolf claimed that but one man was killed at Rock Creek); Falck to AAG, District of the Clearwater, August 4, 1878. NA, RG 393, Part 3. Entry 105. District of the Clearwater. Box unnumbered. McWhorter, *Yellow Wolf,* 264–70, 285–86, also provides Yellow Wolf's account of the episodes with the Fort Missoula soldiers and his disagreement regarding the Nez Perce casualties. Further mention of the fight on the Middle Clearwater appear in "Report of the Commanding General of the Department of Dakota, General Gibbon commanding," October 4, 1878, in *Report of the Secretary of War, 1878,* 68; McRae, "The Third Regiment of Infantry," 449; and in *The Oregonian,* July 30, 1878. Yellow Wolf believed that no Indians were killed in this incident. See McWhorter, *Yellow Wolf,* 260–70 (quotation, 267). Black Eagle believed that three horses had been killed. "Questions to Black Eagle." Box 10, folder 59. McWhorter Collection, WSU. Captain William Falck reported that the Nez Perces captured numbered twenty-four: eleven men, eight women, two boys, and three children. Falck to AAG, Department of the Columbia, August 1, 1878, in *Report of the Secretary of War, 1878,* 180. In 1932, Many Wounds provided McWhorter with the names of fifteen Nez Perces who left Sitting Bull's camp

along with four Lakotas, probably in 1878. They became engaged in combat with unidentified opponents in which three Nimiipuu were killed. It is uncertain whether this engagement was the same as one of those mentioned here. See Many Wounds to McWhorter, February 10, 1932, and McWhorter to Many Wounds, August 11, 1932. Box 11, folder 79. McWhorter Collection, WSU.

19. *The Oregonian*, August 3, 1878.

20. Falck to AAG, Department of the Columbia, August 1, 1878, in *Report of the Secretary of War, 1878*, 180–81 (See also Falck's dispatch from Lapwai, August 1, 1878, in *The Oregonian*, August 6, 1878). Lucy Williams was identified by Peopeo Tholekt as accompanying Wottolen in "Additional Information by Peopeo Tholekt." Box 11, folder 79, McWhorter Collection, WSU.

21. McWhorter, *Hear Me, My Chiefs!* 518–19.

22. McWhorter, *Hear Me, My Chiefs!* 519; Indian Agent John Monteith to Colonel Frank Wheaton, October 31, 1878. NA, RG 393, Part 3. Entry 105. District of the Clearwater. Box unnumbered; McWhorter, *Yellow Wolf*, 283–87 (quotation). For Nimiipuu perspective on the surrenders, see ibid., 270–82. See also what is likely Yellow Wolf's surrender described in Falck to AAG, Department of the Columbia, August 4, 1878, in *Report of the Secretary of War, 1878*, 182.

23. Major Azor H. Nickerson to AG, Division of the Pacific, August 6, 1878, in *Report of the Secretary of War, 1878*, 184; McWhorter, *Yellow Wolf*, 283–84; McWhorter, *Hear Me, My Chiefs!* 519–20; Thompson, *Historic Resource Study*, 86. See Wottolen's exchange with Kipkip Pahliwhkin, who tried to induce his surrender, in Adeline Andres, "Black Eagle's Account of the Return of the Wat-to-len [*sic*] Band of Refugees to the Kamiah Country, Idaho, Summer of 1878." Box 10, folder 59, McWhorter Collection, WSU, and also in McWhorter, *Yellow Wolf*, 271–72; and "The Returned Refugees." Box 11, folder 79, McWhorter Collection, WSU. See also Black Eagle, "The Nez Perce Refugees Subsequent to the Sun Eclipse, as Told in Yellow Wolf(s) [*sic*] Narrative." Box 10, folder 59, McWhorter Collection, WSU; "Refugee Nez Perces Who Returned to Sitting Bull's Camp the Second Time." Box 11, folder 79, McWhorter Collection, WSU; "Wot-to-len," box 9, folder 53, McWhorter Collection, WSU; McDonald to McWhorter, August 24, 1928. Box 28, folder 257, McWhorter Collection, WSU. Wottolen ultimately returned to Idaho, received an allotment, and lived there until his death at age 109. "The Last Fight and Surrender." Box 10, folder 62, McWhorter Collection, WSU; Greene, *Nez Perce Summer*, 357. The spectacular eclipse of the sun that affected the entire Rocky Mountain region occurred on July 29, 1878, thereby precisely positing the date of Wottolen's recollected activities at that time. Regional coverage appeared in *The New North-West*, August 2, 1878. The official record detailing the scientific observations is in *Reports of the Total Solar Eclipses*.

24. Finerty, *War-Path and Bivouac*, 283; Wottolen, "The Last Fight and Surrender." Box 10, folder 62. McWhorter Papers; "Phillip Williams Returned Refugee."

Box 10, folder 62, McWhorter Papers; Camille Williams to McWhorter, September 30, 1942. Box 10, folder 62, McWhorter Papers.

25. Lieutenant Colonel John R. Brooke to AAG, Department of Dakota, November 9, 1878; Ilges to AAAG, District of Montana, November 4, 1878; AAAG, District of Montana, to Gibbon, November 19, 1878; Moale to AAG, Department of Dakota, April 25, 1879; Secretary of the Interior Carl Schurz to Secretary of War George W. McCrary, May 29, 1879; Acting Commissioner of Indian Affairs Edward J. Brooks to Secretary of the Interior Schurz, May 23, 1879; Brooks to McCrary, May 29, 1879; Special Orders No. 65, Headquarters, Department of Dakota, June 21, 1879 (sending Second Lieutenant Daniel A. Frederick to escort the Indians from Benton to Leavenworth); Frederick to AAG, Department of Dakota, August 13, 1879; Second Lieutenant Addis M. Henry to Post Adjutant, Fort Benton, August 1, 1879; Moale to AAG, Department of Dakota, June 13, 1879; AAG to Frederick, June 24, 1879; Sheridan to AG Edward D. Townsend, August 8, 1879; Colonel Charles H. Smith, Nineteenth Infantry, to AAG, Department of the Missouri, August 19, 1879; all the above are contained in National Archives Microfilm Publications M666, roll 362, Letters Received by the Office of the Adjutant General. Main Series, 1871–1880. The arrivees in Idaho in spring and summer 1879 are mentioned in Second Lieutenant Charles W. Rowell, Second Infantry, AAAG, to Commanding Officer, Camp Howard, Mt. Idaho. NA, RG 393, Part 3. Entry 102. Letters Sent, District of the Clearwater, April 1, 1879–July 28, 1879 (ledger), 66. At the same time, the group of Nez Perces headed by Red Heart, who had been imprisoned at Fort Vancouver, Washington Territory, since 1877, was freed by General Howard. For fear of retaliation by angry whites against these people, Howard decreed that they "should not be permitted to range at will, even on the Reservation, over roads frequented by whites. He believes this to be a military necessity, and hopes that you will find it convenient and advisable to locate these Nez Perces very near the agency or between it and the Lapwai Post." Colonel Frank Wheaton to Indian Agent John Monteith, undated. NA, RG 393, Part 3. Entry 102. Letters Sent, District of the Clearwater, April 1, 1879–July 28, 1879 (ledger), 37.

26. Greene, *Nez Perce Summer*, 336–38. See also Pearson, *The Nez Perces in the Indian Territory*, 266–93.

Chapter 6

1. "The Last Fight and Surrender, by Wottolen," box 10, folder 62. McWhorter Collection, WSU.

2. Miles to AAG, Department of Dakota, April 11, 1878. NA, RG 393, Part 3. Entry 886. District of the Yellowstone, Letter Book from September 4, 1877 to December 25, 1877 (ledger); Miles to AAG, April 4, 1878. NA, RG 393, Part 3. Entry

889. District of the Yellowstone, Letters Sent, vol. February, 1878–August, 1878 (ledger) (first two quotations); Miles to AAG, Department of Dakota. NA, RG 393, Part 3. Entry 886. District of the Yellowstone. Letter Book, District of the Yellowstone, from September 4, 1877 to December 25, 1877 (ledger) (last quotation).

3. Irvine to Ilges, March 29, 1878, in "Papers Relating to the Nez Perce Indians," 19–20 (first quotation); Macleod to Scott, June 11, 1878, in "Papers Relating to the Sioux Indians," 116 (second quotation).

4. Special Orders No. 71, Headquarters, Department of the Missouri, April 27, 1878. Copy provided by Bob Rea, Fort Supply, Oklahoma; *Army and Navy Journal*, May 11, 1878; Ben Clark interview in Walter M. Camp Field Notes, box 2, folder 3. Camp Manuscripts, Hammer Collection. Clark was known to the Indians as Red Neck; a Civil War veteran, he was described as "honest, quiet, and modest, but brave and forceful to a degree." Camp Mss Field Notes, Walter Mason Camp Unclassified Envelope 122. (Hammer, *Biographies of the 7th Cavalry June 25th 1876*, 566.) Clark believed that Joseph had wanted him to go to White Bird to retrieve Joseph's daughter. Ben Clark interview in Walter M. Camp Field Notes, box 2, folder 3. Camp Manuscripts, Hammer Collection; Yellow Bull Interview, February 13, 1915. Walter M. Camp Manuscripts, Lilly Library, Indiana University, Bloomington.

5. Material on Yellow Bull, Husis Kute, and Estoweaz is from *The New North-West*, March 28, 1879; McWhorter, *Yellow Wolf*, passim; McWhorter, *Hear Me, My Chiefs!* passim; Greene, *Nez Perce Summer*, passim; and *Army Navy Journal*, May 11, 1878. Estoweaz's name was also spelled Auskehwush, Askeeis, and Ashhawus. McWhorter, *Hear Me, My Chiefs!* 254n35.

6. Telegram, Terry to Miles, May 7, 1878. "Papers Relating to the Nez Perce Indians." Governor General's Office. Governor General's Numbered Files. RG 7, G21, vol. 323, file 2001-1, prints 1875–1879, 7 (quotation).; Miles to AAG, Department of Dakota, June 1, 1878. NA, RG 393, Part 3. Entry 886. District of the Yellowstone. Letter Book, District of the Yellowstone, from September 4, 1877 to December 25, 1877 (ledger); Miles to Baird, May 24, 1878. NA, RG 393, Part 3. Entry 886. District of the Yellowstone. Letter Book, District of the Yellowstone, from September 4, 1877 to December 25, 1877 (ledger) (quotation), (also in "Papers Relating to the Nez Perce Indians," 7–8); Miles to Macleod, June 6, 1878. "Papers Relating to the Nez Perce Indians," 6.

7. Heitman, *Historical Register and Dictionary*, vol. 1, 183; Greene, *Nez Perce Summer*, 276, 277, 316; Miles to President Ulysses S. Grant, December 10, 1873, endorsing Baird for the position of Army Paymaster (quotation). George W. Baird ACP (Appointment, Commission, and Personal) File. NA, RG 94. Records of the Office of the Adjutant General. Baird's left arm had been shattered in the fighting on September 30, 1877, at Bear's Paw, only eight months previous, and he was likely yet undergoing treatment for the wound to some degree in the spring of 1878. Surgeon Henry Tilton had endorsed Baird's application for

absence for disability as recently as March 24, 1878, and had described his wound as follows: "The left ulna was fractured and the flexor muscles badly torn by an explosive bullet. The destruction of soft parts has resulted in adhesion which limits the action of the muscles and at present the left hand is of limited use." Tilton concluded that "[he is] unfit for duty." Contained in ibid.

8. Miles to Macleod, May 24, 1878. NA, RG 393, Part 3. Entry 886. District of the Yellowstone. Letter Book, District of the Yellowstone, from September 4, 1877 to December 25, 1877 (ledger) (first quotation) (also in "Papers Relating to the Nez Perce Indians," 5); Baird to Macleod, June 21, 1878 (second quotation). "Papers Relating to the Nez Perce Indians," 6–7.

9. Baird to Macleod, June 21, 1878 (first quotation), and Macleod to Baird, June 22, 1878 (second quotation), in "Papers Relating to the Nez Perce Indians," 6–8. See also, Macleod to Scott, June 23, 1878, in which Macleod reports that "I deemed it advisable that neither Lieut. Baird, who came here in charge of the three Indians, nor the two American scouts, who accompanied them, should proceed to the camp, as the Sioux and the Nez Perces' Chief, White Bird, have expressed so strongly their antipathy to any Americans, and their strong objections to any of them visiting their camps." "Papers Relating to the Sioux Indians," 116.

10. *The New North-West,* March 28, 1879. MacDonald's figures for the number of Nez Perces with White Bird were given in *The New North-West,* July 26, 1878. He stated that White Bird "looks rather young for his age [given as fifty]," but was "the oldest man in the Nez Perces' camp." Ibid.

11. MacDonald reported that eight warriors accompanied White Bird to Fort Walsh. He stated that the proceedings took place in "the officers' hall." *The New North-West,* March 28, 1879. A transcript of the meetings, July 1–2, 1878, appears in "Papers Relating to the Nez Perce Indians," 9–16. Manzione stated that a Mounted Police officer recorded the proceedings in shorthand for later transcription into this form. *"I Am Looking to the North for My Life,"* 120n34. There exist slight textual variances, often imperceptible in meaning, in selections presented in ibid. (120–24), compared with the transcription published in "Papers Relating to the Nez Perce Indians."

12. MacDonald paraphrased and abbreviated Baird's initial remarks, with some differences from the above, as follows: "An officer of the Queen wrote to the American authorities stating that the escaped Nez Perces were tired of their treatment by the British and wished to return to American soil. The officer to whom the complaint was made told them he would communicate with the American authorities and find out on what terms they would be allowed to return. The letter was received by the U.S. authorities and I was sent with these three members of your tribe to meet you and take you to Joseph. I want you to come with me. You will be treated well and taken down the river on a steamer." *The New North-West,* March 28, 1879.

13. *The New North-West,* March 28, 1879.

14. MacDonald's paraphrased version of these remarks by Baird follow: "You may possibly imagine that you may return, one by one, to Idaho from this place, and be safe in doing so. But you are mistaken in this, and should you attempt it will be arrested. If you return with me you will have no trouble whatever. I come for you on the representations made by the officers of the Queen that you and your people had tired of your home and desired to return." *The New North-West*, March 28, 1879.

15. MacDonald's synopsis of White Bird's comment follows: "I do not want to go where Joseph is. The country is unhealthy. Let Joseph come back here, and together we will return to Idaho of our own accord." *The New North-West*, March 28, 1879.

16. No Hunter, also known as Hunter No More (Tukalikshimei), was brother to Looking Glass, killed at Bear's Paw in October, 1877. *The New North-West*, December 5, 1879.

17. MacDonald further identified this youth as Henry Tavahvour (referenced earlier as Tabador), one of those "in the band of Nez Perces which passed through Montana last year [during the war]." *The New North-West*, March 28, 1879.

18. As a pre-surrender term at Bear's Paw, Miles had told Joseph he would keep them at Fort Keogh through the winter and escort them back to Idaho the next spring. Later, Commanding General Sherman instead insisted that the Nez Perces be transferred to Fort Leavenworth as punishment, as an example to other tribes. Greene, *Nez Perce Summer*, 310, 334.

19. *The New North-West*, March 28, 1879.

20. "Duncan McDonald [*sic*] and Chief White Bird," box 11, folder 79, McWhorter Collection, WSU. McWhorter noted on this item: "The following fragmentary sentences were obtained in a personal interview with McDonald under difficulties in his home at Dixon, Montana, July 1928." McWhorter solicited information from MacDonald in a letter of around January 15, 1928, preceding his visit to MacDonald's home in July. See MacDonald to McWhorter, February 1, 1928, box 8, folder 40, McWhorter Collection, WSU. McWhorter's material, including that quoted above (though edited with slight differences) was used in *Hear Me, My Chiefs!* 522. Journalist Martha E. Plassman, who apparently interviewed MacDonald a few years earlier than McWhorter did, stated that MacDonald was the one who convinced White Bird, after three days of talking with him, to go to Fort Walsh and meet Baird. As Plassman related, White Bird "feared that once at Ft. Walsh he would be arrested and turned over to the United States authorities. . . . Were the Canadians going to betray him? It looked like it. Else why had they come for him? . . . . It was only when he learned that MacDonald was a connection of his [being part Nez Perce], would he agree to accompany him to the assigned meeting place, yet still doubtful of the wisdom of his going." Evidently, Mac-Donald quoted White Bird as telling Baird something different in his concluding

remarks from what he later told McWhorter, and without the dramatic gesture, too. Plassman, conceding that the words were not literally as recorded, stated that, according to MacDonald, the chief addressed Baird as follows: "I came here to escape from your soldiers, and I was not received as an enemy, but as a friend. I am protected. Even you dare not touch me. Henceforth this is my home, and that of my people, and here would we be buried. These, my words, you may take to your Great Father in Washington. He is no longer mine. I have spoken." *Hill County Democrat*, August 13, 1925. (Plassman's piece was reprinted in *Winners of the West* [April 1940]). It must be stated that nothing contained in either the official Canadian transcript or MacDonald's contemporary account of the proceedings in any way intimates the histrionics of the renditions he later provided.

21. Macleod to Scott, July 9, 1878, in "Papers Relating to the Sioux Indians," 118–19; Frederick White to Macleod, October 5, 1878; Irvine to White, November 10, 1878; and Walsh to Macleod, December 12, 1878, in "Papers Relating to the Nez Perce Indians," 17–21; Manzione, *"I Am Looking to the North for My Life,"* 123.

22. Ben Clark interview in Walter M. Camp Field Notes, box 2, folder 3. Camp Manuscripts, Hammer Collection. Documentation on Baird's telegram as cited in McWhorter, *Hear Me, My Chiefs!* 522–23: "Baird to Adjutant General, Division of Missouri, July 11, 1878. National Archives, Records of the War Department, 495 (AGO) 1878" (quotation). Author Merrill Beal cited the same document, identifying it as Document No. 2608-78, AGO 3464, National Archives. *"I Will Fight No More Forever,"* 338. While this telegram doubtless exists, it was not encountered during research for this study at the National Archives. See also the account of Baird's mission in Turner, *North-West Mounted Police,* vol. 1, 395–98.

Chapter 7

1. *The New North-West*, August 9, 1878 (quotations).

2. *The New North-West*, December 5, 1879. Background on Eagle from the Light is in Josephy, *Nez Perce Indians*, 573.

3. Dewdney to Sir John A. McDonald, Superintendent General of Indian Affairs, January 2, 1880. NAC, RG 10, vol. 3704, file 17858, microfilm reel C-10123, 64.

4. Beyond occasional mention of numbers in the Mounted Police records, there was no formal accounting for either the Nez Perce or Lakota populations because these tribes were not considered legally recognized Canadian Indians. In 1885, the *Macleod Gazette* (May 23, 1885) referenced "about 34,408" Indians in the North-West Territories, including Crees, Chippewas, Assiniboines, Piegans, Bloods, Blackfeet, Sarsis, and Saulteaux. "The above," explained the paper, "include 1,109 non-treaty Indians, but not foreign Indians like the Nez Perces or remnants of the Sioux from the other side." Nor was there mention of Nez Perces

in a report on Catholic missions for destitute Indians in the North-West Territories and Manitoba in 1889–90. NAC, RG 10, vol. 3708, file 19502, microfilm reel C-10124. For a succinct overview of Canadian Indian administration, including the various tribes, lands, treaties, and administrators, see, G.M. Matheson, "Historic Sketches on Indian Affairs," NAC, RG 10, vol. 768a, microfilm reel C-13491.

5. Maclean, *Canadian Savage Folk*, 36–37; Hugh A. Dempsey, "The Tragedy of White Bird," 25 (including quotations attributed to a "pioneer"); Painter, *White Bird*, 95; Paul Raczka to Shirley Crowshoe, September 5, 1995. Copy in file "Nez Perce in Canada," in the library/archives of Nez Perce National Historical Park, Spalding, Idaho (hereafter cited as Raczka letter, 1995); *Lethbridge Herald*, March 5, 1995 (article contents based on an interview with Canadian historian George Kush); *North-West Mounted Police Force Commissioner's Report, 1880*, appendix, 18. Pincher Creek was settled in 1878 as a breeding area for horses for the Mounted Police at Fort Macleod. Reference to the "Nez Percy camp" at Pincher Creek appears in NAC, RG 13 (Ministry of Justice), Series C-1, vol. 1427, file 254, "1892—Trial of Sam, Nez Perce Indian." The Nez Perces' selection of the area of Pincher Creek because the nearby mountains reminded them of Oregon was suggested by Faye Morning Bull in an interview with the author, February 15, 2006.

6. Dempsey, "Tragedy of White Bird," 25–26 (including first quotation); *The Fort Macleod Gazette*, May 4, 1883 (second quotation); Crozier to Commissioner, North-West Mounted Police, January 29, 1883. NAC, RG 18 (Royal Canadian Mounted Police), vol. 1005, file 146a (third quotation); *Report of the Commissioner of the North-West Mounted Police Force, 1888*, appendix, 206; *Report of the Commissioner of the North-West Mounted Police Force, 1894*, appendix ff, 237.

7. Jefferson, "Fifty Years on the Saskatchewan," 140 (quotation); Light, *Footprints in the Dust*, 225, 372; Clayton T. Yarshenko, Maple Creek, Saskatchewan, to the author, November 5, 2005, and August 22, 2006. An overview of the North-West Rebellion is in Beal and Macleod, *Prairie Fire*.

8. "Anecdotes of Chief Peo-peo Hi-hi: 'White Bird,'" contributed by Yellow Wolf, July, 1926. McWhorter Collection, WSU, box 11, folder 79.

9. Macleod to Minister of Justice John S.D. Thompson, June 28, 1892. NAC, RG 13 (Ministry of Justice), Series C-1, vol. 1427, file 254, "1892—Trial of Sam, Nez Perce Indian"; Raczka letter, 1995.

10. McWhorter, *Hear Me, My Chiefs!* 524; Dempsey, "Tragedy of White Bird," 26–27. The motive for the killing—that the medicine man had threatened Sam's family—was debated in the Canadian press, and some people believed that the murder was culturally inspired, and that the murderer therefore should not be judged by the standards of white Canadians. Justice James F. Macleod, however, did not accept the view "that if a Medicine Man failed to cure the children of an Indian whom he was called upon to treat, he was, according to Indian custom, liable to be killed by the father. I have been living amongst the Indians now for 18 years & I never heard of such a thing, and others, including The Rev. Father

LaCombe, who have lived with the Indians for a much longer time tell me the same thing." Macleod to Thompson, June 28, 1892.

11. This account of the murder of White Bird and the trial of Nez Percee Sam, including quotations, is digested from NAC, RG 13 (Ministry of Justice), Series C-1, vol. 1427, file 254, "1892—Trial of Sam, Nez Perce Indian." Graphic descriptions of White Bird's wounds are included in Dr. Smith's testimony in ibid. See also Justice Macleod's handwritten notes in "Fort Macleod Court Records. Court Records of Southern Alberta and Sask., 1879–1941, including Col. J. F. Macleod Notebooks, 1889–1894; from Fort Macleod, Pincher Creek, Lethbridge, Medicine Hat, Maple Creek and Drumheller." Microfilm M-179, BE, Glenbow Archives. On the day after the murder, an inquest concluded that Sam was guilty of "willful murder" and that his sons had assisted him in the deed. *Lethbridge News,* March 23, 1892. Obviously, that verdict changed during the interim leading to the trial. Historian Hugh Dempsey identified Mrs. Sam's name as Sarah. "Tragedy of White Bird," 28.

12. The press likely neither knew who White Bird was nor what his history had been among his people. One source stated that in Canada he had changed his name to Blue Earrings. Raczka letter, 1995.

13. *The Macleod Gazette and Alberta Live Stock Record,* March 10, 1892; *Lethbridge News,* March 16, 1892.

14. *The Macleod Gazette and Alberta Live Stock Record,* March 17, 1892; *Lethbridge News,* March 23, 1892. The outcome of the trial appeared in *The Macleod Gazette and Alberta Live Stock Record,* June 2, 1892 under the headline, "Guilty of Murder." The paper explained that "Nez Percee Sam" had no counsel, but "the evidence against the prisoner was long, and the jury brought in a verdict of willful murder." Sam "pleaded not guilty, but when asked if we would like to say anything to the jury, he explained how he killed the victim and why he did it."

15. Macleod to Thompson, June 28, 1892.

16. *Manitoba Daily Free Press,* June 9, 1892; *Lethbridge News,* June 15, 1892; *Manitoba Daily Free Press,* June 10, 1892 (quotations); Telegram, Clifford Sefton to Robert Sedgwick, June 12, 1892 (quotation), in NAC, RG 13 (Ministry of Justice), Series C-1, vol. 1427, file 254, "1892—Trial of Sam, Nez Perce Indian."

17. *Lethbridge News,* June 15, 1892 (quotations); *Manitoba Daily Free Press,* June 11, 1892.

18. *The Macleod Gazette and Alberta Live Stock Record,* June 23, 1892; John Summers and Maclean to Minister of the Interior Edgar Dewdney, June 10, 1892; Andrews to Dewdney, June 11, 1892; and Dewdney to Thompson, June 15, 1892, all in NAC, RG 13 (Ministry of Justice), Series C-1, vol. 1427, file 254, "1892—Trial of Sam, Nez Perce Indian"; Maclean, *Canadian Savage Folk,* 42; Dempsey, "Tragedy of White Bird," 27–28. On Sam's baptism, the *Manitoba Daily Free Press,* June 28, 1892, observed: "A profound sadness pervaded the entire congregation as the poor unfortunate stood by the font and took the solemn vow through an interpreter. The

name preferred by himself was Arthur Wm. Goulding, after his much admired spiritual adviser, Rev. A. W. Goulding. In the course of his sermon, Mr. Goulding referred in feeling terms to his experience with poor Sam, who when asked if he wished to be baptized privately said through his interpreter, 'No, why should I be ashamed of the white man's God, if he is to be my God.' The poor fellow seems to fully realize his dreadful position but keeps up bravely."

19. *Macleod Gazette and Alberta Live Stock Record,* June 23, 1892 (quotations); *Manitoba Daily Free Press,* June 20, 1892 (quotation).

20. *Manitoba Free Press,* July 8, 1892 (quotations). The Mounted Police reported on the murder and ensuing trial without once mentioning the name of the victim, and with accusation directed not only against Sam but against his sons: "On the 6th March a brutal murder was committed in the Pincher Creek district by three Nez Perces, a father and two sons, on an old man a member of their band. They were promptly arrested and after waiting for a considerable time, owing to the difficulty in obtaining an interpreter, were tried and found guilty. The father, 'Nez Percee Sam,' was sentenced to be hanged, but this was afterwards commuted to imprisonment for life. The two sons, on account of their extreme youth, were released." *Report of the Commissioner of the North-West Mounted Police Force, 1892,* appendix C, 37.

21. Order of Governor General, July 7, 1892, in NAC, RG 13 (Ministry of Justice), Series C-1, vol. 1427, file 254, "1892—Trial of Sam, Nez Perce Indian"; Macleod to Thompson, June 28, 1892, in ibid.; *Manitoba Daily Free Press,* July 9, 1892; *Lethbridge News,* July 13, 1892; Dempsey, "Tragedy of White Bird," 28.

22. McWhorter, *Hear Me, My Chiefs!* 524; Miscellaneous notes, 3, and Yellow Bull Interview, February 13, 1915, B22, Walter M. Camp Manuscripts, Lilly Library, Indiana University, Bloomington, 3 (first quotation); Camp Papers, Little Bighorn Battlefield National Monument, BYU-168, BYU-719 (second quotation); MacDonald to McWhorter, August 1, 1928. Box 28, folder 257, McWhorter Collection, WSU; Duncan MacDonald, "Wot-to-len and Party Returns to Idaho," and Starr Maxwell, "Killing of White Bird." Box 11, folder 79, McWhorter Collection, WSU; John M. Webster to Camp, November 9, 1911, and Theodore Sharp to Camp, July 3, 1911. Camp Collection, BYU, box 1, folders 19, 20.

23. "Story of Peo-Peo Hih-Hih 'White Bird.'" Box 8, folder 43, McWhorter Collection, WSU; Dempsey, "Tragedy of White Bird," 29.

24. Dempsey, "Tragedy of White Bird," 28; Painter, *White Bird,* 92, 95; Inspector A. Ross Cuthbert to Assistant Commissioner J. H. McIllree, August 21, 1895. NAC, RG 10 (Indian Affairs), vol. 3952, reel C-10198, file 133933, "Peigan Agency—Correspondence regarding the Admission to Treaty of the Family of the Late Nez Perce Sam" (quotation). Dempsey indicated that Sam had a third daughter, age 1 in 1892. "Tragedy of White Bird," 27. According to Painter, *White Bird,* 95, probate hearings regarding White Bird's estate took place in 1915 and

1918. A discussion of elements of White Bird's family genealogy as derived from the hearings and other sources appears in ibid. See also the charts on 97, 98.

25. Indian Agent H. H. Nash to the Indian Commissioner, September 27, 1895 (first quotation); Cuthbert to McIllree, August 21, 1895 (second quotation); NAC, RG 10 (Indian Affairs), vol. 3952, reel C-10198, file 133933, "Peigan Agency—Correspondence regarding the Admission to Treaty of the Family of the Late Nez Perce Sam"; Dempsey, "Tragedy of White Bird," 28–29.

26. The informants were John Yellowhorn and Joe Crowshoe. Raczka letter, 1995; author's telephone interviews with Faye Morning Bull, Brocket, Alberta, February 15, 2006, and March 28 and 29, 2006. In 1897, "Mrs. Warrior" received $5 as a member of Band C at the Piegan Agency. In 1898, she (listed as "Mrs. Warrior or The Woman never holds") received a like amount, and in 1899, she and her husband (apparently allowed into treaty coverage) received $10. In 1902, besides the parents, the Warrior family numbered two boys and one girl, and received $25. This latter record suggests that one child was born in 1901–1902, and that the other two were born between 1899 and 1901. Piegan treaty annuity payment lists for 1897, 1898, 1899, and 1902. Photocopies provided by Faye Morning Bull and enclosed in letter to Robert West, National Park Service, Bear Paw Battlefield, Montana, November 22, 2005.

27. Faye Morning Bull, "Closing the Circle," 18; e-mail, Superintendent Frank Walker, Nez Perce National Historical Park, to files, October 10, 1995. Copy in file "Nez Perce in Canada," archive and library, Nez Perce National Historical Park, Spalding, Idaho; e-mail copy of news article in the *Lethbridge Herald*, undated but circa October, 1995, in file "Nez Perce in Canada," in ibid.

BIBLIOGRAPHY

Manuscript Materials and Collections

Bloomington. Indiana University. Lilly Library. Walter M. Camp Manuscripts.

Brocket, Alberta. Faye Morning Bull Materials. Photocopies of Piegan treaty annuity payment lists, 1897, 1898, 1899, and 1902.

Calgary, Alberta. Glenbow Museum Library and Archives.
Microfilm M-179, BE. "Fort Macleod Court Records."
James M. Walsh letter to daughter, Cora, May 21, 1890.
James Morrow Walsh Scrapbook #11.

Carlisle, Pennsylvania. Army War College. U.S. Army Military History Institute.
Manuscripts Division. Nelson A. Miles Papers.

Crow Agency, Montana. Little Bighorn Battlefield National Monument.
Walter M. Camp Papers.
Kenneth Hammer Collection.

Denver, Colorado. Denver Public Library. Western History Department. Walter Mason Camp Papers.

Helena, Montana. Montana Historical Society. Manuscript Archives.
J. H. Jones Reminiscences. SC 914.
Martha Edgerton Plassman Papers. MC 78.
Statement of Moccasin. SC 489.
Statement of Speak Thunder. SC 767.

Norman. University of Oklahoma Library. Western History Department. Walter Stanley Campbell Collection.

Ottawa, Ontario. Library and Archives Canada.
Record Group 7. Records of the Governor General's Office.
Record Group 10. Records of the Department of Indian Affairs.
Record Group 13. Records of the Ministry of Justice.
Record Group 15. Records of the Department of the Interior.
Record Group 18. Records of the Royal Canadian Mounted Police.

Provo, Utah. Brigham Young University Library. Manuscripts Division. Walter
    Mason Camp Collection (microfilm).
Pullman. Washington State University Library. Lucullus V. McWhorter Collec-
    tion.
Spalding, Idaho. Nez Perce National Historical Park. Library and Archives.
    James Magera Files.
    Jerome A. Greene Collection.
    Nez Perce History Files.
Washington, D.C., National Archives.
    File Microcopies of Records in the National Archives, No. 99. "Notes to For-
        eign Legations in the United States from the Department of State, 1834–
        1906."
    Microfilm Publication M50, "Notes from the British Legation in the United
        States to the Department of State, 1791–1906."
    Microfilm Publication T24, "Despatches from United States Consuls in Win-
        nipeg, 1869–1906."
    Microfilm Publication M666. Letters Received by the Office of the Adjutant
        General.
    Microfilm Publication M666. 3464 AGO 1877. Nez Perce War Papers.
    Microfilm Publication M666. 4163 AGO 1876. Sioux War Papers.
    Microfilm Publication M666. Letters Received by the Office of the Adjutant
        General. Main Series, 1871–1880.
    Record Group 94. Records of the Office of the Adjutant General.
    Record Group 393, Records of United States Army Continental Commands.

                            Government Publications

Annual Report of the Department of the Interior for the Year ended 30th June 1877.
    Ottawa, 1878. In Sessional Papers (No. 10).
Heitman, Francis B., comp. Historical Register and Dictionary of the United States
    Army, 1789–1903. 2 vols. Washington, D.C.: Government Printing Office,
    1903.
"North West Mounted Police, Reports, 1875–1878." Collected from Sessional
    Papers, Ottawa, 1876–1882. Bound copy in the library/archives of the
    Glenbow Museum, Calgary.
"North-West Mounted Police Force: Commissioner's Report, 1879." Copy in the
    library/archives of the Glenbow Museum, Calgary.
North-West Mounted Police Force Commissioner's Report, 1880. Copy in the
    library/archives of the Glenbow Museum, Calgary.
Papers Relating to the Foreign Relations of the United States, 1878. Washington, D.C.:
    Government Printing Office, 1878.

Papers Relating to the Foreign Relations of the United States, 1879. Washington, D.C.: Government Printing Office, 1879.

Papers Relating to the Foreign Relations of the United States, 1881. Washington, D.C.: Government Printing Office, 1881.

"Papers Relating to the Nez Perce Indians of the United States, Who Have Taken Refuge in Canadian Territory." Governor General's Office. Public Archives of Canada, Ottawa, n.d. [ca. 1879].

"Papers Relating to the Sioux Indians of the United States, Who Have Taken Refuge in Canadian Territory." Governor General's Office. Public Archives of Canada, Ottawa, n.d. [ca. 1879].

Report of the Commission Appointed by Direction of the President of the United States, under Instructions of the Honorables the Secretary of War and the Secretary of the Interior, to Meet the Sioux Indian Chief, Sitting Bull, with a View to Avert Hostile Incursions into the Territory of the United States from the Dominion of Canada. Washington, D.C.: Government Printing Office, 1877 [cited in notes as *Report of the Sitting Bull Commission*].

Report of the Commissioner of the North-West Mounted Police Force, 1888. Ottawa, 1889.

Report of the Commissioner of the North-West Mounted Police Force, 1892. Ottawa, 1893.

Report of the Commissioner of the North-West Mounted Police Force, 1894. Ottawa, 1895.

Report of the Deputy Superintendent-General of Indian Affairs, 1879. Ottawa, 1880.

Report of the Secretary of the Interior, 1877. Washington, D.C.: Government Printing Office, 1877.

Report of the Secretary of the Interior, 1878. Washington, D.C.: Government Printing Office, 1878.

Report of the Secretary of the Interior, 1879. Washington, D.C.: Government Printing Office, 1879.

Report of the Secretary of the Interior, 1880. Washington, D.C.: Government Printing Office, 1880.

Report of the Secretary of the Interior, 1881. Washington, D.C.: Government Printing Office, 1881.

Report of the Secretary of War, 1877. Washington, D.C.: Government Printing Office, 1877.

Report of the Secretary of War, 1878. Washington, D.C.: Government Printing Office, 1878.

Report of the Secretary of War, 1879. Washington, D.C.: Government Printing Office, 1879.

Report of the Secretary of War, 1880. Washington, D.C.: Government Printing Office, 1880.

Reports of the Total Solar Eclipses of July 29, 1878, and January 11, 1880. Issued by the United States Naval Observatory. Washington, D.C.: Government Printing Office, 1880.

Sessional Papers. 1878. 1879. 1882. Dominion of Canada.

Thompson, Erwin N. *Historic Resource Study, Fort Lapwai, Nez Perce National Historical Park, Idaho.* Denver, Colo.: National Park Service, 1973.

Books and Articles

Anderson, Frank W. *Fort Walsh and the Cypress Hills.* Saskatoon, Sask.: Published by the author, 1989.

Anderson, Harry H. "A Sioux Pictorial Account of General Terry's Council at Fort Walsh, October 15–16, 1877." *North Dakota History* 22 (July 1955): 93–116.

Anderson, Ian. *Above the Medicine Line with James Morrow Walsh.* Surrey, B.C.: Heritage House, 2000.

Beal, Bob, and Macleod, Rod. *Prairie Fire: The 1885 North-West Rebellion.* Toronto: McClelland and Stewart, 1984.

Beal, Merrill. *"I Will Fight No More Forever": Chief Joseph and the Nez Perce War.* Seattle: University of Washington Press, 1963.

Black Elk, *The Sixth Grandfather: Black Elk's Teachings Given to John G. Neihardt,* edited by Raymond J. DeMallie. Lincoln: University of Nebraska Press, 1984.

Bray, Kingsley M. "We Belong to the North: The Flights of the Northern Indians from the White River Agencies, 1877–1878." *Montana: The Magazine of Western History* 55 (Summer 2005): 28–47.

Brimlow, George F. *The Bannock War of 1878.* Caldwell, Idaho: The Caxton Printers, 1938.

Brown, Joseph Epes, ed. *The Sacred Pipe: Black Elk's Account of the Seven Rites of the Oglala Sioux.* Norman: University of Oklahoma Press, 1953. Reprint 1989.

Curtis, Edward S. *The North American Indian.* 20 vols. Reprint, New York: Johnson Reprint Corporation, 1976.

DeMallie, Raymond J. "The Sioux in Dakota and Montana Territories: Cultural and Historical Background of the Ogden B. Read Collection." In *Vestiges of a Proud Nation: The Ogden B. Read Northern Plains Indian Collection,* 19–69. Burlington, Vt.: Robert Hull Fleming Museum, 1986.

Dempsey, Hugh A. "The Tragedy of White Bird: An Indian's Death in Exile." *The Beaver* 73 (February–March 1993): 23–29.

Denny, Cecil E. *The Law Marches West.* Toronto: J. M. Dent and Sons, 1939. Reprint 1972.

Diehl, Charles Sanford. *The Staff Correspondent.* San Antonio, Tex.: The Clegg Company, 1931.

Dobak, William A. "Killing the Canadian Buffalo, 1821–1881." *The Western Historical Quarterly* 27 (Spring 1996): 33–52.

Dorrity, Mrs. James. "Mrs. James Dorrity's Story." In Alva J. Noyes, *In the Land of the Chinook, or the Story of Blaine County,* 80–81. Helena, Mont.: State Publishing Company, 1917.

Fahey, John. *The Flathead Indians.* Norman: University of Oklahoma Press, 1974.

Finerty, John F. *War-Path and Bivouac; or, The Conquest of the Sioux.* Norman: University of Oklahoma Press, 1961.

Frazer, Robert W. *Forts of the West.* Norman: University of Oklahoma Press, 1961.

Fritz, Henry E. *The Movement for Indian Assimilation, 1860–1890.* Philadelphia: University of Pennsylvania Press, 1963.

Garcia, Andrew. *Tough Trip through Paradise, 1878–1879,* edited by Bennett H. Stein. Boston: Houghton Mifflin Company, 1967.

Graham, William A., comp. and ed. *The Custer Myth: A Source Book of Custeriana.* Harrisburg, Pa.: Stackpole, 1953.

Greene, Jerome A. *Fort Randall on the Missouri, 1856–1892.* Pierre: South Dakota State Historical Society, 2005.

———. *Nez Perce Summer, 1877: The U.S. Army and the Nee-Me-Poo Crisis.* Helena: Montana Historical Society Press, 2000.

———. *Yellowstone Command: Colonel Nelson A. Miles and the Great Sioux War, 1876–1877.* Lincoln: University of Nebraska Press, 1991; Norman: University of Oklahoma Press, 2006.

Grindle, Lucretia. "Pride and Prejudice." *Canadian Geographic* 119 (November–December 1999): 55–68.

Hammer, Kenneth. *Biographies of the 7th Cavalry June 25th 1876.* Fort Collins, Colo.: The Old Army Press, 1972.

Haines, Francis. *The Nez Perces: Tribesmen of the Columbia Plateau.* Norman: University of Oklahoma Press, 1955.

———, ed. "Letters of an Army Captain on the Sioux Campaign of 1879–1880." *Pacific Northwest Quarterly* 39 (January 1948): 39–64.

Hedren, Paul L. *Sitting Bull's Surrender at Fort Buford: An Episode in American History.* Williston, N.Dak.: Fort Union Association, 1997.

Hoig, Stan. *Perilous Pursuit: The U.S. Cavalry and the Northern Cheyennes.* Boulder: University Press of Colorado, 2002.

Howard, James H. *The Canadian Sioux.* Lincoln: University of Nebraska Press, 1984.

Hutton, Paul A. *Phil Sheridan and His Army.* Lincoln: University of Nebraska Press, 1985.

Jackson, Helen Hunt. *A Century of Dishonor: The Early Crusade for Indian Reform.* New York: Harper and Brothers, 1881.

Jefferson, Robert. "Fifty Years on the Saskatchewan." In *Canadian North-West Historical Society Publications: Chapters in the North-West History Prior to 1890 Related by Old Timers,* vol. 1, no. 5, 1–160. Battleford, Sask.: The Canadian North-West Historical Society, 1929.

Jennings, John. "The Plains Indians and the Law." In *Men in Scarlet,* edited by Hugh A. Dempsey, 50–65. Calgary: Historical Society of Alberta / McClelland and Stewart West, 1974.

Johnson, Virginia W. *The Unregimented General: A Biography of Nelson A. Miles.* Boston: Houghton Mifflin, 1962.

Joseph (Heinmot Tooyalakekt). "An Indian's View of Indian Affairs." *North American Review* 128 (April 1879): 412–33.

Josephy, Alvin M., Jr. *The Nez Perce Indians and the Opening of the Northwest.* New Haven, Conn.: Yale University Press, 1963.

Joyner, Christopher C. "The Hegira of Sitting Bull to Canada: Diplomatic Realpolitik, 1876–1881." *Journal of the West* 13 (April 1974): 6–18.

LaDow, Beth. *The Medicine Line: Life and Death on a North American Borderland.* New York: Routledge, 2001.

Light, Douglas W. *Footprints in the Dust.* North Battleford, Sask.: Turner-Warwick, 1987.

Manzione, Joseph. *"I Am Looking to the North for My Life": Sitting Bull, 1876–1881.* Salt Lake City: University of Utah Press, 1991.

Marquis, Thomas B. *Memoirs of a White Crow Indian.* New York: The Century Company, 1928.

MacDonald, Duncan. "The Nez Perces: The History of Their Troubles and the Campaign of 1877." In *In Pursuit of the Nez Perces: The Nez Perce War of 1877,* compiled by Linwood Laughy, 211–73. Wrangell, Alaska: Mountain Meadow Press, 1993.

Maclean, John. *Canadian Savage Folk: The Native Tribes of Canada.* Toronto: William Briggs, 1896. Reprint, Toronto: Coles, 1971.

Macleod, Roderick C. "James Farquharson Macleod." In *Dictionary of Canadian Biography Online.* Retrieved December 5, 2008, from www.biographi.ca/index-e.html.

———. "James Morrow Walsh." In *Dictionary of Canadian Biography Online.* Retrieved December 5, 2008, from www.biographi.ca/index-e.html.

McCrady, David G. *Living with Strangers: The Nineteenth-Century Sioux and the Canadian-American Borderlands.* Lincoln: University of Nebraska Press, 2006.

McRae, James H. "The Third Regiment of Infantry." In *The Army of the United States: Historical Sketches of Staff and Line with Portraits of Generals-in-Chief,* edited by Theophilus F. Rodenbough and William L. Haskin, 432–51. New York: Maynard, Merrill, and Company, 1896.

McWhorter, Lucullus V. *Hear Me, My Chiefs! Nez Perce History and Legend,* edited by Ruth Bordin. Caldwell, Idaho: The Caxton Printers, 1952; revised printing, 1992.

———. *Yellow Wolf: His Own Story.* Caldwell, Idaho: The Caxton Printers, 1940; revised edition, 1986.

Meyer, Roy W. "The Canadian Sioux: Refugees from Minnesota." *Minnesota History* 41 (Spring 1968): 13–28.

———. *History of the Santee Sioux: United States Indian Policy on Trial.* Lincoln: University of Nebraska Press, 1967.

Monnett, John H. *Tell Them We Are Going Home: The Odyssey of the Northern Cheyennes.* Norman: University of Oklahoma Press, 2001.

Morning Bull, Faye. "Closing the Circle: An Historic Reunion Links Nez Perce Descendants in Alberta with Relatives in the U.S." *Legacy, Alberta's Cultural Heritage Magazine* 6 (Spring 2001): 16–18.

Nichols, Roger, and George R. Adams, eds. *The American Indian: Past and Present.* Waltham, Mass.: Xerox College Publishing, 1971.

Noyes, Alva J. *In the Land of the Chinook, or the Story of Blaine County.* Helena, Mont.: State Publishing Company, 1917.

Painter, Bob. *White Bird: The Last Great Warrior Chief of the Nez Perces.* Fairfield, Wash.: Ye Galleon Press, 2002.

Pakes, Fraser J. "Sitting Bull in Canada, 1877–81." *The Brand Book* 20 (October 1977–January 1978): 1–25. London: The English Westerners' Society.

Papandrea, Ronald J. *They Never Surrendered: The Lakota Sioux Band that Stayed in Canada.* Warren, Mich.: Published by the author, 2003.

Pearson, J. Diane. *The Nez Perces in the Indian Territory: Nimiipuu Survival.* Norman: University of Oklahoma Press, 2008.

Pennanen, Gary. "Sitting Bull: Indian Without a Country." *The Canadian Historical Review* 51 (June 1970): 123–40.

Pinkham, Ron. *Hundredth Anniversary of the Nez Perce War of 1877.* Lapwai, Idaho: Nez Perce Printing, 1977.

Poitevin, Norman, comp. *Captain Walter Clifford: A 7th Infantry Officer's Career in the Indian Wars.* Santa Cruz, Calif.: Privately published, 2002.

St. Germain, Jill. *Indian Treaty-Making Policy in the United States and Canada, 1867–1877.* Lincoln: University of Nebraska Press, 2001.

Scott, Hugh L. *Some Memories of a Soldier.* New York: The Century Company, 1928.

Sharp, Paul F. *Whoop-Up Country: The Canadian-American West, 1865–1885.* Minneapolis: University of Minnesota Press, 1955. Reprint, Norman: University of Oklahoma Press, 1973.

Slaughter, Linda W. "Leaves from Northwestern History." *Collections of the State Historical Society of North Dakota* 1 (1906): 274–76.

Stonechild, Blair. "Indian-White Relations in Canada, 1763 to the Present." In *Encyclopedia of North American Indians,* edited by Frederick E. Hoxie, 277–79. Boston and New York: Houghton Mifflin Company, 1996.

Surtees, Robert J. "Canadian Indian Policies." In *History of Indian-White Relations,* edited by Wilcomb E. Washburn, 89–91. *Handbook of North American Indians,* edited by William C. Sturtevant, 4. Washington, D.C.: Smithsonian Institution, 1988.

Thompson, Scott M. *I Will Tell of My War Story: A Pictorial Account of the Nez Perce War.* Seattle and Boise: University of Washington Press and Idaho State Historical Society, 2000.

Titley, E. Brian. "Edgar Dewdney." In *Dictionary of Canadian Biography Online.* Retrieved December 5, 2008, from www.biographi.ca/index-e.html.

Trout, M. D., ed. *Joseph Culbertson's Indian Scout Memoirs, 1876–1895.* Anaheim, Calif.: Van-Allen Publishing Company, 1984.

Turner, G. Frank. "Sitting Bull Tests the Mettle of the Redcoats." In *Men in Scarlet,* edited by Hugh A. Dempsey, 66–76. Calgary: Historical Society of Alberta/McClelland and Stewart West, 1974.

Turner, John Peter. *The North-West Mounted Police, 1873–1893.* 2 vols. Ottawa: Edmond Cloutier, 1950.

Utley, Robert M. *Frontier Regulars: The United States Army and the Indian, 1866–1890.* New York: Macmillan, 1973.

———. *Frontiersmen in Blue: The United States Army and the Indian, 1848–1865.* New York: Macmillan, 1967.

———. *The Indian Frontier of the American West, 1846–1890.* Albuquerque: University of New Mexico Press, 1985.

———. *The Lance and the Shield: The Life and Times of Sitting Bull.* New York: Henry Holt, 1993.

Vaughn, Robert. *Then and Now; or, Thirty-Six Years in the Rockies.* N.p.: Published by the author, 1900. Reprint, Helena, Mont.: Farcountry Press, 2001.

Vestal, Stanley. *New Sources of Indian History, 1850–1891: A Miscellany.* Norman: University of Oklahoma Press, 1934.

———. *Sitting Bull: Champion of the Sioux.* Norman: University of Oklahoma Press, 1957.

Walker, Deward, Jr. "Nez Perce." In *Plateau,* edited by Deward Walker, Jr., 420–38. *Handbook of North American Indians,* edited by William C. Sturtevant, 12. Washington, D.C.: Smithsonian Institution, 1998.

West, Elliott. *The Last Indian War: The Nez Perce Story.* New York: Oxford University Press, 2009.

Woodruff, Thomas M. "'We have Joseph and all his people. . . .': A Soldier Writes Home about the Final Battle," *Montana: The Magazine of Western History* 4 (October 1977): 30–33.

Wooster, Robert. *The Military and United States Indian Policy, 1865–1903.* New Haven, Conn.: Yale University Press, 1988.

Zimmer, William F. *Frontier Soldier: An Enlisted Man's Journal of the Sioux and Nez Perce Campaigns, 1877,* edited by Jerome A. Greene. Helena: Montana Historical Society Press, 1998.

Newspapers

Army and Navy Journal, 1877, 1878

Benton Record (Fort Benton, Mont.), 1877

Bismark Tribune, 1879

Bozeman Times, 1877

Chicago Inter Ocean, 1877

Chicago Times, 1877

Chicago Tribune, 1890

Fort Benton Record, 1878

Fort Macleod Gazette, 1883

Hill County Democrat (Havre, Mont.), 1925

Idaho Statesman (Boise), 1877

Lethbridge Herald (Alta.), 1995

Lethbridge News (Alta.), 1892

Macleod Gazette and Alberta Live Stock Record, 1885

Manitoba Daily Free Press, 1892

National Republican, 1876, 1877

New North-West, 1878, 1879

New York Herald, 1877, 1890

Oregonian (Portland), 1878

Winners of the West, 1940

Personal Communications

Telephone interviews with Faye Morning Bull. February 15, 2006; March 28 and 29, 2006.

Letters from Clayton T. Yarshenko. November 5, 2005; August 22, 2006.

Index

CPSIA information can be obtained
at www.ICGtesting.com
Printed in the USA
FFOW03n0330020318
45320247-45970FF